LOST TO SERVICE

A Summary of Accidents to RAF Aircraft and Losses of Personnel – 1959 to 1996

Compiled and Edited

by

Colin Cummings

N

Nimbus Publishing

Nimbus Publishing,
October House,
Yelvertoft,
Northamptonshire
NN6 6LF

ISBN 0 9526619 0 X

Profits from the sale of this book will be donated
to the Royal Air Force Benevolent Fund

Produced by

Axxent Ltd,
The Old Council Offices
The Green
Datchet
Berkshire, SL3 9EH

Contents

Acknowledgements

I am indebted to a considerable number of people for their assistance and advice in the preparation of this book.

Sarah Sharman, author of 'Sir James Martin', and Brian Miller of Martin-Baker Aircraft Ltd for permission to quote from Appendix 4 of Mrs Sharman's book.

Wing Commander J M Henderson RAF provided advice and guidance on useful sources of information. Mr John Williams, currently Director of Support Management 4(RAF), for his recollections of a Vulcan accident in 1963. Mr Chris Bartle, Secretary of the 80 Squadron Association, for details of the Berriedale Canberra loss in 1966.

Group Captain Charles Ness RAF, Wing Commander Dick Johnson RAF, Wing Commander David Woodman, Wing Commander Veronica Thompson, Squadron Leader Huw Morris, Squadron Leader Viv Walker, Squadron Leader Geoff Roberts and Flight Lieutenant Jim Anderson helped in running to earth details of particular incidents or the names of crew members.

Group Captain Ken Parfitt and his daughter, Wing Commander Wendy Vose RAF, provided a summary about the loss of a Hercules at RAF Fairford in March 1969. Colonel Angelo Pacifico, Italian Military Attache London, gave me details of the Italian military personnel lost off Pisa in November 1971. Robert and Anne Smith of Barby, researched some accidents to aircraft operating from RAF Chivenor. I am also grateful to members of the Shackleton Association, particularly John Botwood, their president, for their comments and recollections about the 'Old Growler'.

The staff of the RAF Air Historical Branch were most helpful with my persistent enquiries and extremely tolerant of my questions. The staff of the RAF Museum Library at Hendon, particularly Ray Funnell, provided me with access to the basic source data for accidents in the early part of this account.

The staffs of The Records and Research Department of Shrewsbury Library, the Reference Section of Northampton Library and Stamford Public Library. Mr Tim Warren of Newark Public Library, Gillian Spokes of Hull Central Library and Jennie Mooney of the Local Studies Department of Grimsby Library.

Mr Raymond D Holdich of the London Collectors Centre, Whitcomb Street, whose researchers looked through various records at the Public Record Office relating to accidents in the 1960s.

Mr Ken Allen, St Clement Danes Church, London (The Royal Air Force church).

In acknowledging the help of these and others, I accept that any mistakes and ommissions in this account are my responsibility. I should be grateful to learn of inaccuracies in this account and also information to complete the record.

Introduction

In the period 1959 to 1996 the RAF lost through accident, enemy action or as a result of irreparable damage sustained, nearly 1100 aircraft. In addition, these accidents claimed the lives of several hundred crew members or passengers: the youngest a 15 year old air cadet and the oldest a 60 year old gliding instructor. Some lives were also lost outside the aircraft when debris fell to earth.

This account records the losses of these aircraft, including those RAF types being operated by other Defence agencies such as the Empire Test Pilots' School (ETPS), the Royal Aircraft Establishment (RAE) and the Aircraft and Armament Experimental Establishment (A&AEE). It also records, where possible, the casualties suffered and in some cases details those who escaped, increasingly as the period progressed using Martin-Baker or Folland ejection seats - some on more than one occasion!

Inevitably in a service like the RAF, the majority of losses occurred to the fighter and light bomber fleets. In the early years of this account, therefore, the Hunter, Javelin and Canberra all feature regularly, with the Harrier, Jaguar and Lightning taking over as the period advanced. There was a a steady attrition of training aircraft throughout and so Provost and Vampire and later Jet Provost appear in the pages. The relative fragility of helicopters means that they were often damaged beyond repair after fairly minor accidents.

By their very nature, transport aircraft losses account for a proportionately higher number of personnel casualties. Fortunately, they are rare with only four significant losses in the review: three Hastings aircraft in the early to mid 1960s and a Hercules in 1971.

The maritime aircraft fleet, with crews often numbering a dozen, have contributed with the Shackleton losing five aircraft and their crews between the end of 1965 and early 1968 followed by a sixth serious loss in 1990.

Behind the raw statistics there are many poignant stories, which this account cannot expose, and others of considerable skill being displayed by crews in exceptionally difficult conditions.

Perhaps to illustrate that there can be a lighter side to the serious business of miltary aircraft safety, one story might be worth recording.

An experienced fast jet pilot was returning to base in a twin engined, two seat training version of an attack aircraft. The passenger was the squadron senior engineering officer: SEngO. Unfortunately, for some reason or another the undercarriage was not lowered and the aircraft landed on the drop tanks (fortunately empty) and slid along the runway. However, as it swerved off the side of the runway and onto the grass, the danger that it might turn over increased and so the pilot ejected, leaving a somewhat alarmed SEngO alone in the aircraft. With the famed speed of uptake, for which officers of the Engineer Branch of the RAF are supposedly endowed (not always supported in reality), the engineer followed his pilot. Some months later the engineer officer left the squadron at the end of his tour of duty and as is the custom, was dined out by his peers. After the speeches, he was presented with a Flying Log Book, recording his sorties flown with the squadron. One of the entries, legend maintains, records: Captain and 1st Pilot - one and half seconds!!!!!!!!!!

The Royal Air Force Flight Safety Scene

At the start of the first full year of peace following the end of the Second World War; 1946, the Royal Air Force, in common with the other services was undergoing a rapid demobilisation and period of retrenchment. Nonetheless, there were still some 400 squadrons listed in the Order of Battle and a substantial number of aircraft used by Station Flights, Communication flights and squadrons and as general 'hacks'. To this figure must be added the training and operational conversion units. The precise number of aircraft 'on the books' is not clear and also the existing statistics are subject to various interpretations as to what was or was not, an active flying machine.

What is clear, however, is that 1946 saw a total of nearly 1000 aircraft destroyed or damaged beyond repair in accidents and almost 700 people killed. This accident rate of almost three per day, when set against the number of hours flown, amounted to about 9 accidents per 10000 flying hours. Some of the statistics and facts would cause the most enormous alarm if experienced today. For example, Dakota transport aircraft suffered an average of more than one loss per week and one squadron; No: 10, lost three aircraft of this type in a single day.

There were of course many reasons for this situation. First, the aircraft were not as reliable nor robust as they are now. Coupled with this was the more rapid obsolescence of aircraft: significant improvements to an aircraft's design or capability resulted in a new Mark of the type being introduced rather than retro-fitting of the capability to existing airframes. This in turn led to comparatively minor damage being classified as beyond economic repair on anything but the latest version of a type. Navigation aids were not as sophisticated as now and consequently there was a significant attrition caused by aircraft being off course or lost, with all that this entailed. Training of crews was not always as rigorous as it might have been and there was a relative youth and inexperience of crews and less stringent regulation.

The listing of losses in this account begins in 1959. By that time the RAF had settled down from the effects of the post-war decline and reorganisation, the effects of Korea, Suez and the Malayan campaign had worked through. The Hunter and Javelin were established as the main fighter aircraft types and the Canberra as the light bomber. In the transport role the Hastings, Beverley and Valetta were all matured and the Shackleton held sway in the maritime role with the demise of the Neptune and the retirement of the Sunderland. Training aircraft were mainly Provosts or increasingly Jet Provosts, and Vampires were the principal advanced trainer. Increasing numbers of 'V' bombers; Valiant, Victor and Vulcan were coming into service; the last Washingtons had gone from Signals Command and the Lincoln was to all intents finished.

At the start of this survey there were the ubiquitous 'station flights' and senior officers filling ground appointments were still allowed to keep in flying practice, mainly using the Meteor T7, and these officers often flew communications types, such as the Anson, if visiting other units.

By the end of the period the RAF had rid itself of most of the second and third generation jet powered aircraft; 'V' bombers were no more, Phantom, Buccaneer, Jet Provost and Hunter were all gone. Notwithstanding, the average age of the RAF's aircraft remained significantly high. The fleets of Hercules, VC10s, and Nimrods go back to the late 1960s or early 1970s. It was only the large numbers of second generation Harriers and Tornado aircraft which dragged the age down to respectable levels. However, age is not of real consequence anymore because the 'air vehicle' can be reworked with fatigue damage redressed and the systems within the aircraft constantly updated.

Greater reliability, improved training, higher skill levels and enhanced navigational equipments all contribute to an improved safety position over that of 50 years ago. Inevitably, of course there is always the instant expert or 'auto babble' politician ready to spring forward with the condemnation of RAF low flying training whenever an aircraft crashes or worse they collide. Notwithstanding, the accident rate can now be measured in terms of losses per 100000 flying hours and, with the exception of the period from 1975 to 1981, when the accident rate expressed in terms of flying hours moved upwards, there has been a steady reduction in accidents and the inevitable loss of life or injury.

The RAF and the other services, are not complacent about their accident record and continue to invest substantially to ensure that the rate improves, although it is of course unrealistic to expect it ever to be eliminated.

The RAF Categorisation System

The RAF system of classifying aircraft for damage assessment or maintenance purposes has followed the same general principles for many years. However, the precise categorisation has varied as circumstances within the service have changed.

Basically, aircraft are categorised into five groups; Categories 1 to 5. The groups equate for maintenance and damage assessment purposes to the levels of repair or maintenance performed at certain locations within the RAF and industry. The table below outlines the meanings of the categories.

This account, with a very few exceptions, relates to those aircraft which were determined to be Category 5.

Category	Maintenance	Structural Damage
1	The aircraft and its systems require only to be checked and consumables replenished before it is available for further use	The damage is such that it can be repaired without withdrawing the aircraft from service
2	The aircraft requires to undergo maintenance which is beyond the capacity of the operating squadron. This maintenance can either be scheduled periodic maintenance or the correction of a random failure requiring facilities or equipment held by the station but not the squadron	The damage requires the aircraft to be taken out of use and returned to the specialist station staff for repair.
3	The aircraft requires maintenance support from a specialist maintenance unit, usually for a pre-arranged periodic service which is conducted at a dedicated facility.	The damage cannot be repaired at a unit and requires a specialist team to visit or for the aircraft to be taken to the specialist repair facility. It could fly there under certain circumstances which impose an operating restriction eg leave the undercarriage down. In this example the aircraft would be said to be 'Cat 3 - Fly'.

4	Maintenance would be conducted by a contractor	The repairs would be undertaken at a contractor's works or by a contractor's working party because the RAF facilities were inadequate or not available in time.
5	The aircraft is not subject to the normal maintenance schedules because it is no longer in current use. If being used for training, it would be subject to a specific range of maintenance checks to ensure it was safe to use in its specific role.	The aircraft is beyond repair. The category allows for a number of sub-types to be used. For example: Cat 5 (Scrap) Cat 5 (Components) Cat 5 (Ground Instructional Aircraft) Cat 5 (Missing)

Date Serial Aircraft Unit Place Casualties
Brief Circumstances of Accident
Casualty Details (If Applicable)

14-Jan-59 VW817 Valetta C1 84 Sqn Firq Oman 0

Tipped over after tyre burst on landing and aircraft swung off runway

---

16-Jan-59 WJ818 Canberra PR7 13 Sqn RAF Akrotiri 0

Belly landed after hydraulics failure and undercarriage would not lower

---

19-Jan-59 VZ302 Vampire FB5 CAACU 0.75 miles from Exeter Airport 1

Aircraft approached to land from 70 degrees off the runway with an angle of bank of about 40 degrees. At about 100 feet the port wing dropped and the angle of bank increased to 75 degrees. Immediately afterwards the aircraft rolled to starboard and struck the ground inverted. The cause was excessive corrective action when the port wing dropped (hard right aileron and pull back on stick) causing the aircraft to stall. There was a strong crosswind which caused the pilot to misjudge his approach; he should have overshot before the situation got out of control.

Flight Lieutenant Kenneth Albert Oriel MUNSON 36 RAuxAFRO

20-Jan-59 WH206 Meteor T7 SF Khormaksar Mogadishu Somalia 1

The crew were unable to locate their precise position on the coastline and when the fuel state ran down to 40 gallons each side they broadcast a distress call but there was some confusion over the steering information they were given. It was decided to bail out when the fuel supplies were exhausted and the canopy was jettisoned. The aircraft glided from 20000 to 12000 feet and then the crew abandoned the aircraft which continued in a shallow dive until it crashed. Although the co-pilot, Flight Lieutenant A Bradshaw, survived the captain was killed and it is surmised that his rip cord fouled as he left the aircraft causing his parachute to deploy early and for his body to strike the tailplane. The accident was caused by faulty flight planning, poor navigation, failure to divert early enough when the arrival airfield had no

---

VHF homer, premature descent, use of both engines when fuel state low. The level of supervision exercised was also inadequate.

Flight Lieutenant Filmete BRIDGLAND 28 Pilot

20-Jan-59 WX978 Meteor FR9 Station Flt Sharjah 0

Swung on take off after a tyre burst, struck an obstruction and the undercarriage collapsed

---

26-Jan-59 KJ810 Dakota C4 209 Sqn Kuala Lumpar Malaya 0

Stalled and crashed after the aircraft took off with the elevators locked

---

31-Jan-59 WR194 Vampire 9 RAFC 0.5 miles east of RAF Cranwell 1

This aircraft returned to the airfield and joined the dead side of the circuit whilst another aircraft was completing an overshoot. As the other aircraft turned starboard it collided with this aircraft, which was crossing the upwind end of the runway. Both aircraft immediately crashed. The pilot of this aircraft failed to make a call that he was joining the circuit and maintained an inadequate lookout.

Flight Cadet Michael DICKINSON 21

31-Jan-59 XE936 Vampire T11 RAFC 0.5 miles east of RAF Cranwell 2

Mid air collision with WR194 as outlined above.

Flight Lieutenant Donald Gilliland MURCHIE 28 Pilot Instructor
Flight Cadet Peter David KEELING 20 Student Pilot

02-Feb-59 WV676 Provost T1 2FTS RAF Shawbury 0

Tipped over in a forced landing necessitated because the aircraft ran out of fuel

---

17-Feb-59 XE619 Hunter F6 1 Sqn RAF Honington 0

Whilst approaching RAF Stradishall the aircraft hit trees and it subsequently made a crash landing at RAF Honington where it was written off as beyond economic repair.

18-Feb-59 XA569 Javelin FAW1 87 Sqn Near RAF Bruggen 1

The aircraft was flying level but with a slight nose up attitude and a little negative 'g' applied with a speed of 0.75 Mach. The pilot, Flight Lieutenant R A V Carey, felt the ejection seat begin to move and it then fired; at 10000 feet the separation sequence worked but the pilot found he was upside down and supported only by his right thigh strap and on landing he was injured. The navigator was found strapped into his seat and did not survive. It is believed that the pilot's ejection was caused by the top latch being left undone and the navigator's face blind was probably operated by blast and cockpit turbulence. The drogue line was not connected to the drogue gun piston. The navigator had also failed to remove the secondary firing handle safety pin and thereby prejudiced his ejection

Flight Lieutenant Alec COOPER Navigator

19-Feb-59 WL478 Meteor T7 RAFFC Theddlethorpe All Saints Lincolnshire 1

The pilot was intending to carry out a double flame out practice and to follow this with an asymetric overshoot. However, with the flaps and undercarriage down the aircraft did not accelerate and it stalled and dived into the ground.

Pilot Officer Alan Gerald TREASURE 27 Student Pilot

21-Feb-59 XE319 Sycamore HR14 194 Sqn 6 miles south of Kuala Lumpur Malaya 2

Date Serial Aircraft Unit Place Casualties
Brief Circumstances of Accident
Casualty Details (If Applicable)

The aircraft was undertaking a training sortie when in level flight and at approximately 400 feet, pieces were seen to fall from the aircraft which promptly spiralled down, oscillating in all directions and crashed. It seems probable that the cause of the crash was the failure of the main rotor blade trailing edge near its root and subsequent break up of the tail rotors and tail boom as the fuselage was cut through

Flight Lieutenant Arthur George MITCHELL 41 Pilot & instructor
Flight Lieutenant Terence HILLMAN 27 Student pilot

28-Feb-59 XD967 Swift FR5 2 Sqn Jever 0

Belly landed after undercarriage could not be lowered

04-Mar-59 XH207 Canberra B(I)8 59 Sqn 3 miles south of Sorpe Dam 2

The aircraft crashed in hilly country about 50 to 90 miles from its briefed course, striking the ground in an inverted position starboard wing first before cartwheeling and exploding. It seems probable that, having flown in an area he was briefed to avoid, the pilot then flew below his briefed minimum altitude of 2000 feet in order to stay below the cloud which was at 1500 feet and that he subsequently stalled.

Flying Officer Michael John HARROP 24 Pilot
Flying Officer Anthony John Seymour BROWN Navigator

09-Mar-59 XE854 Vampire T11 1 FTS Near Rotherham 1

Having completed a detail at Full Sutton the aircraft was seen heading towards Rotherham very low and fast. It entered cloud and was next seen in a dive which developed into a spiral left hand dive before striking the ground. The cause was that the pilot indulged in unauthorised low flying and departed from his briefed exercise and encountered conditions with which he could not cope. It seems that the pilot may have been low flying in the vicinity of his parents' home.

Midshipman I F WILSON 19 Royal Navy

09-Mar-59 XA802 Javelin FAW2 46 Sqn RAF Sylt 0

Engine explosion on start up damaged aircraft beyond repair

18-Mar-59 WJ761 Canberra B6 9 Sqn RAF Luqa 0

Overshot at night but touched the ground and undercarriage raised to stop. Struck another aircraft in the process

---

20-Mar-59 WV410 Hunter F4 229 OCU RAF Chivenor 0

Caught fire after hitting the sea wall in the undershoot

24-Mar-59 XG208 Hunter F6 26 Sqn 3 miles west of RAF Gutersloh 0

Abandoned by the pilot, Flight Lieutenant R V Boult, after loss of engine power coupled with radio problems

---

08-Apr-59 XM287 Twin Pioneer CC1 78 Sqn 30 miles west of RAF Khormaksar 0

Overturned in forced landing after both engines failed

08-Apr-59 XM288 Twin Pioneer CC1 78 Sqn near RAF Khormaksar 0

Ditched in the sea after double engine failure

09-Apr-59 XD928 Swift FR5 2 Sqn near RAF Sylt 0

Abandoned by the pilot, Flight Lieutenant B J St Aubyn, after engine failure

Date Serial Aircraft Unit Place Casualties
Brief Circumstances of Accident
Casualty Details (If Applicable)

10-Apr-59 XH264 Vampire T11 28 Sqn Tat Hong Channel Hong Kong 0

Abandoned after engine failure. Flight Lieutenant B A Lewis and Flying Officer P M Dickenson escaped without serious injury.

24-Apr-59 VM308 Anson C19 RAFTC Comms Flt , Roborough 0

The pilot was landing at Roborough which was a small badly marked airfield. After a dummy run, the pilot lined up on the wrong heading (20 degrees out). Due to the rise in the airfield surface the pilot did not realise until too late that he was heading towards a parked ambulance and he swung to port over rough ground coming to rest in a cutting on the boundary. The passenger was slightly injured but the aircraft was a write-off.

27-Apr-59 XF267 Sycamore HR14 194 Sqn 3.5 miles north of Kuala Lumpur 3

Shortly after take off and at a height of about 600 to 800 feet the engine was heard to falter and a rotor blade detached followed by the rotor head. The initial failure is thought to be near the root on the blade trailing edge.

Flight Lieutenant Peter de Burgh DALEY 33 Pilot
Flight Lieutenant Ian William David DRAY Pilot
Squadron Leader John Edwin SCOTT

04-May-59 XF882 Provost T1 RAFC near Londonthorpe Lincolnshire 0

Abandoned after entering uncontrolled spin

05-May-59 TX189 Anson C19 Station Flt RAF Colerne 0

Undercarriage collapsed during landing after the aircraft swung due to over correction. The pilot (instructor) over corrected after the student allowed the aircraft to swing. The check pilot did not have his own brake lever and was reaching across the student. It appears that there was confusion amongst the crew as to precisely who was flying the aircraft!!!

06-May-59 XF996 Hunter F4 229 OCU near RAF Chivenor 0

Whilst approaching to land the pilot, Flying Officer N H J Ferguson, experienced a control restriction and ejected from the aircraft.

11-May-59 WN318Meteor T7 BCCS RAF Benson 0

Aircraft belly landed after the under carriage failed

20-May-59 VV955 Anson T21 CCCF 7 miles west south west of Llandudno 3

En route from RAF Bovingdon to RAF Ballykelly, the aircraft was diverted to RAF Valley to pick up another passenger but nothing further was heard from its crew and it was discovered to have crashed. The cause was the pilot's decision to let down in mountainous country below safety height in IMC conditions and his failure to obtain a fix before descending.

Flight Lieutenant Ernest Alfred HART 36 Pilot
Flying Officer Pran Nath HANDA Navigator
Group Captain John Eley PRESTON AFC : Passenger HQ Coastal Command staff officer

---

25-May-59 WP828 Chipmunk T10 Glasgow UAS 2 miles west of Newburgh Fife 0

Struck water in River Tay whilst in a turn at low level and cartwheeled

29-May-59 TG522 Hastings C1 36 Sqn 1 mile south of Khartoum 5

Shortly after take off the No 2 engine failed and was feathered. Fuel was dumped and the aircraft returned to land but on the finals turn the port wing centre section stalled. The pilot mistook this for a No 1 engine failure and feathered this one as well. The pilot was then compelled to make a forced landing short of the runway and the aircraft crashed and caught fire. Although the flight deck crew lost their lives, the AQM and 25 passengers survived.

Flight Lieutenant Alan Bertram EYRE 32 Pilot Captain
Flying Officer Anthony Lambert MILLARD Co-Pilot
Flight Sergeant Frank Melville JONES Navigator
Master Engineer Mansel ATYEO Flight Engineer
Flight Sergeant Arthur DOBSON Air Signaller

02-Jun-59 WT304 Canberra B6 139 Sqn Near RAF El Adem 3

Whilst on a night target marking exercise the aircraft struck the ground and was destroyed. At the time of impact the aircraft was at a very shallow angle and considerable speed and attempting a pull out. It seems possible that the pilot may have been anxious to remark the target quickly and to have turned into his final attack from an unfavourable position.

Squadron Leader Henry George COUSINS 36 Pilot and Flight Commander
Flying Officer Raymond Peter ROGERS Navigator
Flight Lieutenant David BLACKERY Observer

03-Jun-59 WL481 Meteor T7 RAFFC 6.5 miles south east of RAF Driffield 0

Elevators failed and aircraft abandoned

07-Jun-59 WZ880 Chipmunk T10 Bristol UAS 2.5 east north east of RAF Filton 1

At 5500 feet the pilot demonstrated a stall and at the point of the stall the right wing dropped and the aircraft entered a spin. As it passed through 2500 feet the captain, Flight Lieutenant Alec Shannon, the Air Experience Flight commanding officer, ordered the cadet to abandon the aircraft and then jumped himself. However the cadet did not escape and was killed on impact. The cause was failure to recover from the spin.

Cadet Sergeant Francis DEVONSHIRE 17 Air Training Corps

08-Jun-59 WG217 Balliol T2 School of FC Hurn Airport 0

Undercarriage collapsed whilst landing

12-Jun-59 VV640 Vampire FB5 Ferry Wg In the Bristol Channel near RAF St Athan 1

The aircraft was being flown from Oakington to St Athan and arrived overhead Llandow at 29000 feet when the pilot was advised of the let down aids available and the prevailing weather conditions. The pilot elected to make a controlled descent through cloud to the CRDF beacon because of the amount of cloud and sea fog. All proceeded normally until the pilot reported he was at 2000 feet on the inbound leg when contact was lost and wreckage was subsequently located in the sea off RAF St Athan. No satisfactory explanation for the accident could be found although it is possible that the altimeter was not functioning properly and gave a false reading.

Flying Officer Derek Ashley MANNING 25

16-Jun-59 WH256 Meteor F8 Malta TTS Takali Malta 0

Struck a wall after aborting the take-off run

18-Jun-59 VZ357 Vampire FB5 5 FTS RAF Oakington 0

Brake failure on landing and collided with other aircraft

Date Serial Aircraft Unit Place Casualties
Brief Circumstances of Accident
Casualty Details (If Applicable)

18-Jun-59 WE846 Vampire FB5 5 FTS RAF Oakington 0

Struck by VZ357

18-Jun-59 XD463 Vampire T11 5 FTS RAF Oakington 0

Struck by VZ357

20-Jun-59 XA750 Javelin FAW4 3 Sqn 2 miles north west of Norvenich 2

After a normal take off, the aircraft began a climbing turn to starboard. At about 500 feet it started to roll to port and when inverted the nose dropped, the roll rate reduced and the pilot then appeared to attempt a 'pull through'. The aircraft stalled and spun into the ground. The cause was that the pilot attempted an unauthorised and unrehearsed slow roll and was unable to recover from the inverted position.

Flight Lieutenant Wilfred Smith JACQUES 35 Pilot
Flying Officer David Alexander RITCHIE Navigator

22-Jun-59 WR475 Venom FB4 Ferry Wg RAF Khormaksar 1

On take off for a flight to Eastleigh the starboard side ammunition door came open and the pilot announced that he would return to land immediately. He made a tight starboard turn but because of its high all up weight, the aircraft stalled and the pilot had insufficient height to recover.

Flight Sergeant Andrew Horace SINCLAIR 34

03-Jul-59 TG580 Hastings C1 48 Sqn RAF Gan 0

Undercarriage collapsed on landing

03-Jul-59 WA681 Meteor T7 81 Sqn RAF Tengah 0

Belly landed at night

05-Jul-59 WT331 Canberra B(I)8 88 Sqn RAF Sharjah 0

Struck the water whilst attempting to overshoot in poor weather conditions. The aircraft came to rest in an upright position and the crew were able to evacuate it safely, however, it was beyond repair and struck off charge.

07-Jul-59 XA722 Javelin FAW4 72 Sqn RAF Leconfield 0

Struck off charge because of damage received after engine failure in flight

---

08-Jul-59 WJ649 Canberra B2 231 OCU 1/2 mile north east of RAF Bassingborne 3

After the starboard engine RPM dropped, the pilot shut down the engine and returned to base. On final approach the aircraft yawed to port, the nose lifted and the aircraft rolled to starboard on to its back and then dived into the ground. The primary cause of the accident was the lack of skill by the student pilot in allowing the airspeed to drop below a level which would allow him to retain lateral and directional control. The engine fluctuations were caused by a loose article jamming the rocker lever in a fuel tank.

Flying Officer David John ROGERS 22 Pilot
Pilot Officer Malcolm Joyner MAULE Navigator
Flying Officer John Arend BRINK Observer

09-Jul-59 XH750 Javelin FAW7 33 Sqn 5 miles west of RAF Horsham St Faith 0

Caught fire and abandoned by Flight Lieutenant Jack Buckley and his navigator Sergeant D U Epe, after being struck by lightning

Date Serial Aircraft Unit Place Casualties
Brief Circumstances of Accident
Casualty Details (If Applicable)

09-Jul-59 WV745 Pembroke C1 Stn Flt El Adem RAF Akrotiri 0

Taxied into a ditch when the brakes failed

13-Jul-59 XD955 Swift FR5 79 Sqn RAF Gutersloh 0

Struck off charge as a consequence of damage to the rear fuselage after an hydraulics fire

---

15-Jul-59 WL480 Meteor T7 12 Gp Comms Flt, near RAF Leconfield 1

The aircraft had taken off from RAF Horsham St Faith and was overshooting Leconfield to burn off fuel when it flew along the runway heading at about 100 to 150 feet but at a lower than normal overshoot speed. The aircraft yawed, the nose lifted and it rolled to port on to its back and dived into the ground. The likely cause was the loss of control during a flapless stall with the undercarriage down because the pilot failed to increase power, raised the flaps whilst the undercarriage was still down and did not increase power to maintain flying speed. In late 1942, Embling, at that stage a 29 year old Wing Commander, bailed out of an aircraft over Germany and evaded capture before returning to UK.

Air Vice Marshal John Robert Andre EMBLING CBE DSO 46 Air Officer Commanding No 12 Group

---

17-Jul-59 XD961 Swift FR5 79 Sqn 2 miles east of RAF Gutersloh 0

Flight Lieutenant J H Turner was compelled to abandon the aircraft after engine failure.

20-Jul-59 XD627 Vampire T11 RAFC off Lincolnshire coast 0

Struck off charge from damage received when aircraft struck the sea recovering from a simulated rocket dive attack

30-Jul-59 XH789 Javelin FAW7 64 Sqn RAF Akrotiri 0

Whilst attempting an emergency landing the aircraft overshot the runway and was damaged beyond repair

---

31-Jul-59 XJ766 Whirlwind HAR2 22 Sqn Constantine Bay Cornwall 0

Ditched in the sea after engine failed during an SAR sortie

04-Aug-59 WL142 Meteor F8 APS Sylt off the coast at RAF Sylt 0

Lost its tail unit after a mid-air collision with WK864 and the pilot, Flight Lieutenant R S McCarty, abandoned aircraft

---

05-Aug-59 VM306 Anson T22 A&AEE RAF Boscombe Down 0

Crashed into the undershoot whilst coming in to land

07-Aug-59 XF986 Hunter F4 229 OCU Near Sutton North Devon 0

Aircraft entered a spin during aerobatics and the pilot, Flight Lieutenant A J B Barnetson, ejected after failure to recover

---

20-Aug-59 XH668 Victor B2 A&AEE off Milford Haven 5

The aircraft was on a test flight when it lost the starboard pressure head. This gave incorrect airspeed readings and the aircraft was then allowed to dive and became out of control before breaking up. A massive search was conducted to recover the wreckage of this aircraft from the sea and to identify the cause of the loss.

Squadron Leader Raymond James MORGAN 34 Pilot Captain
Squadron Leader George Breakspear STOCKMAN 29 Co-Pilot

Date Serial Aircraft Unit Place Casualties
Brief Circumstances of Accident
Casualty Details (If Applicable)

Flight Lieutenant Lewis Nicholas WILLIAMS Navigator
Flight Lieutenant Ronald John HANNAFORD Air Electronics Officer
Mr Robert H WILLIAMS Handley Page Flight Test Observer

24-Aug-59 WP982 Chipmunk T10 1 FTS RAF Linton on Ouse 0

Damaged beyond repair after striking a ground support trolley

---

25-Aug-59 XF502 Hunter F6 74 Sqn Cantley Norfolk 1

Having taken off to carry out practice GCAs at Sculthorpe, the pilot of this aircraft formated on XF425 and then collided with it. The cause of the accident was the deliberate disregard of their briefing by both pilots who intended to meet up and undertake aerobatics at night!!!

Flying Officer Peter Roland BUDD 25

25-Aug-59 XF425 Hunter F6 74 Sqn Cantley Norfolk 0

Mid air collision with XF502, Flight Lieutenant Peter R Rayner 25 the squadron adjutant, ejected safely.

26-Aug-59 WT540 Canberra PR7 13 Sqn RAF Akrotiri 0

Made a belly landing after an engine was shut down and the aircraft yawed on the final approach

---

27-Aug-59 WN124Swift FR5 2 Sqn 5 miles west of Rinteln 0

Abandoned after the engine failed. Flight Lieutenant R Rimington, on his 28th birthday, ejected!!!!

01-Sep-59 XH775 Javelin FAW7 23 Sqn Brundall Norfolk 0

Mid air collision at night with XH781 and abandoned by Flight Lieutenant F H B Stark and Flying Officer P Baigent.

01-Sep-59 XH781 Javelin FAW7 23 Sqn Brundall Norfolk 2

During practice interceptions at night and at a height of 40000 feet, this aircraft was following XH775 when they began a return to base. Height and speed were gradually reduced by use of airbrakes and reduced engine power and at about 26000 feet this aircraft flew into the rear of the other.

Flight Lieutenant Christopher Stamp Tulloch Constable BROOKSBANK 29 Pilot
Sergeant Graham Anthony John SPRIGGS Navigator

07-Sep-59 WR400 Venom FB4 208 Sqn Eastleigh Kenya 0

Ran into a ditch after the brakes failed whilst taxying

08-Sep-59 WT335 Canberra B(I)8 88 Sqn Hochneukirch 2

The aircraft had completed its sortie and was returning to base at about 1000 feet. It entered a port turn normally but this steepened to a high angle of bank during which the aircraft lost about 400 feet. It levelled out but then rolled onto its back and dived into the ground. The cause was not positively determined but three spanners were found in the wreckage which suggests the possibility of a loose article jamming the controls or throttles.

Flying Officer David Norman MAY 22 Pilot
Flying Officer Clive Aubrey DEAKIN Navigator

09-Sep-59 XE648 Hunter F6 56 Sqn RAF Nicosia 0

Ran into a fence after overshooting a landing

Date Serial Aircraft Unit Place Casualties
Brief Circumstances of Accident
Casualty Details (If Applicable)

11-Sep-59 XD869 Valiant B1 214 Sqn 3 miles north east of RAF Marham 6

Just under 3 miles from the end of the runway the aircraft struck the ground after taking off at night en route to Nairobi. Although not determined it is thought likely that the accident was caused by a Tail Plane Incidence reversal. After take off the pilot would have selected nose down trim to compensate for the retraction of the flaps but the pilot's TPI selector switch operated in the reverse direction making him think that he had runaway trim. The emergency drill would have been to reduce power and move the control column forward. With the pilot disoriented on a dark night and realising the proximity of the ground he would have called for power and pulled back on the stick but not soon enough to prevent the aircraft striking the ground in a tail down attitude. It was considered that the relatively inexperienced crew should not have taken off on such a night with a very heavy aircraft and that the aircraft had not been air tested despite being in maintenance for the previous 3 weeks.

Flight Lieutenant Thomas Cledwyn WATKINS 28 Pilot Captain
Flying Officer Peter Edward WORMALL 22 Co-Pilot
Flight Lieutenant Donald HOWARD Navigator Radar
Flight Lieutenant Murray Frederick HYSLOP Navigator Plotter
Flying Officer Christopher CANDY Air Electronics Operator
Chief Technician Robert Vernon SEWELL Crew Chief

14-Sep-59 WH982Canberra B6 9 Sqn 1.25 miles south south west of Idris 0

Both engines failed and the aircraft was seriously damaged in a forced landing

---

17-Sep-59 XE307 Sycamore HR14 103 Sqn Tymbou Cyprus 0

Rotors struck the ground after the engine had cut out in the hover and the aircraft rolled over

---

23-Sep-59 WJ514 Anson T21 Stn Flt Binbrook RAF Leeming 0

Tailwheel failed on landing

24-Sep-59 XF884 Provost T1 RAFC RAF Barkston Heath 0

Undercarriage collapsed after a swing on landing got out of control

---

26-Sep-59 VM322 Anson C19 Stn Flt North Coates RAF Jurby Isle of Man 0

Following a tyre burst during the take off, the aircraft swung and suffered severe structural damage

---

29-Sep-59 XA662 Javelin FAW5 228 OCU 30 miles west of RAF Leeming 0

The crew, Flying Officer C P Cowper and Captain R E Nietz, abandoned the aircraft after it became impossible to restart a failed engine

---

02-Oct-59 WF835 Meteor T7 5 FTS 1 mile east north east of RAF Oakington 1

The pupil pilot pulled out of a loop at high level and was climbing at about 0.6 Mach when the aircraft flicked into a spin and began to descend rapidly, spinning to the right. As the pupil could not recover the pilot took control and attempted recovery but was unsuccessful and so called for the aircraft to be abandoned as it approached the cloud tops. Although the pilot, Flying Officer D Skinner 37, landed safely, the student did not open his parachute. The cause could not be determined although the pilot might have suffered the effects of anoxia and not taken the correct recovery action.

Pilot Officer Paul SALTMARSH Student Pilot

04-Oct-59 WR421 Venom FB4 60 Sqn RAF Tengah 0

Belly landed after undercarriage became jammed

Date Serial Aircraft Unit Place Casualties
Brief Circumstances of Accident
Casualty Details (If Applicable)

06-Oct-59 WV566 Provost T1 1 FTS 0

Mid air collision with WV578

06-Oct-59 WV578 Provost T1 1 FTS 0

Mid air collision with WV566

14-Oct-59 XH720 Javelin FAW7 33 Sqn RAF Nicosia 0

Undercarriage collapsed after a swing on landing

15-Oct-59 XE897 Vampire T11 5 FTS 5 miles west of RAF Oakington 0

Damaged beyond repair following a mid air collison with WZ495

15-Oct-59 WZ495 Vampire T11 5 FTS 5 miles west of RAF Oakington 1

Collided with XE897 and dived into the ground. It seems possible that the collision was caused because of some confusion about the arrangements for changing formation.

Flight Sergeant Henry Walter GIBSON AFM 35

23-Oct-59 XG561 Pioneer CC1 209 Sqn Near Ipoh Malaya 2

The aircraft took off in heavy rain and turned left rather than right, probably to avoid a storm approaching. The aircraft levelled out and then almost immediately climbed steeply away. The starboard wing struck a wire stay attached to a radio mast and the wing was torn off. The aircarft rolled twice and crashed to the ground. The cause was that the pilot, in his hurry to get airborne and avoid the storm, forgot about the presence of the radio masts and when advised of their position by ATC was too close to avoid them. In addition, the pilot was not wearing his corrective spectacles.

Flight Lieutenant Albert Elliott JOHNSON 42 Pilot
Senior Aircraftman James William Motton DOUGLAS

26-Oct-59 WK304 Swift FR5 2 Sqn 4 miles east south east of RAF Jever 0

Abandoned after power decayed during GCA approach. Flight Lieutenant A Martin was rescued without serious injury after ejecting.

29-Oct-59 WE377 Venom FB1 28 Sqn RAF Kai Tak Hong Kong 0

Crashed into the sea after overshooting a flapless landing when the brakes failed

---

01-Nov-59 WZ870 Chipmink T10 Stn Flt Duxford RAF Duxford 0

Struck runway lights whilst taking off and then tipped over during the subsequent forced landing

---

10-Nov-59 XF953 Hunter F4 RAFFC 0

Damaged beyond repair after a severe bird strike

11-Nov-59 XJ641 Hunter F6 93 Sqn off the Friesian Islands 1

The pilot took off despite poor RT reception and had frequent problems in flight with radio communications. Despite being given numerous calls by RT at various stages, the pilot lost all communications and the aircraft disappeared and was never found.

Flying Officer Roger Moncrieff WEST 22

17-Nov-59 WA413 Vampire FB5 3 CAACU 0

Damaged beyond repair

Date Serial Aircraft Unit Place Casualties
Brief Circumstances of Accident
Casualty Details (If Applicable)

18-Nov-59 WL424 Meteor T7 APS Sylt 2 miles south east of Grinsted Denmark 1

En route from RAF Wildenrath to Sylt the aircraft suffered an RT failure but the pilot, Flight Lieutenant C Hyam 25, pressed on. The passenger was told that the hood would be jettisoned if there was a need to bale out and so when this was done in preparation for a forced landing, he abandoned the aircraft at only 250 feet.

Flight Lieutenant Christopher Hugh Francis D'ALBIAC Passenger

---

28-Nov-59 WH699 Canberra B2 RAFFC 2 miles west south west of RAF Strubby 1

The canopy misted over after take off and the pilot went on to instruments. However, he experienced a serious nose up attitude change because of the failure of a balance weight and the crew ejected when they realised the proximity of the ground. It seems likely the navigator was incapacitated and could not release himself from his seat. Squadron Leader P M Walker AFC 37 and Wing Commander C E W Ness survived. Ness subsequently became the first navigator to serve on the Air Force Board and retired after a tour as Air Member for Personnel. The aircraft was named 'Aries IV' and was one of several aircraft to bear the Aries marking. A gate guardian at RAF College Cranwell painted to represent this aircraft is in fact WJ637.

Wing Commander Frank Geoffrey WOOLLEY DFC AFC Navigator

04-Dec-59 WJ481 Valetta T3 RAFC RAF Barkston Heath 1

Ground crew walked into propeller of aircraft which was undamaged. The crew of 5, captained by Flight Lieutenant J Davidson 36, were uninjured.

Leading Aircraftman Ernest John CREASEY

18-Dec-59 XL828 Sycamore HR14 SAR Flt 23 miles north north east of Aden 0

Destroyed by ground resonance

30-Dec-59 XE830 Vampire T11 1 FTS 1.5 miles south west of RAF Linton on Ouse 1

At the end of a sortie of circuits and roller landings the aircraft was at about 300 feet when it ceased to climb and entered a left hand diving turn from which it did not recover. There was some evidence that the pilot had experienced problems with his instrument flying and had admitted to being disorientated in formation and when flying solo.

Lieutenant M H ATKINS 22 Royal Navy

05-Jan-60 WV537 Provost T1 6FTS High Ercall 0

Hit by XF905 whilst Taxying

08-Jan-60 XJ675 Hunter F6 93 Sqn Near Aurich West Germany 0

Abandoned after engine fire. The pilot, Squadron Leader D S White, landed safely.

11-Jan-60 VW472 Meteor T7 RAF College RAF Cranwell 0

Bellylanded after jammed undercarriage

19-Jan-60 WV664 Provost T1 1FTS Pocklington Yorks 1

Dived from cloud into the ground. Although not positively determined, it is possible that the pilot was disorientated.

Midshipman A L VARNEY 19 Royal Navy

20-Jan-60 XJ728 Whirlwind HAR2 22 Sqn off Padstow Cornwell 0

Spun into sea after tail rotor control cable broke

Date Serial Aircraft Unit Place Casualties
Brief Circumstances of Accident
Casualty Details (If Applicable)

21-Jan-60 WF926 Canberra PR3 39 Sqn 19miles East North East of RAF Luqa 2

During continuation training the pilot overshot and climbed to height in order to carry out a let down with GCA pickup. On turning starboard he stated he would fly asymetric for practice. The outbound leg was completed successfully and the pilot confirmed that he was turning on the inbound leg as instructed. Nothing further was heard from the aircraft and wreckage was subsequently found at the approximate position the aircraft would have turned in bound. The Board of Enquiry believed that the pilot had misread his altimeter on the outbound leg and that his subsequent actions were based on this incorrect height reading.

Flying Officer Brian James MCGEE 23 Pilot
Flight Lieutenant Aubrey Richard HUDSON 29 Navigator

02-Feb-60 XD520 Vampire T11 8FTS RAF Swinderby Approach 0

Struck ground whilst descending and subsequently struck off charge

---

04-Feb-60 XM377 Jet Provost T3 2FTS RAF Syerston 0

Instrument failure and subsequent crash landing on grass

05-Feb-60 WK298 Swift FR5 79 Sqn Fallingbostel West Germany 0

Engine ran down on low level cross country and aircraft abandoned by Flight Lieutenant E J E Smith

---

15-Feb-60 VP535 Anson C19 Station Flt RAF Gutersloh 0

Undercarriage collapsed whilst taxying and aircraft not repaired

16-Feb-60 WT334 Canberra B(I)8 16 Sqn Nordhorn Range 2

The aircraft carried out two dummy bombing attacks on the Nordhorn Range followed by a LABS manoeuvre. The aircraft was seen to pull up into a climb into cloud and then re-emerged on a reciprocal heading in a starboard turn and flew on for about one mile in a gentle descent until it flew into the ground. The most probable cause was that the pilot became disorientated in cloud and in weather conditions which were more turbulent than expected.

Flying Officer Michael James WATTS 22 Pilot
Flight Lieutenant Graham George BYFORD Navigator

01-Mar-60 TG579 Hastings C1 48 Sqn 1.5 Miles off RAF Gan Maldive Islands 0

Crashed into the sea on approach after pilot blinded by lightning

---

01-Mar-60 WR504 Venom FB4 208 Sqn Eastleigh Kenya 0

Hit a tree whilst recovering from a dive and found beyond economic repairon return to base

---

04-Mar-60 VW423 Meteor T7 13 Gp Comms RAF Ouston 0

Structural damage in flight and not repaired

05-Mar-60 XG334 Lightning F1 AFDS Wells Next The Sea Norfolk 0

The pilot, Squadron Leader R Harding, abandoned the aircraft after the undercarriage failed to lower.

07-Mar-60 XD969 Swift FR5 79 Sqn RAF Gutersloh 0

Engine flamed out and aircraft was abandoned on approach by Flight Lieutenant J E Nevill.

Date	Serial	Aircraft	Unit	Place	Casualties
Brief Circumstances of Accident					
Casualty Details (If Applicable)					
08-Mar-60	XM385	Jet Provost T3	2FTS	RAF Syerston	0
Engine failed during an overshoot and aircraft crashed into undershoot.					
09-Mar-60	XH988	Javelin FAW8	41 Sqn	Dalston Cumberland	0
Electrical failure led to aircraft being abandoned when unable to find airfield.					
09-Mar-60	XM941	Twin Pioneer CC1	209 Sqn	West of Patoh Malaya	0
Double engine failure, aircraft tipped over during forced landing					
11-Mar-60	XG520	Sycamore HR14	CFS (H)	RAF South Cerney	0
Ground resonance developed on landing and aircraft rolled over. The only satisfactory way to deal with this condition was to lift off again otherwise the aircraft would, literally, shake itself to pieces.					
29-Mar-60	XF424	Hunter FGA9	8 Sqn	Sharjah United Arab Emirates	0
Severely damaged by bird strike and declared beyond repair					
08-Apr-60	XA640	Javelin FAW4	3 Sqn	RAF Geilenkirchen West Germany	0
Overshot into a wood after the nosewheel jammed on landing					
09-Apr-60	XF434	Hunter F6	43 Sqn	South south east of RAF Nicosia	0
Engine flamed out and pilot ejected. This pilot, Flying Officer John Cleaver, was killed subsequently in another Hunter aircraft accident.					

29-Apr-60 XL555 Pioneer CC1 230 Sqn RAF Upavon 0

Stalled whilst taking off and dived into the ground

30-Apr-60 WP774 Chipmunk T10 Hull UAS Brough 2

Shortly after take off the instructor called that he was to practice an engine failure and the aircraft was seen to glide and then enter a right hand turn which steepened and tightened into a spin. The aircraft did not recover and struck a shed killing both crew. The probable cause was that the student misused the controls and the instructor failed to take control soon enough.

Squadron Leader Peter Norman BOYLE 38 Pilot
Officer Cadet Neil Fred CLAVERDON 21 Student Pilot

07-May-60 WA445Vampire FB5 CAACU Weston Zoyland Somerset 0

Struck off charge following extensive bird strike damage

10-May-60 WT321 Canberra B(I)6 213 Sqn Varrelbusch West Germany 3

The aircraft was seen to pull up into cloud as if to loop and a minute later it was seen in a steep descent and crashed. It seems possible that the pilot who was inexperienced in the LABS role may have expected to recover in clear air above the clouds but on finding himself still in clouds and on reverting to instruments, may have become disorientated and tried to pull through the bottom of the loop instead of rolling out.

Flight Lieutenant Peter Legge CROSSLEY 35 Pilot
Flight Lieutenant John Frederick William KEATY Navigator
Flying Officer Frederick Eugene BRIGGS Navigator

17-May-60 XE612 Hunter F6 74 Sqn RAF Horsham St Faith 0

Power lost on take off and aircraft overshot and destroyed by fire

Date Serial Aircraft Unit Place Casualties
Brief Circumstances of Accident
Casualty Details (If Applicable)

21-May-60 XA823 Javelin FAW6 29 Sqn North East of Scarborough 0

Mid air collision with Javelin XA835 of the same squadron. abandoned over sea by the crew of Flight Lieutenants D J Wyborn and J S Wilson.

21-May-60 XA835 Javelin FAW6 29 Sqn North West of Hartlepool 0

Collided with XA823 and abandoned by crew over the coast. Flying Officer E Wood and Flight Lieutenant D J S Clark ejected safely.

30-May-60 XF507 Hunter F6 65 Sqn Thrapston Northants 1

During air combat manouvering at about 20000 feet the aircraft was following another in a steep dive. When told to pull out there was no acknowledgement and the aircraft was not seen again The pilot made no attempt to eject and made no radio calls and it is thought that he may have been incapacitated, perhaps with a reduced 'g' tolerance because he had not eaten any breakfast.

Flight Lieutenant Gerald Brumhead THORNALLEY 26 Pilot

31-May-60 XF901 Provost T1 RAF College 2 Miles North East of RAF Spitalgate 1

Engine failed after overspeed and pilot crashed during forced landing

Flight Cadet Peter Robin TOMES 20 Pilot

01-Jun-60 VV298 Anson T21 Bomber Command Comms Sqn RAF Northolt 0

Crashed into a dairy after engine failed on take off

01-Jun-60 XL615 Hunter T7 8 Sqn 13.5miles From RAF Khormasksar 2

About 15 minutes into the sortie the aircraft was at 20000 feet and began to let down for a controlled descent. It completed a final turn on to the outbound heading after which RT contact was lost. The aircraft struck ground in a shallow dive. The Board of Enquiry was unable to establish the cause of the accident but it may have been that one pilot was paying too much attention to heading and insufficient to height and the other may have been inattentive.

Flight Lieutenant Colin David George DEVINE 31
Flying Officer Michael John WALLEY 23

10-Jun-60 XE883 Vampire T11 8FTS RAF Swinderby 1

Lost power after take off and crashed into rising ground

Pilot Officer David Edward PEARCE 24

10-Jun-60 XG193 Hunter F6 111 Sqn Near RAF Wattisham 1

Mid air collision with another Hunter of the same squadron. The two aircraft involved were part of a nine aircraft formation making a downward break at the end of an air display sequence. Shortly after the break they passed through cloud at about 2000 feet and on emerging they collided. Although the pilot initiated ejection the sequence did not complete.

Flight Lieutenant Stanley Wentworth WOOD 26

16-Jun-60 XK626 Vampire T11 RAF College 2 Miles West of RAF Cranwell 0

Skidded onto a road after engine failed on take off.

17-Jun-60 VW803 Valetta C1 84 Sqn Mukerias Aden Protectorate 0

Overshot runway after brakes failed on landing and undercarriage collapsed.

Date Serial Aircraft Unit Place Casualties
Brief Circumstances of Accident
Casualty Details (If Applicable)

17-Jun-60 XM382 Jet Provost T3 2FTS Near Melton Mobray 0

Abandoned by the student pilot, Acting Pilot Officer O M J Kendrick after uncontrolled spin developed.

23-Jun-60 XD913 Swift FR5 79 Sqn RAF Gutersloh 0

Damaged beyond repair after nose wheel failed to lower and the aircraft made a forced landing.

29-Jun-60 XA706 Javelin FAW5 228OCU RAF Leeming 0

Forced landed after electrical failure and not repaired

29-Jun-60 WK299 Swift FR5 2 Sqn RAF Jever 0

Undercarriage did not lower properly and aircraft landed on two wheels, swung off the runway and damaged beyond repair

---

01-Jul-60 WG473 Chipmunk T10 London UAS RN Air Station Brawdy (UAS Camp) 0

Struck an electrical supply point whilst taxiing and damaged beyond repair

---

07-Jul-60 XD549 Vampire T11 5FTS 7 Miles South West of RAF Oakington 2

Collided with Varsity WJ914 and dived into the ground

Flying Officer Albert John LAKEMAN
Pilot Officer Joseph Jarvis BALL

07-Jul-60 WJ914 Varsity T1 RAF College 4 Miles South south west of Oakington 6

Collided with Vampire XD549 and dived into ground

Flight Lieutenant Zenon Waclaw KAYE Captain
Flight Lieutenant William Henry JACKSON Co-Pilot
Flight Lieutenant Malcolm Beauchamp WHITE Navigator
Flight Sergeant Walter Leslie HANNANT Air Signaller
Flying Officer Lewis Stanley Roy UTTON Engineer
Flight Lieutenant Brian WALKER

12-Jul-60 WP895 Chipmunk T10 Southampton UAS, Hamble 0

Damaged beyond repair after sinking heavily into the ground whilst landing

---

14-Jul-60 XE827 Vampire T11 8FTS RAF Swinderby 0

Damaged In Forced Landing After Engine Failure And Control Restrictions

---

19-Jul-60 XH617 Victor B1A 57 Sqn 3 Miles South East of Diss Norfolk 3

Abandoned on fire after alternator drive failed and penetrated fuel tank. The Captain, Flight Lieutenant J Mudford and the Air Electronics Operator, Flying Officer G C Stewart, survived the accident

Flying Officer Michael John WILKES Co-Pilot
Flight Lieutenant John Bernard Paul WILDING Navigator (Radar)
Flight Lieutenant Rodney Syd BRISTOW Navigator (Plotter)

19-Jul-60 WP836 Chipmunk T10 3AEF Weston-Super-Mare 0

Struck by civilian Miles Messenger aircraft G-AKBM whilst parked

Date	Serial	Aircraft	Unit	Place	Casualties
20-Jul-60	WD305	Chipmunk T10	Cambridge UAS	RAF Martlesham Heath	0
24-Jul-60	XL699	Pioneer CC1	209 Sqn	Bareo Sarawak	0
27-Jul-60	XJ761	Whirlwind HAR4	228 Sqn	off Great Yarmouth	0
04-Aug-60	WZ472	Vampire T11	5FTS	1.5 Miles from RAF Wattisham	1
09-Aug-60	XL557	Pioneer CC1	230 Sqn	Watchfield	0
12-Aug-60	XD864	Valiant BK1	7 Sqn	Spanhoe Airfield Lincolnshire	5

Brief Circumstances of Accident

Casualty Details (If Applicable)

20-Jul-60 WD305 Chipmunk T10 Cambridge UAS RAF Martlesham Heath 0

Damaged beyond repair after taxing over an obstruction

24-Jul-60 XL699 Pioneer CC1 209 Sqn Bareo Sarawak 0

Sank back onto ground after take off and overturned

27-Jul-60 XJ761 Whirlwind HAR4 228 Sqn off Great Yarmouth 0

Engine ran down and aircraft crashed into the sea and sank

04-Aug-60 WZ472 Vampire T11 5FTS 1.5 Miles from RAF Wattisham 1

Abandoned in uncontrolled spin. Although the student pilot, Flying Officer E J Shere aged 21 survived the instructor did not. (Flight Lieutenant Garwood should not be confused by another of the same name who was a very distinguished rotary wing pilot of the 1950s and 60s).

Flight Lieutenant Roy Edward GARWOOD 27 QFI

09-Aug-60 XL557 Pioneer CC1 230 Sqn Watchfield 0

Wing dropped after being struck by a heavy wind gust and the undercarriage broke

12-Aug-60 XD864 Valiant BK1 7 Sqn Spanhoe Airfield Lincolnshire 5

Stalled and crashed shortly after take off.

Flight Lieutenant Brian John WICKHAM 38 Captain
Flight Lieutenant William Russell HOWARD 29 Co-Pilot

Flight Lieutenant Henry George BULLEN 40 Navigator (Plotter)
Flight Lieutenant Arthur John IRESON 30 Navigator (Radar)
Sergeant Roy Harvey JOHNSON 26 Air Electronics Operator

15-Aug-60 WP865 Chipmunk T10 Oxford UAS Milcombe Oxfordshire 0

Spun into the ground

15-Aug-60 XF614 Provost T1 CFS RAF Little Rissington 0

Overshot on landing and nosed over

16-Aug-60 WZ587 Vampire T11 5FTS 6 Miles North West of Methwold 0

Abandoned in a spin when recovery could not be effected. Pilot Officer V Faulkner and Flying Officer F W Mitchell ejected safely.

26-Aug-60 XG560 Pioneer CC1 209 Sqn Rengah Malaya 0

Hit trees during forced landing after engine lost power

05-Sep-60 VZ521 Meteor F8 5 CAACU RAF Woodvale 0

Swung off the runway after tyre burst taking off

14-Sep-60 XG538 Sycamore HR14 110 Sqn Na Plang Thailand 0

Rolled over whilst lifting off and rotors struck the ground

20-Sep-60 XH838 Javelin FAW7 33 Sqn RAF Middleton St George 0

Undercarriage leg collapsed after tyre burst on take off

Date Serial Aircraft Unit Place Casualties
Brief Circumstances of Accident
Casualty Details (If Applicable)

26-Sep-60 WH169 Meteor T7 RAF Flying College, RAF Cranwell 0

Ran off the runway whilst carrying out a single engine overshoot

---

03-Oct-60 XJ693 Hunter F6 20 Sqn RAF Gutersloh 0

Aircraft belly landed after undercarriage jammed up

04-Oct-60 XJ450 Pioneer CC1 209 Sqn Fort Kemar Malaya 0

Tipped over after being struck by a squall whilst landing

11-Oct-60 XL151 Beverley C1 84 Sqn 15 Miles North East of RAF Khormaksar 7

The aircraft was diverted to take part in a search for a missing C45 believed en-route to Aden. The pilot was briefed to fly initially at 300 feet and later at 500 feet and he subsequently flew into rising ground at 570 feet.

Flight Lieutenant Ronald Ernest EVANS Captain
Flying Officer Anthony Richard WEST Co-Pilot
Flying Officer Michael Frederick PIKE Navigator
Flight Sergeant John Smith BAIRD Air Signaller
Senior Aircraftman Keith Wreford BAGULEY
Senior Aircraftman Eric Walter GABLE
Leading Aircraftman James HENTHORN

17-Oct-60 WD415 Anson T19 229 OCU RAF St Athan 0

Undercarriage selected up instead of flap!!!!

24-Oct-60 WT504 Canberra PR7 58 Sqn 11.5 Miles North North East of RAF Wyton 0

Abandoned after false fire warning with the crew of Flight Lieutenant J P Wighton and Flying Officer R G Braithwaite escaping successfully.

24-Oct-60 XE953 Vampire T11 8FTS RAF Swinderby 0

Undercarriage raised to stop the aircraft after overshooting with fire warnings

---

25-Oct-60 WZ417 Vampire T11 RAF College 2.5 Miles North of RAF Scampton 0

Abandoned after engine flamed out above cloud. The instructor, Flight Lieutenant John Badham and his pupil, Flight Cadet P J Headley ejected safely. Badham was subsequently a very well regarded helicopter pilot who served as a flight commander with 103 Squadron during the Indonesian Confrontation later in the decade.

26-Oct-60 XN463 Jet Provost T3 A&AEE Teffont Evias Wiltshire 0

Crash landed into trees after engine lost power

27-Oct-60 XA754 Javelin FAW4 72 Sqn RAF Leconfield 0

Jet pipe split during engine run up and severely damaged by heat build up

---

09-Nov-60 XE590 Hunter F6 4 Sqn Near RAF Jever 0

Damaged beyond repair after bird strike in flight

11-Nov-60 WF766 Meteor T7 A&AEE 3 Miles North West of Lyme Regis Dorset 1

Date Serial Aircraft Unit Place Casualties
Brief Circumstances of Accident
Casualty Details (If Applicable)

Broke up in the air

Flight Lieutenant John Stewart DUNCAN AFC 32

17-Nov-60 WK278 Swift FR5 79 Sqn Near RAF Gutersloh 0

Struck off charge after colliding with trees in poor visibility

---

21-Nov-60 XA825 Javelin FAW6 29 Sqn Bowbeet Hill 4 Miles North East Peebles 2

Flew into side of a hill whilst descending in cloud

Flight Lieutenant Victor Leslie HILL 30 Pilot
Flight Lieutenant John Michael KNIGHT Navigator

24-Nov-60 WJ759 Canberra B6 9 Sqn Tarhuna Libya 3

During LABS manoeuvre the aircraft pulled up into cloud and was then seen in a very steep dive into the ground. It is probable that the pilot became disorientated in cloud and attempted to pull through instead of rolling out.

Flying Officer John Malcolm PRATLEY 25 Pilot
Flying Officer William Angus SCOTT Navigator
Sergeant Clive Ernest SMITH Navigator

07-Dec-60 XG511 Sycamore HR14 103 Sqn off Famagusta Cyprus 0

Rotor struck the mast of a ship during a rescue sortie and aircraft crashed

16-Dec-60 XM138 Lightning F1 AFDS RAF Coltishall 0

Caught fire after landing when fire bottle exploded causing fuel leak. The pilot; Flight Lieutenant Eric Hopkins was unhurt.

09-Jan-61 XD431 Vampire T11 5FTS 18m North of Scunthorpe 0

Abandoned on fire

13-Jan-61 XG128 Hunter FGA9 8 Sqn Wadi Yahar Aden 1

Flew into rising ground in a wadi

Flight Lieutenant Leslie Ronald Gerald SWAIN 33

23-Jan-61 WJ342 Hastings C2 36 Sqn Eastleigh Kenya 0

Engine failure on take off, swung onto grass and undercarriage collapsed

---

23-Jan-61 XE593 Hunter F6 65 Sqn Duxford 0

Engine explosion on start up

23-Jan-61 XE882 Vampire T11 1FTS Aysgarth Yorkshire 0

An uncontrolled spin led the instructor, Flight Lieutenant G Richards and his student, Lieutenant M J M Wilkin RN to eject.

01-Feb-61 XN460 Jet Provost T3 2FTS Castle Bytham Lincs 0

Abandoned in spin by the student pilot, Pilot Officer I F Mitchenson

Date Serial Aircraft Unit Place Casualties
Brief Circumstances of Accident
Casualty Details (If Applicable)

07-Feb-61 XF893 Provost T1 6FTS Great Witley Worcestershire 1

Control lost and dived into ground at night

Sub Lieutenant A ABBAS MASRY Lebanese Air Force

20-Feb-61 VI312 Anson C19 Tech Trg Comman Comms Flt N Barrule Isle of Man 6

Crashed into hill whilst flying in cloud. At this time it was possible for aircrew undertaking ground appointments to fly 'communications' type aircraft providing they were judged to be in current flying practice

Wing Commander John Leonard ARON MBE Pilot
Squadron Leader Charles HESELTINE MBE
Flight Lieutenant Humphrey David FURNESS
Flight Lieutenant Bryan Heaton MILLER
Master Technician Eric Newton ROBINSON
Flight Sergeant Russell James BRIDGEMAN

01-Mar-61 XA904 Vulcan B1A 44 Sqn RAF Waddington 0

Power controls failed and aircraft landed on grass where undercarriage collapsed

---

02-Mar-61 XE604 Hunter FGA9 1 Sqn Cowden Range 1

Stalled recovering from dive and crashed into ground

Flying Officer Barrie John DIMMOCK 22

02-Mar-61 XA752 Javelin FAW4 72 Sqn RAF Leeming 0

Barrier raised in error and aircraft struck it after which undercarriage failed on landing

---

02-Mar-61 XL966 Twin Pioneer CC1 21 Sqn Mount Meru Tanganyika 1

Flew into rising ground whilst dropping supplies. Although the navigator was killed the others on board survived.

Flight Lieutenant Ronald Albert NORTON-CRAIG 36 Navigator

08-Mar-61 XE602 Hunter F6 229 OCU RAF Chivenor 0

Throttle jammed open and aircraft overshot into the barrier

16-Mar-61 WK295 Swift FR5 2 Sqn In Flight 0

Damaged by bird strike and written off

20-Mar-61 XE322 Sycamore HR14 110 Sqn Malaya 0

Failed to take off from clearing and sank back into a jungle river

---

22-Mar-61 WD144 Lincoln B2 23MU South East of RAF Aldergrove 0

During a three-engineed approach, the aircraft lost height and crashed into trees. This was the last Lincoln to be lost in RAF service as the type was at the end of its days.

23-Mar-61 XM347 Jet Provost T3 2FTS Near Wragby Lincs 0

The student pilot, Pilot Officer J B Fardell abandoned the aircraft after the engine failed.

Date Serial Aircraft Unit Place Casualties
Brief Circumstances of Accident
Casualty Details (If Applicable)

24-Mar-61 WZ513 Vampire T11 8FTS 4 Miles South of RAF Binbrook 0

Mid air collision with XE944. Squadron Leader L A Boyer ejected safely

---

24-Mar-61 XE944 Vampire T11 8FTS 4 Miles South of RAF Binbrook 1

Mid air collision with WZ513

Flight Lieutenant Maurice Thomas CHAPMAN 27

28-Mar-61 XM477 Jet Provost T3 1FTS 2 Miles South of RAF Dishforth 0

Abandoned on fire in the air. The crew, comprising the instructor Flying Officer A F Marshall and a Royal Navy student, Midshipman M Dugan

---

04-Apr-61 XG522 Sycamore HR14 110 Sqn 0524N 1030E Cameron Highlands Malay 0

Sank back after take off and rolled over. The power margin in a Sycamore when 'hot and high' was non-existant and vertical take offs needed to be very finely judged and a transition to forward flight completed as soon as practical but CAREFULLY!!!.

12-Apr-61 XA813 Javelin FAW2 46 Sqn RAF Waterbeach 0

Jet pipe fracture caused irreparable heat damage

19-Apr-61 XD507 Vampire T11 5 CAACU Exeter 0

Lost drop tank during dive and subsequent stresses left aircraft beyond repair

---

24-Apr-61 XD584 Vampire T11 4FTS Wanddeusant Anglesey 0

Abandoned in a spin. Flight Lieutenant Winspear and his student Pilot Officer Greenland ejected safely.

02-May-61 XA803 Javelin Circumstances of loss not known

04-May-61 XG238 Hunter F6 92 Sqn 2m off Pomos Point Cyprus 1

Abandoned after fire warning but pilot did not survive. Cleaver ejected from Hunter XF434 in April 1960.

Flight Lieutenant John CLEAVER 24

04-May-61 XH692 Javelin FAW5 228 OCU RAF Leeming 0

Caught fire on landing and not repaired

05-May-61 XM469 Jet Provost T3 1FTS 5miles Nort north east of York 0

Abandoned in a spin. Flight Lieutenant W A Langworthy and Midshipman C A Skillett RN survived. Bill Langworthy appears to have ejected on a number of occasions during his career. He is the brother of Squadron Leader Richard Ulrich Langworthy who was awarded the DFC for his efforts as a Chinook pilot in the Falklands conflict and who subsequently died of natural causes whilst serving in the islands post the conflict.

15-May-61 XG188 Hunter F6 19 Sqn Thixendale Yorkshire 0

Abandoned in a spin by Flying Officer P A Bacon.

26-May-61 WV737 Pembroke C1 18 Gp Comms Flt South West of North Berwick Lothian 0

Engine fire on take off from east fortune; crashed in a field.

29-May-61 WD497 Hastings C2 48 Sqn RAF Seletar Singapore 13

The aircraft had completed one pass of a supply dropping detail over Seletar airfield. As it turned to make another pass it was seen to lose height and to crash port wing low. The No 2 engine was stopped and the propeller was feathered. but the other three were operating normally. The most likely cause of the crash was the failure of the No 2 engine and the loss of control under asymetric conditions.

Flight Lieutenant Anthony LYNE 36 Pilot Captain
Flight Lieutenant George Ernest HICKMAN 28 Co-Pilot
Flight Lieutenant Peter George TARLING 29 Navigator
Sergeant John Anthony WELLS 40 Flight Engineer
Sergeant John Joseph McCONNELL 31 Air Signaller
Corporal George P BARNARD 22 Royal Army Service Corps Air Despatchers
Corporal Albert C HOWITT 38
Lance Corporal Harry W SMITH 26
Driver David WROE 19
Driver Anthony C KING 21
Driver Anthony D J BOX 26
Driver Frank E SMITH 24
Driver David M TENNANT 22

01-Jun-61 XJ765 Whirlwind HAR2 225 Sqn 1/2 Mile South of RAF Upavon 2

Control rod broke and control lost. Merrifield was a distinguished wartime Mosquito pilot who had subsequently commanded 684 Squadron in the Far East. He had also served with distinction in Korea.

Flying Officer Barrie Milton Lodge ARMITAGE 36 Pilot & QHI
Group Captain John Roy Hugh MERRIFIELD DSO DFC AFC 46 Pilot

16-Jun-61 XL664 Pioneer CC1 A&AEE 6m West north west of Kidderminster 0
Engine failed and aircraft overshot into a wood during forced landing

---

28-Jun-61 XM185 Lightning F1A 111 Sqn 1m North of Lavenham 0
Abandoned after undercarriage and airbrakes jammed and Flying Officer Pete Ginger was forced to eject.

29-Jun-61 XE848 Vampire T11 5 CAACU Exeter 0
Overshot runway after abandoned take off

29-Jun-61 XM373 Jet Provost T3 2FTS RAF Syerston 0
Stalled on take off, sank back & undercarriage collapsed

11-Jul-61 XG134 Hunter FGA9 208 Sqn Mutla Ridge Kuwait 1
Flew into ground whilst recovering from a dive in hazy weather

Flying Officer Flavian Neol HENNESSY 24

13-Jul-61 XG271 Hunter FGA9 54 Sqn RAF Sylt Germany 0
Failed to become airborne & caught fire after crashing into barrier

---

18-Jul-61 WG319 Chipmunk T10 UAS RAF Valley 0
Hit obstruction & damaged beyond repair

05-Aug-61 XH791 Javelin FAW9 12 Gp Comms Flt Ganges Delta Pakistan 1
Abandoned in a spin after engine explosion. Although the pilot was killed, apparently after surviving the ejection, the navigator, Master Navigator A D Mellion survived.

Flight Lieutenant Edward Nicholas OWENS 33

Date Serial Aircraft Unit Place Casualties
Brief Circumstances of Accident
Casualty Details (If Applicable)

05-Aug-61 XL113 Whirlwind HAR4 228 Sqn Cullercoats Bay Northumberland 0

Engine cut during winching practice and ditched in sea

08-Aug-61 XE579 Hunter FR10 8 Sqn 6m East of Zinjibar Aden 1

Flew into ground approaching gunnery range. Johnnie Volkers was on his first tour after leaving RAF College Cranwell and was thought to have had a bright career in front of him.

Flying Officer John Frederick Cyril VOLKERS 22

29-Aug-61 WP841 Chipmunk T10 RAF Tech College, RAF Henlow 0

Struck marker on take off and damaged beyond repair

29-Aug-61 XH971 Javelin FAW8 41Sqn RAF Geilenkirchen 2

Broke up during formation break, possibly due to severe overstressing of the structure

Flight Lieutenant John Lawrence HATCH 26 Pilot
Flight Lieutenant John Charles Patrick NOTHALL 29Navigator

30-Aug-61 XG454 Belvedere HC1 BTU RAF Farnborough 0

Undercarriage collapsed in heavy landing

30-Aug-61 XM423 Jet Provost T3 CFS 3m South-east Kidderminster 0

Abandoned after engine failed during night navigation exercise by Flight Lieutenant I K McKee and Pilot Officer J Armstrong.

04-Sep-61 XD592 Vampire T11 1FTS 7m North north west RAF Acklington 0
Abandoned out of fuel after radio aids failed and could not locate base. Flight Lieutenant G D Lambert and his student Midshipman J M Heath escaped.

12-Sep-61 XE583 Hunter F6 19 Sqn 16m South-west Skydstrup Denmark 1
Rolled over and dived into ground
Flight Lieutenant David Martin NICHOLLS 24

18-Sep-61 WV623 Provost T1 6FTS RAF Acklington 0
Ground looped at night whilst landing

23-Sep-61 VP946 Devon C1 Air Attache Caracas Kobbermindbugt Greenland 0
Ditched after radio contact lost in bad weather

25-Sep-61 WV564 Provost T1 6FTS Acklington 0
Heavy Landing

29-Sep-61 XD602 Vampire T11 RAF College In Flight 0
Overstressed and not repaired

06-Oct-61 XM110 Beverley C1 84 Sqn Bahrain 0
Aircraft severely damaged by an explosive device in the cargo hold and not repaired

---

10-Oct-61 WD498 Hastings C2 70 Sqn RAF El Adem 17

As the aircraft was about to become airborne the flying pilot's seat slid back on its runners. The pilot called to the captain to take control and then released hold of the control column. However, the aircraft had become prematurely airborne and had stalled. The captain attempted to regain control by lifting the port wing but the starboard wing then dropped steeply and the aircraft struck the ground, caught fire and came to rest at 90 degrees to the runway. Although the flight deck crew escaped unhurt as did 18 passengers, the AQM and 16 others were killed. The cause of the crash was that the aircraft stalled, the recovery action by the pilot was incorrect, the flying pilot handed over control unnecessarily, and there was no positive handover of control. Furthermore, the flying pilot was only a 'D' category pilot and should not have been allowed to attempt the take off with passengers.

Sergeant John Michael HUGHES 26 Air Quartermaster
Captain Francis J BOATWRIGHT 35
10 other ranks of the Malta Artillery
5 other passengers

11-Oct-61 XJ725 Whirlwind HAR2 22 Sqn off Ramsgate 0

Engine cut whilst practising winching

13-Oct-61 XG521 Sycamore HR14 118 Sqn RAF Aldergrove 0

Rotor struck ground whilst landing and aircraft rolled over

13-Oct-61 XF940 Hunter F4

Circumstances of the loss of this aircraft are not known

20-Oct-61 WR968 Shackleton MR2 210 Sqn RAF Ballykelly 0

Undercarriage collapsed when aircraft yawed & wing tip hit ground during 3 engine landing

---

23-Oct-61 WZ559 Vampire T11 5FTS Oakington 0

Abandoned take off after power loss and hit barrier

25-Oct-61 XK861 Pembroke C1 2ATAF RAF Bruggen 0

Bellylanded by mistake during asymetric landing

26-Oct-61 WD995Canberra B2 32 Sqn 2.5 miles North RAF Akrotiri 3

Collided with Javelin XH906 during practice night interceptions

Flight Lieutenant Norman Bowan YOUD 26 Pilot
Flying Officer John GELDHART 24 Navigator
Flying Officer Michael Frederick HARRIS 22 Navigator

26-Oct-61 XH906 Javelin FAW9 25 Sqn 2.5 miles North RAF Akrotiri 1

Collided with Canberra WD995. The only survivor of this accident was the Javelin pilot, Flight Lieutenant R H Lloyd.

Flight Lieutenant John Harry MORRIS 31 Navigator

03-Nov-61 WZ399 Valiant B(PR)1 543 Sqn Offutt Air Force Base Nebraska 0

Abandoned take off and overshot railway line. The crew survived mainly because when the aircraft struck the railway embankment, the cockpit broke off and was catapulted across the line and away from the burning fuselage.

Date Serial Aircraft Unit Place Casualties
Brief Circumstances of Accident
Casualty Details (If Applicable)

08-Nov-61 WT511 Canberra PR7 31 Sqn 5miles North-west Munster 2

The crew was authorised for a low level sortie across country and to take photographs. The aircraft was seen to hit tree tops and crash about 300 yards further on. It was found that both engines had flamed out about 1.5 minutes before the crash due to fuel starvation. There was some evidence that the starboard rear fuel cock had been closed and it is possible that the pilot made an incorrect selection after the first engine flamed out.

Flying Officer David Glyn Alan RICHARDS 25 Pilot
Master Navigator Peter Bertram SANDERS 36 Navigator

21-Nov-61 VM372 Anson C19 3Gp Comms Flt 1mile South west of RAF Mildenhall 0

Engine cut, undercarriage jammed down crash landed into trees and hit pole and building

---

21-Nov-61 XM266 Canberra B(I)8 3 Sqn 2miles East of Tiverton 2

Engine failed at night and aircraft dived into ground

Flight Lieutenant Roger Johnson MOORE 29 Pilot
Flying Officer Martin Edward James ARCHARD Navigator

22-Nov-61 XE581 Hunter FGA9 8 Sqn 28m South west Diha Aden 1

Abandoned for reasons unknown

Flying Officer Richard Austin GAIGER 24

27-Nov-61 XH878 Javelin FAW9 64 Sqn 11 1/2m South-east RAF Waterbeach 0

Hydraulics failed and aircraft abandoned with seized controls. Fortunately, Squadron Leader D A P Saunders-Davies and Flight Lieutenant P Dougherty survived.

09-Dec-61 XE643 Hunter FGA9 208 Sqn Mombasa Airport 0

Abandoned take off and overshot, undercarriage raised to stop aircraft

---

14-Dec-61 XG500 Sycamore HR14 225 Sqn Bender Somalia 0

Tail rotor failed on landing. Aircraft not repaired because of difficult access and abandoned in situ.

22-Dec-61 WK623 Chipmunk T10 UAS 1 1/2m Perth Airfield 1

Rolled over and dived into the ground

Acting Pilot Officer Gordon Richard GOUDIE 25

27-Dec-61 TG624 Hastings Met 1 202 Sqn RAF Aldergrove 0

After about 400 yards of the take off run and with the tail wheel off the ground the aircraft developed a marked swing to port. The pilot took corrective action as the aircraft left the runway, using rudder, brakes and engine power but the aircraft became airborne in a stalled condition and was heading for some parked Shackleton aircraft. The pilot retracted the undercarriage and as the aircraft slide to halt the No 3 engine caught fire. The main cause was the failure to correct the swing quickly enough

---

04-Jan-62 WB532 Devon C1 70 Sqn 6m South-East Asmara Ethiopia 0

Belly landed after power loss on take off

15-Jan-62 WT310 Canberra B(I)6 213 Sqn 1m E Elbergen Germany 3

The two aircraft involved in this accident were carrying out an exercise under the lead of the captain of WT315. At 2000 feet the pilot of WT310 advised that he was going to fly above WT315 for the purpose of taking photographs. It appears possible that the pilot of WT310 then lost sight of the other aircraft although he was seen by the pilot of WT315 to above and to the port. The pilot of WT315 instructed WT310 to break away and then WT310 stated that he was two miles away and would continue taking photographs. Shortly afterwards WT310 collided with WT315. Although the crew of WT310 was killed, the pilot of WT315 and one of the navigators escaped (Flight Lieutenant G Willis and Flying Officer M F Whittingham). A second navigator and a supernumery pilot in WT315 were, however, unable to escape and were killed.

Flying Officer John William HULLAND 23 Pilot
Flying Officer David Robert CLARK 20
Flying Officer Ronald William Marshall LEAR 31

15-Jan-62 WT315 Canberra B(I)6 213 Sqn 1m E Elbergen Germany 2

Mid air collison with WT310 during photographic run

Flying Officer Kenneth Brian WILLINGS
Flight Lieutenant James Elial ABRAHAM 27

16-Jan-62 XG192 Hunter F6 DFLS RAF Nicosia 0

Abandoned take off and overshot an escarpment

16-Jan-62 WV607 Provost T1 6FTS RAF Acklington 0

Overstressed and not repaired

17-Jan-62 WL465 Meteor T7 5FTS RAF Stradishall 0

Undercarriage collapsed after stall on approach caused by both engines failing

---

29-Jan-62 WF771 Meteor T7 RAFFC East Halton Lincs 2

Crashed into hill for unknown reason

Flight Sergeant William Henry BLACK AFM 39 Pilot QFI
Wing Commander Francis Michael HEGARTY AFC 40 Pilot student

30-Jan-62 XE621 Hunter FR10 2 Sqn Papenburg Germany 1

Stalled and dived into hill

Flight Lieutenant Stuart Cyril BARNES 28

05-Feb-62 WP854 Chipmunk T10 1FTS Rufforth 0

Undercarriage fractured in heavy landing and aircraft damaged beyond repair

---

13-Feb-62 XG509 Sycamore HR14 CFS RAF Tern Hill 0

Struck ground in a turn and rolled over

21-Feb-62 WJ582 Canberra B2 Met R 1 1/4m East of RAF Leuchars 0

Flew into sea on approach in bad weather

Date	Serial	Aircraft	Unit	Place	Casualties
Brief Circumstances of Accident					
Casualty Details (If Applicable)					
01-Mar-62	XD379	Vampire T11	5FTS	Graveley	0
Crashed on airfield after being abandoned by Pilot Officer R E Turner following fire warning					
07-Mar-62	TG508	Hastings C1	242OCU	RAF Thorney Island	0
Yawed on landing and wing tip struck ground followed by fire					
09-Mar-62	XH794	Javelin FAW9	33 Sqn	RAF Wildenrath	0
Hydraulic failure, overshot landing and undercarriage collapsed					
14-Mar-62	WL470	Meteor T7	85 Sqn	RAF West Raynham	0
Bellylanded and damaged beyond repair					
23-Mar-62	XL159	Victor B2	A&AEE	Stubton Notts	2
Stalled and dived into house killing 2 on ground					
Mr M EVANS 25 Navigator Handley Page Flight Test Crew					
Mr P ELWOOD 26 Flight Test Observer Handley Page Flight Test Crew					
Mr P Murphy (Captain), Mr J Tank and Flight Lieutenant J Waterton all survived the accident)					
27-Mar-62	XN599	Jet Provost T3	6FTS	RAF Acklington	0
Skidded into a bank after swinging off runway when landing					

30-Mar-62 XE607 Hunter FGA9 8 Sqn RAF Khormaksar Aden 1

Dived into ground during air display. Three aircraft, two from one direction and the other from the opposite end of the airfield, were supposed to fly past each other. However, the singleton did not complete the crossover and crashed. The most likely cause of this accident was the nose trim ran away downwards and the pilot had insufficient time to rectify or to recover from this.

Flying Officer Peter John Humphrey BLACKGROVE 23

05-Apr-62 XM452 Jet Provost T3 RAF College 1m S Rauceby 0

Control lost after tip tank struck by lightning. Flight Lieutenant Peter R C Jones ejected and landed safely and, clearly undaunted by the experience went on to be a successful Hunter pilot.

09-Apr-62 XH977 Javelin FAW8 41Sqn RAF Gutersloh 0

Engine explosion on start up

13-Apr-62 XH844 Javelin FAW9 64 Sqn RAF Waterbeach 0

Engine explosion after start up

16-Apr-62 WJ605 Canberra B2 45 Sqn 26m E RAF Changi Singapore 2

Broke up during run over bombing range

Flying Officer Michael John MOY 25 Pilot
Flight Lieutenant David Tyne Armstrong LANSLEY 40 Navigator

24-Apr-62 WE111 Canberra T4 Station Flight Akrotiri Bay Cyprus 2

The aircraft was at about 20000 feet and requested a controlled descent with the pilot asking if ATC would accept a 'u/t pilot'. About ten miles from Akrotiri and after an otherwise satisfactory approach, the aircraft disappeared from radar and contact was lost. The cause could not be determined although the comments about 'u/t pilot' making the approach was taken to mean that the navigator might have been flying the aircraft! Although this was possible, it was considered unlikely because the flying was generally accurate up to the time the aircraft disappeared from radar.

Flight Lieutenant Donald William CROFTS 26 Pilot
Flying Officer Andrew Ernest MARSHALL 23 Navigator

08-May-62 XM422 Jet Provost T3 6FTS 1/2m West-south-west RAF Acklington 1
Flew into ground during display practice

Flight Lieutenant David Donald WYMAN 31

09-May-62 XN604 Jet Provost T3 6FTS 5 M S RAF Acklington 0
False fire warning led to abandonment by Flight Lieutenant W D E Eggleton and his student Pilot Officer M Hyland.

10-May-62 XA760 Javelin
Circumstances of loss not known

12-May-62 XL667 Pioneer CC1 230 Sqn 1/2m S Kingussie Fife 0
Wing dropped and engine failed to pick up and wing tip struck ground

---

15-May-62 VP294 Shackleton MR1 205 Sqn RAF Gan 0
Destroyed in forced landing

17-May-62 XL132 Beverley C1 242OCU Chichester Harbour 2

Engine caught fire on approach and aircraft ditched

Flight Lieutenant Edward Thomas HOLLINS Navigator
Sergeant Nigel Duncan McLEOD Flight Engineer

18-May-62 XH755 Javelin FAW9 33 Sqn 7m E Tynemouth Northumberland 1

Control lost and abandoned in a spin the pilot; Master Pilot J E Crowther was rescued after ejecting.

Master Navigator John Albert FAREY BEM Navigator

02-Jun-62 WK516 Chipmunk T10 UAS Thornbury Bristol 0

Struck cables during practice forced landing and crashed

07-Jun-62 XL610 Hunter T7 56 Sqn 4m West-south-west Sleaford Lincs 2

Stalled and rolled into ground

Flight Lieutenant Robert Alfred FOULKS 31 Pilot
Flight Lieutenant Robert Henry Thomas BAKER

07-Jun-62 XA645 Javelin FAW5 5 Sqn 4m North-west Wesel West Germany 0

Flight Lieutenants J H Adam and C M Pinker abandoned the aircraft after an in-flight fire.

14-Jun-62 XH613 Victor B1A 15 Sqn 5miles North East of RAF Cottesmore 0

Whilst approaching RAF Cottesmore at the end of the sortie, all four engines ran down because the electrical connectors became disconnected on the throttle box. The aircraft was being flown by the squadron commander; Wg Cdr Matthews with Flying Officer Lowther as his co-pilot. On the order to abandon the aircraft, it is believed that the rear crew left the aircraft in less than half a minute and, although one man left the rubber of his flying boots along the fuselage, the entire crew survived. It was particularly tragic, therefore, that a few days later another Victor from the Cottesmore sister squadron should crash with the loss of all on board. (Crew: Captain - Wg Cdr J G Matthews, Co-Pilot - Fg Off W B Lowther, Navigator Plotter - Flt Lt G B Spencer, Navigator Radar - Flt Lt B H Stubbs, Air Electronics Operator - Flt Lt E W Anstead). In June 1983, the author joined Bill Lowther for a drink to celebrate his second 21st birthday!

16-Jun-62 XA929 Victor B1 10 Sqn RAF Akrotiri Cyprus 6

Incorrect flap reading led to wrong selection on take off. By the time the pilot had realised the possible reason for the aircraft not becoming airborne it was too late to avoid the crash. The co-pilot ejected shortly before the crash but his ejection was outside the design limits of the seat and he did not survive.

Flight Lieutenant George Alfred GOATHAM 27 Pilot Captain
Flight Lieutenant David Cairns BROWN 28
Flight Lieutenant John GRAY 36
Flying Officer Anthony William MITCHELL 21 Co-Pilot
Flying Officer Albert Peter PACE 24
Master Technician Donald Arthur SMITH 40 Crew Chief

17-Jun-62 WP976 Chipmunk T10 UAS RAF Filton 0

Overturned after severe bounce on landing

20-Jun-62 XP392 Whirlwind HAR10

Circumstances of loss not known

25-Jun-62 XE600 Hunter FGA9 8 Sqn Khormaksar Ranges Aden 1

The pilot had been warned by the Range Safety Officer; Flight Lieutenant Gordon Talbot for infringements of the height limits in the range area. The pilot then asked for permission to make a pass to check height calibration and when this was granted he 'beat up' the range office. However, he encountered a dust and sand cloud from his own jet wash and in attempting to pull up he stalled the aircraft and it crashed into the range area and he was killed.

Flying Officer John Martin WEBBON 20

26-Jun-62 WG962 Meteor T7 CFS RAF Little Rissington 2

Rolled into the ground after engine failure on take off and failure to correct quickly the asymetric condition. The Meteor was notorious for problems in asymetric flight if the speed and lateral control were not monitored very carefully and if the correct use of flaps and undercarriage were not followed

Flight Lieutenant Trevor James DOE 38 Pilot
Flight Lieutenant Henry William CARTER 24 Navigator

27-Jun-62 XF943 Hunter F4 CFS RAF Kemble 0

Crashed into a wall having overshot after hydraulics failed

09-Jul-62 XJ382 Sycamore HR14 110 Sqn 15m E Kuala Lumpur 0

Hit obstruction during forced landing after fire warning

12-Jul-62 XF451 Hunter F6 229 OCU RAF Chivenor 0

Overshot forced landing after power loss and struck barrier

12-Jul-62 XJ128 Javelin FAW8 85 Sqn RAF West Raynham 0

Engine fire on start up

Date	Serial	Aircraft	Unit	Place	Casualties
Brief Circumstances of Accident					
Casualty Details (If Applicable)					
17-Jul-62	VP191	Mosquito TT35	CAACU	Weston Super Mare	0
Abandoned take off and crashed into a hedge					
25-Jul-62	XA646	Javelin FAW5	FCSCH	RAF West Raynham	0
Engine Fire On Start Up					
30-Jul-62	XG465	Belvedere HC1	72 Sqn	4miles North-west RAF Gutersloh	6
Lost power and dived into ground. Watson was the commanding officer designate of 21 Squadron which was to operate the Belvedere in Aden					
Squadron Leader Bryan WATSON 30 Pilot Flight Lieutenant Colin Kennedy ROSS 29 Senior Technician Roy MITCHELL 26 Flying Officer Colin George CROCKER 27 Corporal Dennis OTTEWELL 23 Flying Officer John Hubert BRUNDLE 22					
08-Aug-62	XD620	Vampire T11	4FTS	4 1/2m South East of Mona Airfield	1
Stalled on approach and dived into ground					
Acting Pilot Officer Francis John MARRIOTT 22					
14-Aug-62	XF684	Provost T1	6FTS	1 1/2m W RAF Ouston	1
Collided with XF903 whilst overshooting at night					
Acting Pilot Officer James Frank THOMAS 21					

14-Aug-62 XF903 Provost T1 6FTS 1 1/2m W of RAF Ouston 1

Collided with XF684 after taking off at night

Acting Pilot Officer Barry Robert Powell HYDE 18

22-Aug-62 XM456 Jet Provost T3 on loan Histon Cambridgeshire 0

Whilst on loan to Hunting Aircraft Ltd the aircraft crashed but Squadron Leaders R A Lees and J D Barwell ejected safely.

28-Aug-62 WJ480 Valetta T3 2ANS 5m West North West of Chippenham 3

The pilot carried out a normal asymetric overshoot with the starboard engine feathered and the aircraft then proceeded westerly with both propellers turning and with the undercarriage retracted. It turned north and in a flatish turn before crashing into the ground and cartwheeling. The main cause was that the starboard engine master fuel cock was left shut off and hence the engine could not be restarted and speed decayed.

Flight Lieutenant David Robert KENWARD 39 Pilot Captain
Flight Lieutenant Donald Harrison BLUNDY 39 Pilot
Sergeant Ivor Patrick MEW 28 Air Signaller (died of injuries sustained 5 September 1962)

04-Sep-62 XD448 Vampire T11 8FTS RAF Swinderby 0

Abandoned take off after multiple bird strike and hit barrier

---

17-Sep-62 XE544 Hunter FGA9 208 Sqn Nairobi 0

Abandoned take off after fire warning, tyre burst and undercarriage raised to stop

---

20-Sep-62 XP622 Jet Provost T3 2FTS Wymeswold 0

Engine cut during a roller landing and undercarriage collapsed when aircraft went onto grass

Date Serial Aircraft Unit Place Casualties
Brief Circumstances of Accident
Casualty Details (If Applicable)

25-Sep-62 XG523 Sycamore HR14 CFS RAF Tern Hill 0

Heavy landing caused serious damage which was not worth repairing.

28-Sep-62 XL825 Sycamore HR14 110 Sqn Malakoff Estate Malaya 1

Main rotor struck tail and aircraft became uncontrollable and crashed

Flying Officer John William MARTIN 22

02-Oct-62 XA934 Victor B1 232OCU 3m South-west RAF Gaydon 3

Engine failed on take off and the aircraft was abandoned after two others failed

Flight Lieutenant Noel Edward COOKE 39 Pilot Captain
Pilot Officer John Anthony COTTRIDGE
Flying Officer Douglas Frank HAYNES

(the co-pilot; Flight Lieutenant E B C Gwinnel, a former Canberra pilot with 45 Squadron was saved)

04-Oct-62 XA701 Javelin FAW5 Conv RAF West Raynham 0

Engine exploded on start up

05-Oct-62 XG462 Belvedere HC1 72 Sqn 3m South-west Bomba Libya 0

Crashed after rear engine caught fire in the air

12-Oct-62 XM696 Gnat T1 A&AEE RAF Boscombe Down 0

Bellylanded after tyre lost at take off

16-Oct-62 XN601 Jet Provost T3 6FTS 1/2m W RAF Acklington 0
Power loss when taking off and the aircraft sank back onto the ground

---

16-Oct-62 XM427 Jet Provost T3 RAF College 1 1/2m Nne RAF Waddington 1
Flew into ground on night approach
Under Officer B S PERERA 22 Royal Ceylon Air Force

25-Oct-62 WJ730 Canberra B2 ETPS RAE Farnborough 0
Crashed following loss of control during practice engine failure on take off

---

28-Oct-62 XG253 Hunter FGA9 1 Sqn 37 miles North-east RAF Khormaksar 0
Abandoned after engine flamed out. Pilot - Flight Lieutenant B L Scotford.

29-Oct-62 XA661 Javelin FAW5 11 Sqn RAF Geilenkirchen 0
Engine exploded after start up

02-Nov-62 WP922 Chipmunk T10 UAS 3 M South-east Newport Shropshire 1
Crashed during roll
Cadet Pilot Christopher Charles BUTLER 20

04-Nov-62 WD372Chipmunk T10 UAS 2m South-east Reading 2
Mid air collision with Beagle Terrier G-ASAE (aircraft operating from RAF White Waltham)
Flight Lieutenant Brian Michael RIDGWAY DSO DFC 40 Pilot RAFVR(T)
Flying Officer Charles Malcolm ROSTRON DFC 40 RAFVR(T)

Date Serial Aircraft Unit Place Casualties
Brief Circumstances of Accident
Casualty Details (If Applicable)

03-Dec-62 XH836 Javelin FAW9 60Sqn 12m S Mersing Malaya 0

Engine explosion and the aircraft was abandoned by Squadron Leader F Jolliffe and Wing Commander Peter Smith after loss of control.

12-Dec-62 XM993 Lightning T4 LCS Middleton St George 0

Undercarriage leg collapsed on landing and the aircraft rolled over. The instructor; Flight Lieutenant Al Turley and the pupil; Wing Commander Charles Gibbs escaped from the upturned wreckage

---

28-Dec-62 XE535 Hunter FGA9 28 Sqn Lion Rock near RAF Kai Tak Hong Kong 1

Whilst diving towards the airfield at RAF Kai Tak the aircraft flew into the northern face of the Lion Rock near to its summit. It was never satisfactorily established why this happened although one theory was that the reinforced windscreen glass could have caused some sort of refraction effect that made the pilot believe he would clear the top of the rock. Creighton was something of a local celebrity with his name appearing in the local papers several times in the week before his tragic death.

Flight Lieutenant David Grant CREIGHTON 26

29-Jan-63 WJ824 Canberra PR7 58 Sqn Caldbeck Cumberland 2

Flew into ground in poor visibility

Flight Lieutenant Peter BROUGHTON 29 Pilot
Squadron Leader John Christopher Charles ALMOND Navigator

29-Jan-63 XM476 Jet Provost T3 7FTS RAF Church Fenton 0

Collided with XN466 whilst landing on same runway in poor visibility

29-Jan-63 XN466 Jet Provost T3 7FTS RAF Church Fenton 0

Collided with XM476

10-Feb-63 XL700 Pioneer CC1 209 Sqn Patik Malaya 0

Failed to clear trees after take off

14-Feb-63 XN318 Twin Pioneer C1 209 Sqn 6m N Long Somado Sarawak East Malaysia 5

Flew into trees on cliff side and crashed into river below. Because of the inaccessibility of the crash site it was never possible to examine the wreckage properly to determine the cause of the accident. The aircraft was one of three searching for a missing Army patrol and its progress shortly before the crash was monitored by a Sycamore helicopter flying nearby. All appeared to be normal shortly before the crash and it can only be assumed that the aircraft was allowed to descend into the valley or was subjected to a gust of wind which caused it to strike the tree tops.

Flying Officer James Edward PEARCE 38 Pilot
Flight Lieutenant Donald BERRY 28 Navigator
Flight Lieutenant Michael Reginald MORLING 31 Supernumery Navigator
Junior Technician John David CRANES 23
Lance Corporal Dennis HARGREAVE 23

19-Feb-63 XN642 Jet Provost T3 3FTS 2m N RAF Leeming 1

Abandoned after engine flame out on take off . Although the instructor, Flight Lieutenant Bill Gambold escaped, his student did not.

Pilot Officer Adrian Keith MacKLEN 19

20-Feb-63 XF385 Hunter F6 229 OCU RAF Chivenor 0

Engine lost power and undercarriage collapsed after overshooting landing

Date	Serial	Aircraft	Unit	Place	Casualties

Brief Circumstances of Accident

Casualty Details (If Applicable)

Date	Serial	Aircraft	Unit	Place	Casualties
27-Feb-63	XJ919	Sycamore HR14	RAFHSqn	RAF Boscombe Down	0

Tail rotor struck ground and aircraft rolled over

Date	Serial	Aircraft	Unit	Place	Casualties
07-Mar-63	XF433	Hunter F6	229 OCU	2m N Hartland Point	0

Collided with XE594

Date	Serial	Aircraft	Unit	Place	Casualties
07-Mar-63	XE594	Hunter F6	229 OCU	2m N Hartland Point	0

Collided with XF433. The two pilots, Flight Lieutenants Chris Strong (who later commanded 20 Sqn) and Pete Tate ejected safely

Date	Serial	Aircraft	Unit	Place	Casualties
13-Mar-63	XM290	Twin Pioneer C2	21Sqn	Kalimikui Kenya	0

Tipped over on landing

Date	Serial	Aircraft	Unit	Place	Casualties
14-Mar-63	XN504	Jet Provost CT3	1FTS	1/2 M N Rufforth	0

Abandoned on approach after engine power loss in the circuit. The two Royal Navy officers flying the aircraft, Lieutenants Ward and Pinney escaped

Date	Serial	Aircraft	Unit	Place	Casualties
20-Mar-63	XM714	Victor B2	100 Sqn	3 1/2 M East-north-east RAF Wittering	5

The aircraft, with a crew of five and a Bomber Command 'umpire' took off in the early evening to fly a bomber night exercise. The weather was good and the aircraft had only recently been delivered new from the factory. After a normal take-off and after passing 800 feet, the co-pilot noticed the No 2 engine fire warning light illuminated. He told the captain that No 1 engine was on fire but the captain contradicted him with the correct engine details and instructed the co-pilot to tell Air Traffic Control and then told the rear crew members to check their parachutes. The co-pilot noticed that the undercarriage warning flag, which is activated if speed drops below 160 knots and the undercarriage has not been lowered, was flashing and he warned the captain to watch his speed. The captain replied that he was climbing for height and despite the severe juddering believed that the aircraft had sufficient speed because, it is thought, he believed he was at 100 knots higher speed than was the case. At around 5000 feet the aircraft flicked over to port and fell away partly inverted. The captain ordered the crew to abandon the aircraft and the rear crew members were unable to do so because of the increasing 'G' forces as the aircraft spun down. The co-pilot ejected and was unharmed. It seems the only possible explanation for an experienced captain losing control in this way was for him to have assumed he had the right speed and that the juddering was not a stall but structural failure caused by the engine fire.

Flight Lieutenant Alexander Douglas GALBRAITH 29 Pilot
Flight Lieutenant Edward Joseph VERNON 32 Navigator Radar
Flight Lieutenant James CHURCHILL 31 Navigator Plotter
Flying Officer Terence Ian SANDFORD 23 Air Electronics Officer
Master Navigator Albert STRINGER 39 (Exercise Umpire, on loan from 139 Squadron)

(co pilot Flight Lieutenant B J Jackson escaped)

27-Mar-63 XP661 Jet Provost T4 6 FTS on recovery 0

Over stressed in flight and not repaired

29-Mar-63 XE309 Sycamore HR14 CFS 4 1/2m S RAF Tern Hill 1

Control lost at low level and crashed into ground

Pilot Officer Arthur Barry WATSON 28

01-Apr-63 WJ994 Canberra B2 ETPS RAE Farnborough 0

Undercarriage collapsed during a roller landing

Date Serial Aircraft Unit Place Casualties
Brief Circumstances of Accident
Casualty Details (If Applicable)

10-Apr-63 XL600 Hunter T7 111 Sqn 8 miles south west of Norwich 1

During a slow role to the left at 370 knots and a height of 8000 feet the captain heard a bang and simultaneous wind noise. He noticed that the co-pilot's seat was almost out of the aircraft with the co-pilot still in it. The captain righted the aircraft and reduced speed but when he next looked the co-pilot had fallen from the seat. The cause was that the top latch had not been correctly engaged during seat replacement. There was also criticism of the support services for not ensuring the correct embodiment of modifications to ejection seats. The pilot during this sortie was Flight Lieutenant A V Thomas, aged 30, who was uninjured

Flying Officer David George ADAM Co-Pilot

(the aircraft was not written-off - aircrew casualty only)

13-Apr-63 XB268 Beverley C1 53 Sqn RAF El Adem Libya 2

About 30 miles from RAF El Adem the crew discussed diversion tactics as they had been informed that landing conditions were poor. However, seeing the airfield lights they decided to land from an ACR7 approach, although the pilot was not informed of fog formation. The aircraft entered cloud below its break-off height and despite the co-pilot's warning that the aircraft was below break-off height, the captain continued. The pilot then initiated an overshoot but the aircraft struck the ground in a nose down attitude with the left wing low and broke up coming to rest about 1500 feet from the runway threshold. The AQM and a supernumery airman aboard were killed when they were thrown from the aircraft because they were not strapped in. The cause was that the pilot lost control on an instrument approach, he left overshoot action too late, he failed to divert and went below break off height in cloud. ATC failed to inform the pilot of the actual landing conditions.

Flight Sergeant Frank DENBY 33 Air Quartermaster
Senior Aircraftman David Edward MARSHALL 23 Air Mechanic (Supernumery crew)

18-Apr-63 XP635 Jet Provost T4 6FTS Whitton Shields Morpeth Northumberland 0

Abandoned following fire warning. Flight Lieutenant Shadbolt and his student Pilot Officer Gladwin ejected

---

18-Apr-63 XL994 Twin Pioneer C1 152 Sqn 1m W Bu Hafafa Oman 8

Dived into ground in circuit. The cause of the accident was not positively determined. One soldier survived the accident

Flight Lieutenant Norman Arthur BULL 37 Pilot
Flight Lieutenant Glyndwr EVANS 30 Navigator
Passengers: Major Raymond LEWIS 37 The 9th/12th Lancers
Trooper Raymond H BRIERLEY 20 The 9th/12th Lancers
4 Arab soldiers of Trucial Oman Scouts whose names are not recorded

---

19-Apr-63 XP623 Jet Provost T4 2FTS Thrussington Lancs 0

Abandoned in a spin after Pilot Officer N J Tillotson was unable to regain control

---

24-Apr-63 WZ612 Vampire T11 4FTS RAF Valley 0

Undercarriage collapsed on landing

24-Apr-63 XE628 Hunter FGA9 1 Sqn off Set Tehami Libya 1

The pilot was flying as Black 4 in a four aircraft formation during practice air combat. Others in the formation lost sight of Black 4 until they saw a splash in the sea. The lack of any real evidence made it impossible to determine the cause of the accident.

Captain F A MATTHEWS 31 United States Air Force

Date Serial Aircraft Unit Place Casualties
Brief Circumstances of Accident
Casualty Details (If Applicable)

26-Apr-63 XM142 Lightning F1 74 Sqn off Cromer Norfolk 0

Abandoned after hydraulics failure. Flight Lieutenant T J Burns ejected

---

29-Apr-63 WJ719 Canberra B2 98 Sqn Samsun Turkey 0

Undercarriage retracted whilst taxying

29-Apr-63 XM368 Jet Provost T3 2FTS 2 1/2m South-west Pateley Bridge Yorks 0

Abandoned in a spin after Flight Lieutenant Chalmers was unable to regain control. The student, Pilot Officer Waterson also ejected safely

---

02-May-63 XP588 Jet Provost T4 CFS 1/2m N Chedworth Airfield 0

Flight Lieutenant Graham Sturt abandoned the aircraft after a fire warning

---

04-May-63 XG473 Belvedere HC1 66 Sqn Long Murarap, Sarawak 8

Yaw cables failed and the aircraft rolled over and crashed out of control into jungle. The yaw cables in a Belvedere ran over pulleys and there was a tendency for them to jump off with obvious and disasterous results. The Belvedere had been rejected by the Royal Navy because, amongst other things, it spilt a large quantity of Avpin (a very explosive starter fuel) all over the floor at regular intervals which did not commend it for aircraft carrier operations!

Flight Lieutenant Arthur Paul John DODSON 32 Pilot Captain
Flight Lieutenant Derek Reginald Watson VINER 38 Co-Pilot

Corporal Technician John Llewelyn WILLIAMS
Major Ronald H D NORMAN MBE MC 43
Major Harry A I THOMPSON MC 41
Corporal Phillip M MURPHY 29
Mr Michael Henry DAY
another unidentified civilian

06-May-63 XL822 Sycamore HR14 110Sqn Near Long Murarap Sarawak 0

Whilst engaged in the search operations for XG473, the aircraft suffered a partial engine failure. With considerable skill the pilot, Master Pilot Eric Leyden, managed to land in a restricted clearing but the undercarriage struck a tree stump and the aircraft turned over.

07-May-63 XK991 Whirlwind 10 228 Sqn Bridlington Bay Yorks 0

Rotor struck mast of vessel whilst lowering winchman onto boat; ditched

---

06-Jun-63 XF449 Hunter F6 CFE RAF Binbrook 0

Caught fire whilst taxying because a leaking fuel valve allowed fuel to leak into the starter area.

06-Jun-63 XM179 Lightning F1A 56 Sqn Great Bricett Suffolk 0

Collided with XM181 during bomb burst and abandoned by the pilot, Flight Lieutenant Mike Cook who sustained a broken neck as a result

---

12-Jun-63 VM388 Anson C19 Odiham Station Flt Cherbourg France 0

Landed on a beach after airfields closed due to fog

Date Serial Aircraft Unit Place Casualties
Brief Circumstances of Accident
Casualty Details (If Applicable)

12-Jun-63 XH477 Vulcan B1A 44 Sqn St Colme Aboyne Aberdeenshire 5

Flew into hill on low level nav ex at night

Flight Lieutenant David Allen BLACKMORE 29 Pilot Captain
Flying Officer Derek George FAULKE Co-Pilot
Flight Lieutenant Arthur David ROPER Navigator
Flight Lieutenant Jerrold Bartley ROSS Navigator
Flight Lieutenant John Rodney CHAPMAN Air Electronics Officer

---

15-Jun-63 WD364Chipmunk T10 UAS 8m South-west Dyce 1

Dived into ground during practice forced landing

Officer Cadet G A EWING 19

24-Jun-63 XF523 Hunter FGA9 54 Sqn Benina Airport Libya 1

The aircraft was on a low level sortie from El Adem to Benina, Derna and then returning to El Adem. Having made two runs over Benina at 400 to 500 feet, during which the pilot carried out a roll on each occasion, the pilot asked to cross the airfield from west to east to set course for Derna. He crossed the west boundary at about 200 feet and at 420 knots and rolled the aircraft on its back where the roll stopped with the aircraft slightly nose down. After a short pause the nose continued to drop and the aircraft struck the ground and disintegrated. The cause was loss of control whilst engaged in unauthorised aerobatics at low level

Flight Lieutenant Robert Edgar WRATHER 29

24-Jun-63 XH962 Javelin FAW9 29 Sqn RAF Nicosia Cyprus 0

Undercarriage collapsed after swing on take off

04-Jul-63 WZ857 Chipmunk T10 UAS Ilfracombe Devon 0

Crashed in forced landing after engine cut during aerobatics

04-Jul-63 XG512 Sycamore HR14 103 Sqn Tobruk Libya 0

Nosewheel collapsed on landing and rotors hit the ground

10-Jul-63 XK633 Vampire T11 1FTS Rufforth 0

Swung off the runway whilst taking off and undercarriage collapsed

---

18-Jul-63 XM186 Lightning F1A 111Sqn 1m W RAF Wittering 1

Abandoned in a spin during aerobatic display

Flight Lieutenant Alan GARSIDE 25

29-Jul-63 XM380 Jet Provost T3 2FTS 1m S Seagrave Leics 0

Abandoned after fire warning and engine flame out. The instructor; Master Pilot A Naismith and his student Pilot Officer Fisher ejected safely

---

02-Aug-63 XH990 Javelin FAW8 41 Sqn RAF Marham 0

Undercarriage leg jammed up and aircraft swung off runway

23-Aug-63 XG517 Sycamore HR14 103 Sqn Tobruk 0

Controls malfunctioned and aircraft rotor struck ground on landing

---

10-Sep-63 XJ428 Whirlwind 10 228 Sqn 2miles South of Bridlington 0

Lost power and destroyed in forced landing

Date	Serial	Aircraft	Unit	Place	Casualties
Brief Circumstances of Accident					
Casualty Details (If Applicable)					
11-Sep-63	XJ113	Javelin FAW8	41 Sqn	RAF Wattisham	0
Engine failure on take off and aircraft swung off runway and caught fire					
30-Sep-63	WZ578	Vampire T11	8FTS	1miles East of Upton Magna Shropshire	0
Abandoned after engine flame out. Flight Lieutenant Peter Callaghan (who subsequently flew the last RAF Dakota at RAE Farnborough) and his student Pilot Officer D Aylward ejected. Dougie Aylward subsequently became one of three 'first tourists' to go to the Lightning force immediately after their ab initio pilot training when he joined No 14 LCC in June 1964					
17-Oct-63	XH758	Javelin FAW9	5 Sqn	2miles West Zonhoven Germany	0
Abandoned after engine explosion which caused serious internal damaged and controls failed					
18-Oct-63	XR536	Gnat T1	4FTS	RAF Sealand	0
Engine fire warning led to forced landing and aircraft struck obstruction on runway					
05-Nov-63	XM336	Javelin T3	FCIRS	Jaujac France	0
Abandoned after double engine failure and although Flight Lieutenant Colin Holman and his navigator escaped there were 4 killed and 8 injured on ground					
05-Nov-63	XH765	Javelin FAW9	64 Sqn	Kalaikunda India	0
Overshot after abandoned take off					

16-Nov-63 WD304Chipmunk T10 1AEF 5miles North-west RAF Manston 2
Dived Into Sea

Flying Officer Ronald Charles WACE 42 RAFVR(T) Pilot
Air Cadet M SHEPHERD Air Training Corps

19-Nov-63 XM187 Lightning F1A 111 RAF Wattisham 0
Undercarriage collapsed after heavy bounce when landing

25-Nov-63 XD164 Whirlwind 10 CFS Holyhead Bay Anglesey 0
Ditched after engine failed

13-Dec-63 XM421 Jet Provost T3 7FTS 2miles North-west RAF Church Fenton 0
Pilot Officer Michaels, the trainee pilot, abandoned the aircraft after control was lost in cloud

---

17-Dec-63 TG610 Hastings C1 242OCU RAF Thorney Island 0
Struck building after a swing on landing. casualty killed on ground.

03-Jan-64 XR698 Jet Provost T4 3FTS RAF Leeming 0
Stalled on approach to practice forced landing and bellylanded

---

10-Jan-64 XG514 Sycamore HR14 CFS RAF Tern Hill 0
Rolled over while practising sloping ground landings and rotor hit ground

---

24-Jan-64 XG519 Sycamore HR14 110 Sqn 8m S Fort Kemar Malaysia 0
Crashed after avoiding trees and destroyed by fire

Date Serial Aircraft Unit Place Casualties
Brief Circumstances of Accident
Casualty Details (If Applicable)

Date	Serial	Aircraft	Unit	Place	Casualties
30-Jan-64	XH723	Javelin FAW9	29 Sqn	RAF Nicosia Cyprus	0

Engine failure on take off and aircraft severely damaged by fire

---

Date	Serial	Aircraft	Unit	Place	Casualties
10-Feb-64	XH747	Javelin FAW9	60 Sqn	off Singapore	0

Tailplane trimming tab detached and as the aircraft became uncontrollable it was abandoned over the sea but Flight Lieutenant G Sykes and T P Burns survived

---

Date	Serial	Aircraft	Unit	Place	Casualties
17-Feb-64	XG166	Hunter F6	229 OCU	4m N Hartland Point	1

Dived into the sea from cloud

Indian Air Force officer student

Date	Serial	Aircraft	Unit	Place	Casualties
20-Feb-64	XJ433	Whirlwind 10	110 Sqn	Pa Umor Borneo	0

Lost power approaching to land and fell short into scrub

Date	Serial	Aircraft	Unit	Place	Casualties
01-Mar-64	XG265	Hunter FGA9	20 Sqn	RAF Labuan	1

Caught fire and abandoned but pilot did not survive

Flight Lieutenant Robert Andrew Fraser SHIELDS 37

Date	Serial	Aircraft	Unit	Place	Casualties
12-Mar-64	XP639	Jet Provost T4	CFS	1m N Morton In The Marsh Gloucestershire	0

Mid air collison with XR670 led to Flight Lieutenant R S S Cox bailing out

25-Mar-64 XN723 Lightning F2 R-R Keyham Leicestershire 0

Abandoned after catching fire whilst on loan to Rolls Royce (Civilian Test Pilot Mr Dennis Witham ejected)

25-Mar-64 XL820 Sycamore HR14 CFS Tern Hill Railway Station 2

Rotor blade failure in flight

Flight Lieutenant Brian Richard GALLETLY Pilot Instructor
Flight Lieutenant Bruce Sinclair NORTHWAY Student

29-Mar-64 XH955 Javelin FAW9 60 Sqn RAF Labuan 0

Undercarriage collapsed when aircraft swung off runway with burst tyre

---

03-Apr-64 XH724 Javelin FAW9 60 Sqn RAF Tengah Singapore 0

Crashed into a monsoon drain after swinging off the runway; caught fire

---

04-Apr-64 XE311 Sycamore HR14 110 Sqn Butterworth 0

Caught fire after landing and destroyed

16-Apr-64 XL594 Hunter T7 19 Sqn 1/4m North North West of Carnaby 1

Hit ground pulling out from a dive

Flight Lieutenant Crawford McGregor CAMERON 26

17-Apr-64 XG136 Hunter FGA9 43 Sqn Haref Libya 1

Wing damaged by drop tank breaking away in dive and aircraft flicked into ground

Flying Officer Martin Stewart HERRING 22

Date Serial Aircraft Unit Place Casualties
Brief Circumstances of Accident
Casualty Details (If Applicable)

21-Apr-64 XG293 Hunter FGA9 20 Sqn RAF Tengah Singapore 0

Abandoned after engine failure whilst doing aerobatics

27-Apr-64 XN785 Lightning F2 92 Sqn Hutton Cranswick North of Leeming 1

Ran out of fuel and destroyed in crash whilst attempting to land at a disused airfield

Flying Officer George Charles DAVIE

06-May-64 WZ363 Valiant B1 148 Sqn Near Market Rasen Station 5

Dived into ground after night overshoot from RAF Binbrook

Flight Lieutenant Francis Christopher WELLES Captain
Flight Lieutenant George Arthur MILLS Co-Pilot
Flight Lieutenant John Robert STRINGER Navigator
Flight Lieutenant Leslie Richard HAWKINS Navigator
Sergeant Richard NOBLE Air Electronics Operator

11-May-64 XH535 Vulcan B2 A&AEE Chute Hampshire 4

Spun into ground after uncontrolled yaw during low speed handling demonstration

Flight Lieutenant Jack DINGLY 44 Navigator
Flight Lieutenant Frank Ashley YOUNG 29
Flight Lieutenant Peter CHILTON 32 Air Electronics Officer
Master Signaller Laurence CHRISTIAN AFM

The captain; Mr Osborne James Hawkins and the co-pilot Flight Lieutenant R L Beeson survived

20-May-64 XH774 Javelin FAW9 29 Sqn RAF Akrotiri Cyprus 0

Caught fire after engine failed on take off

23-May-64 WZ396 Valiant BPR(K)1 543 Sqn Manston 0

Landed on foam carpet after undercarriage jammed up

27-May-64 XR949 Gnat T1 4FTS Nr Bala Merioneth 0

Hood fractured and pilot ejected after losing control

29-May-64 XM942 Twin Pioneer CC1 209 Sqn Long Akah Borneo 0

Undercarriage broke off when aircraft hit soft patch of ground on landing

---

03-Jun-64 XP348 Whirlwind 10 22 Sqn 2m South-west Midhurst Sussex 2

Flew into ground after blade stall. In helicopters the 'retreating' blade stalls because the aircraft is travelling too fast and there is insufficient airflow over the blade. The remedy is to slow down but in this case the pilot dived the aircraft and attempted to increase speed

Flight Lieutenant Reginald Edward YOUNG 35 Pilot
Flight Sergeant Richard William George PECK Winchman

Flight Lieutenant R C Hope the navigator/winch operator survived the accident

---

09-Jun-64 XM191 Lightning F1A 111 Sqn RAF Wattisham 0

Engine fire whilst landing but aircraft damaged beyond repair. The pilot; Flight Lieutenant N Smith was uninjured

Date	Serial	Aircraft	Unit	Place	Casualties
Brief Circumstances of Accident					
Casualty Details (If Applicable)					
11-Jun-64	VW863	Valetta C1	52 Sqn	RAF Labuan	0
Belly landed after undercarriage jammed					
15-Jun-64	XN580	Jet Provost T3	RAF College	Scopwick Lincs	0
Abandoned after catching fire					
24-Jun-64	XJ615	Hunter T7	ETPS	1 1/2m South-east Haslemere	1
Flew into high ground					
Capitaine M BIGOIS Armee de l'Air					
30-Jun-64	XK139	Hunter FGA9	208 Sqn	Dasa Island Persian Gulf	0
Mid air collison with XE647 during practice low level attack					
30-Jun-64	XE647	Hunter FGA9	208 Sqn	Dasa Island Persian Gulf	0
Mid air collison with XK139					
10-Jul-64	XF710	Shackleton MR3	120 Sqn	Culloden Moor Inverness	0

Major uncontained fire and crash landed. Flight Lieutenant John Gladstone and his crew took off from Kinloss but almost immediately the No: 3 engine began to overspeed and caught fire and eventually fell off. At this time the No: 4 engine fire warning lights came on and it had to be feathered. With two engines on the same side out and with the wing ablaze, the aircraft avoided Inverness and was crashed on Culloden Moor under control by Gladstone and his co-pilot - Flight Lieutenant J A W Lee. The local villagers were holding a dance and the crew adjourned to the party to await the rescue services. 'Pop' Gladstone received an exceptionally well deserved second bar to the Air Force Cross.

10-Jul-64 XG597 Sycamore HR14 CFS RAF Tern Hill 0

Damaged in heavy landing

16-Jul-64 WJ771 Canberra B16 6 Sqn 15m S Khartoum Sudan 3

Broke up in the air

Flying Officer John Alan SMITH 28 Pilot
Flying Officer Carmichael Dutch STEWART 23 Navigator
Flying Officer David GIBBON 25 Navigator

16-Jul-64 XA909 Vulcan B1A 101 Sqn 3m E RAF Valley 0

Abandoned after bomb bay explosion damaged controls. The captain; Flight Lieutenant M H Smith, and his co-pilot; Flying Officer C Woods ejected and the Air Electronics Officer; Flying Officer D M T Evans and the navigators parachuted safely

---

22-Jul-64 XR978 Gnat T1 4FTS Near Blaenau Ffestiniog 0

Abandoned in an inverted spin

27-Jul-64 XP682 Jet Provost T4 7FTS Scotton Lincs 1

The pilot was on a sortie near the end of his flying training course and was undertaking a low level navigation exercise. He had been seen to pass overhead RAF Kirton in Lindsey at a very low altitude and he continued to dive off the Lincolnshire Wolds in to the valley below. Shortly afterwards he was seen to fly into a line of high tension cables, a wing was ripped off and the aircraft spun into the ground and the pilot was killed.

Flying Officer David Thomas BURKIE

Date Serial Aircraft Unit Place Casualties
Brief Circumstances of Accident
Casualty Details (If Applicable)

06-Aug-64 WP217 Valiant B1 232OCU 65m North-west RAF Gaydon 0

Rear spar fracture in flight and aircraft not repaired. This accident was probably the start of the troubles which led to the Valiant being withdrawn from service because of severe fatigue problems

---

11-Aug-64 XE623 Hunter FGA9 43 Sqn 1 1/2m North-west RAF Khormaksar Aden 0

Abandoned by Flight Lieutenant R S Burrows after engine failure

---

17-Aug-64 WH958Canberra B15 45 Sqn Kai Tak Airport Hong Kong 0

Abandoned take off after hitting a flock of birds and overshot into sea. The crew, comprising Flight Lieutenant R A Renton, Flying Officer G N Wade, Flying Officer M S Clark and Sergeant I A Ramsey escaped

---

17-Aug-64 XP397 Whirlwind 10 230 Sqn 1/2m N RAF Gutersloh 0

Tail rotor struck ground in forced landing after lost power

19-Aug-64 XH437 Javelin T3 23 Sqn RAF Leuchars 0

Caught fire during start up and damaged beyond repair

25-Aug-64 WF329 Varsity T1 AES RAF Topcliffe 2

Cartwheeled into ground after wing dropped during asymetric approach

Flight Lieutenant James Alexander KENNEDY AFC
Master Pilot Frank William RANDALL 40

28-Aug-64 XH845 Javelin FAW9 23 Sqn RAF Leuchars 0

Caught fire after engine failure on take off

28-Aug-64 XP704 Lightning F3 74 Sqn RAF Leuchars 1

Spun Into ground during aerobatic display practice. Pilot attempted to eject but was too low for the ejection sequence to complete and was probably outside the seat's operating limits anyway.

Flight Lieutenant Glyn Owens

10-Sep-64 XJ760 Whirlwind 10 110 Sqn Lang Banga Borneo 0

Forced landing in jungle after loss of power during approach

11-Sep-64 XM134 Lightning F1 226 OCU off Happisburgh Light House Norfolk 0

Abandoned by Flight Lieutenant Terry Bond after undercarriage would not lower .

11-Sep-64 XP294 Twin Pioneer CC1 209 Sqn Bario Borneo 0

Skidded on wet ground and ran into a ditch where the undercarriage collapsed

---

16-Sep-64 XM943 Twin Pioneer CC1 78 Sqn Manawa Borneo 0

Hit trees on edge of jungle airstrip after swinging off the runway

---

17-Sep-64 XN583 Jet Provost T3 7FTS 2 1/2m S Harrogate 1

Flew into wood at Hill Top Farm Pannel whilst carrying out unauthorised low flying.

Acting Pilot Officer Alan David DENNIS

Date Serial Aircraft Unit Place Casualties
Brief Circumstances of Accident
Casualty Details (If Applicable)

19-Sep-64 XF455 Hunter FGA9 20 Sqn 15m North-east RAF Changi 1

Crashed into the sea in poor visibility

Flying Officer Douglas Stewart Annandale CLAVERING 24

23-Sep-64 WT370 Canberra B16 45 Sqn 1m S RAF Kuantan Malaya 0

Overshot into a rubber plantation after power loss on landing and missed approach. Flying Officer P H Sykes and Flying Officer C G Jefford, the author of the most comprehensive squadron history yet published (Flying Camels) were not seriously injured

---

30-Sep-64 XR664 Jet Provost T4 6FTS 3m North-east Jedburgh Roxburghshire 0

Engine damaged by bird strike and aircraft abandoned

05-Oct-64 WJ820 Canberra PR7 58 Sqn Terhune Range Idris Libya 0

Struck off charge after severe damage from bird strike

07-Oct-64 XM601 Vulcan B2 9 Sqn RAF Coningsby 5

The aircraft was approaching RAF Coningsby at night during asymetric training when, at a very late stage in the approach, the Captain ordered the co-pilot to overshoot. The power was applied to the engines but the aircraft rolled over because of the unequal thrust and control was lost. The two pilots attempted ejection but were unsuccessful because of the angle at which the seats left the aircraft but the three men in the rear had no opportunity to abandon the aircraft at the height involved. Paul Busfield had just returned from his Honeymoon.

Wing Commander Kenneth John Lewis BAKER 39 Captain (Squadron Commander 12 Squadron)
Flying Officer Paul Elliott BUSFIELD 23 Co-Pilot
Flight Lieutenant Charles Vernon BURKARD Navigator (Radar)
Flight Lieutenant Geoffrey BINGHAM Navigator (Plotter)
Flying Officer Alan Hubert JONES 21 Air Electronics Officer

12-Oct-64 XR976 Gnat T1 4FTS Rhosneigr Anglesey 0

Abandoned after undercarriage failed when undershot practice forced landing at RAF Valley

---

16-Oct-64 XE592 Hunter FGA9 8/208 Sqn 3m W RAF Masirah 1

Crashed into the sea

Flying Officer Ian Arthur Marshall STEPHENS 23

19-Oct-64 XK136 Hunter FGA9 20 Sqn 32m West-north-west RAF Tengah 0

Crashed into a swamp after being abandoned in a spin

30-Oct-64 XG463 Belvedere HC1 26 Sqn 20m Nnw RAF Khormaksar Aden 3

The explosion of the front engine is believed to have damaged the control cables or to have incapacitated the pilots. Flt Lt Smith had recently been awarded the Air Force Cross for his skill and courage in saving another Belvedere which suffered a serious in-flight emergency.

Flight Lieutenant Kenneth William WOODCOCK 41 Pilot Captain & Qualified Helicopter Instructor
Flight Lieutenant William Stanley SMITH AFC 34 Co-Pilot
Sergeant John Arthur WHITEHEAD 27

Date Serial Aircraft Unit Place Casualties
Brief Circumstances of Accident
Casualty Details (If Applicable)

14-Dec-64 XM460 Jet Provost T3 CFS RAF Little Rissington 1

Crashed after overshooting and hitting power lines. The Flight Line Controller and Deputy Unit Test Pilot was severely injured and died in January 1965 as a result of his burns.

Flight Lieutenant Edward ROBERTS DFC

31-Dec-64 XG461 Belvedere HC1 26 Sqn RAF Khormaksar 0

Lost cyclic pitch control on rear rotor and rolled over on landing; caught fire

---

11-Jan-65 XG335 Lightning F1 A&AEE Woodborough Wilts 0

The trials pilot, Squadron Leader J Whitaker, ejected after the undercarriage failed to lower.

14-Jan-65 XR568 Gnat T1 4FTS RAF Valley 0

Engine vibration on take off and failed in emergency landing

03-Feb-65 XH231 Canberra B(I)8 3 Sqn Near Osnabruck West Germany 2

Flew into hillside during low level exercise

Flying Officer Sidney TOWNSHEND 33
Flying Officer Neil James TOMPKINS 24

03-Mar-65 XH833 Javelin FAW9 60 Sqn RAF Butterworth Malaya 0

Aborted take off after compressor failure and fire

05-Mar-65 WL680 Varsity T1 CAW Near Stewton Louth Lincolnshire 0
Engine cut during asymetric overshoot from RAF Manby

09-Mar-65 XR542 Gnat T1 4FTS RAF Valley 0
Forced landing following engine failure

11-Mar-65 WH231Meteor T7 ETPS Cove Hants 1
Flew into trees after loss of control during asymetric approach. Indian Air Force pilot

---

11-Mar-65 XP253 Auster AOP9 2Wing AAC Near Middle Wallop, 1 RAF
Flew into ground during low level flying
Squadron Leader Gerald JONAS Officer Commanding 103 Squadron designate killed

---

06-Apr-65 XR985 Gnat T1 4FTS RAF Valley 0
Crashed on landing at Valley

20-Apr-65 XM428 Jet Provost T3 3FTS Northallerton Yorks 1
Mid air collision with XN631
Acting Pilot Officer Laurence MEAD

20-Apr-65 XN631 Jet Provost T3 3FTS Northallerton Yorks 0
Mid air collision with XM428

22-Apr-65 XR950 Gnat T1 4FTS Carmel South of Caernarvon 1

Date Serial Aircraft Unit Place Casualties
Brief Circumstances of Accident
Casualty Details (If Applicable)

Mid air collision with XS108 during formation flying practice

Flight Lieutenant Timothy Francis Haughton MERMEGAN

22-Apr-65 XS108 Gnat T1 4FTS RAF Valley 1

Mid air collision with XR950, cartwheeled trying to land at RAF Valley and broke up in the process killing the student pilot

Flying Officer Gavin Darrell PRIEST

25-May-65 XM576 Vulcan B2 27 Sqn RAF Scampton 0

Crashed into car park during asymetric overshoot. The captain, Flight Lieutenant Derek Vernon and his crew were all saved

---

29-May-65 KJ955 Dakota C4 MECS RAF Khormaksar Aden 0

Blown up by terrorist bomb

01-Jun-65 XG206 Hunter F6 CFE off St Abbs Head 1

Dived into sea from an unknown cause

Wing Commander Harry BENNETT AFC 43 Officer Commanding Central Fighter Establishment

---

02-Jun-65 WT481 Canberra T4 39 Sqn 35 Miles South West of Malta 3

Crashed into the sea on a training sortie from RAF Luqa

Flight Lieutenant Derek ARMSTRONG 33 Captain and 1st pilot
Flying Officer Geoffrey WILLIAMS 28 Pilot
Flight Lieutenant Gerrard Peter EVANS 32 Navigator

11-Jun-65 WP986 Chipmunk T10 7AEF RAF South Cerney 0

Sank back onto ground whilst towing off a glider at the World Gliding Championships

---

22-Jun-65 XH877 Javelin FAW9R 64 Sqn Near Tawau Sabah East Malaysia 0

Port engine exploded and crew; Flight Lieutenant P J Hart and his navigator Flight Lieutenant P E 'Dinger' Dell ejected. Having been sent to investigate a radar contact, the Javelin crew identified the target as a Borneo Airways Dakota being flown by Captain Dave Baker. As the Javelin passed the Dakota one of the former's engines exploded and the crew bailed out. Baker circled his aircraft in the vicinity of the accident until help arrived and subsequently became firm friends with Dell and was the source of many good parties when Baker moved to Cathay Pacific Airways in Hong Kong to fly Convair 880s.

26-Jun-65 XR712 Lightning F3 111 Sqn Watergate Bay Near St Mawgan 0

Fire in jet pipe area and aircraft abandoned after control lost. However, the pilot; Flight Lieutenant Al Doyle who was undertaking an air display, ejected safely

---

29-Jun-65 WG662 Dragonfly HR3 ETPS Near Farnham Hampshire 1

Aircraft crashed during an autorotation landing

Squadron Leader John Sloan HURLL

03-Jul-65 XP402 Whirlwind 10 230 Sqn Port Victoria Labuan 0

During an air display the aircraft's engine failed when in high hover which was essentially outside the Whirlwind's flight envelope. The pilot was unable to control the subsequent ditching and the crewman suffered serious back injuries.

Date	Serial	Aircraft	Unit	Place	Casualties
06-Jul-65	TG577	Hastings C1A	36 Sqn	Little Baldon near Abingdon	41

Brief Circumstances of Accident
Casualty Details (If Applicable)

Fatigue failure of elevator hinge caused loss of control. The aircraft had been flown from RAF Colerne to RAF Abingdon for parachute training. It had completed several sorties that day and was about to drop another group of parachutists. After becoming airborne, the pilot reported control difficulties - 'trim troubles' followed shortly afterward by a call about sloppy controls and requesting an emergency landing. Unfortunately the nearest runway was not available as a Beverley had been parked on it and so the aircraft was continued round the circuit after the pilot said he would make a wide circuit and long approach. Unfortunately, before it was possible to land the aircraft was seen to pitch up from 1200 feet to about 2000 feet, stall turn to port and dive straight into the ground at 1609 hours and all aboard were killed instantly on impact. The Hastings fleet was grounded for several months after the accident whilst repairs were carried out but it was a tragic loss of life.

Flight Lieutenant John AKIN 36 Pilot Captain
Flying Officer Christopher John PAYNE 23 Co-Pilot
Flight Lieutenant Herbert Roy SCOTT 35 Navigator
Sergeant Graham George BLAKE 31 Air Signaller
Flight Sergeant Michael David Charles BOYLES 28 Flight Engineer
Master Air Quartermaster Peter Samual John TIMMS 36 Air Quartermaster
Flight Lieutenant William Peter RODEN 33 : Parachute Jumping Instructors
Sergeant John HURRY 32
Sergeant Peter CLIFTON 28
Sergeant James Ian BORTHWICK 31
Sergeant Philip Michael WAY 27
Sergeant John Joseph McGARTLAND 35
Sergeant Anthony EVANS 29

Sergeant Michael Charles PALMER 27
Flight Sergeant Austin Ralph CASEY 38 511 Squadron : Air Quartermasters
Flight Sergeant Joseph William ROBINSON 36 511 Squadron (recorded as Master AQM in some records)
Sergeant Colin David HOLMES 28 Air Training Squadron RAF Lyneham
Flight Lieutenant David George STEPHENS 29 : Students undergoing short parachuting courses
Flight Lieutenant George Joseph TAYLOR 33
Pilot Officer Alan Frederick CANHAM 19
Pilot Officer Royston John LEGG 20
Pilot Officer Thomas Issac ADAMS 19
Pilot Officer Alan William Henry TURNER 20
Corporal Dennis Joseph BAYLISS 24
Corporal John Raymond SMITH 25
Corporal Anthony Charles LEE 24
Corporal Alexander Morris TELFER 23
Junior Technician Paul Glynne WILLIAMS 20
Senior Aircraftman Anthony John SYKES 18
Leading Aircraftman Michael Raymond IRELAND 18
Colour Sergeant Bernard J HOUGHAM 36 10th Battalion The Parachute Regiment : Regular and Territorial Army
Colour Sergeant Thomas P ALDERSON 40 10th Battalion The Parachute Regiment
Sergeant Harry ELLIS 33 17th Battalion The Parachute Regiment
Private Duncan J STEWART 18 Airborne Forces Training Depot Aldershot
Private William G HILDITCH 21
Private Colin BASSOM 18
Private Terence R BRETT 18

Date Serial Aircraft Unit Place Casualties
Brief Circumstances of Accident
Casualty Details (If Applicable)

Private Robin M ANDREWS 18
Private Michael D WALKER 17
Private Anthony A BLACKMAN 17
Gunner Thomas COOPER 17

14-Jul-65 WT324 Canberra B(I)6 213 Sqn Roermond Netherlands 3

Ingested bird into engine and spun into ground

Flying Officer Thomas Francis CLAPP Pilot
Flight Lieutenant Leslie Dennis DINGLE Navigator
Flying Officer Hugh Mands SIME Navigator

19-Jul-65 XR543 Gnat T1 4FTS Crashed Into Llyn Maelog 1

Dived into Lake Maelog whilst approaching to land on Runway 32 at RAF Valley

Pilot Officer Roger Maxwell COOPER

23-Jul-65 XG540 Sycamore HR14 Met Comms Sqn Chinnor Oxon 0

Crashed in forced landing after engine cut

29-Jul-65 XN603 Jet Provost T3 6FTS Eshott 4 Miles From RAF Acklington 0

Crew ejected after false fire warning

17-Aug-65 XE804 Kirby Cadet TX3 CGS Swanton Morley ?

03-Sep-65 XH911 Javelin FAW9 5 Sqn Geilenkirchen West Germany 0

Scrapped after damage from start up fire

06-Sep-65 XR979 Gnat T1 4FTS Valley ?

21-Sep-65 XJ410 Whirlwind 10 22 Sqn River Torridge Near Bideford ?

Struck high tension cables across the River Torridge whilst on an SAR sortie and rotors ripped off

---

25-Sep-65 XP327 Whirlwind 10 225 Sqn 45m E Kuching Sarawak Borneo 5

Following the disappearance of an Army Scout helicopter, the Whirlwind was despatched to search for it. It carried the three airmen as lookouts. The main rotor blades became disconnected due to maintenance error and the aircraft crashed with the loss of all aboard. A subsequent court martial acquitted the maintenance technician. Jack Canham had been one of the crew of a Whirlwind SAR helicopter who rescued fishermen from a French trawler off Lands End in 1962 for which the pilot; Flight Lieutenant Trevor Eggington received the AFC and the winchman Sergeant Eric Smith the George Medal.

Flying Officer Samuel Philip SMITH 23 Pilot
Squadron Leader John Lorimer Neville (Jack) CANHAM DFC 43 Navigator
Senior Aircraftman Brian John LANGLEY 19
Senior Aircraftman Richard Moore GALBRAITH 19
Senior Aircraftman Paul EVANS 20

29-Sep-65 XD623 Vampire T11 5 CAACU Exeter 0

Struck off charge after a heavy landing

Date *Serial* *Aircraft* *Unit* *Place* *Casualties*
Brief Circumstances of Accident
Casualty Details (If Applicable)

29-Sep-65 XP739 Lightning F3 111 Sqn Battisford Hill Near Wattisham 0

Flight Lieutenant Hedley Molland abandoned the aircraft after engine problems. This was Molland's second enforced abandonment as he had ejected previously from a Hunter

---

13-Oct-65 XE320 Sycamore HR14 CFS Near Peplow Shropshire 1

Crashed in early evening when student pilot lost control. It is considered possible that the aircraft suffered a state known as vortex ring, where the airflow over the blades is effectively stalled and the aircraft becomes uncontrollable. An inexperienced pilot would probably not recognise or be able to react to the vortex ring quickly enough to recover. It was also surmised that the pilot might have reverted to operating the controls as though he was flying a fixed wing aircraft since Harvey did some fixed wing flying at weekends. Thereafter, students were forbidden to fly fixed wing aircraft during their rotary wing training. Flight Lieutenant Harvey was an officer of the Engineer Branch on a flying appointment.

Flight Lieutenant Ian Rennie HARVEY 28

08-Nov-65 XH887 Javelin FAW9R 64 Sqn 5 Miles off RAF Changi 0

Crew ejected after undercarriage failed to lower (Flight Lieutenant K E Fitchew and Flight Lieutenant A Evans were rescued)

08-Nov-65 XH959 Javelin FAW9R 64 Sqn 5 Miles off RAF Changi 1

Flew into the sea whilst engaged in a search for the crew of XH887. The navigator: Flight Lieutenant B G Unsted escaped with severe back injuries and was rescued with the crew of XH887. Poppe had survived an ejection from a Meteor when a student pilot during the early 1950s

Flight Lieutenant Peter John POPPE 36 Pilot

10-Nov-65 WT330 Canberra B(I)8 3 Sqn RAF Akrotiri Cyprus 0

Engine lost power and aircraft overran runway

12-Nov-65 XM406 Jet Provost T3 2FTS Newark Notts 0

Failed to recover from spin forcing the student pilot; Pilot Officer I G Parfit to eject.

15-Nov-65 XP621 Jet Provost T4 3FTS Near RAF Leeming 0

Crew ejected after fire warning; the crew of Flight Lieutenant J Dearden and Pilot Officer G Wheeler ejected safely.

17-Nov-65 XH749 Javelin FAW9 60 Sqn RAF Butterworth 0

Ground looped after tyre burst whilst landing

20-Nov-65 XR480 Whirlwind 10 103 Sqn Near Stass Sarawak 2

Strayed across border and shot down by indonesians

Flight Lieutenant Albert Raymond (Bert) FRASER
Gunner Anthony F MARTIN 24

08-Dec-65 XF704 Shackleton MR3 201 Sqn Moray Firth 8 Miles off RAF Kinloss 7

Flew into sea at night possibly due to loss of control or stall whilst making a finals turn to land in poor weather and visibility

Flight Lieutenant Christopher Brian TAYLOR 28 Pilot Captain & Instructor
Flight Lieutenant David William PERRY 27 Pilot
Flying Officer George William PATRICK 26

Date Serial Aircraft Unit Place Casualties
Brief Circumstances of Accident
Casualty Details (If Applicable)

Master Engineer Brian TIMMS 35
Flight Sergeant Brian Stanley ORME 30
Sergeant Major David Anthony BRAY 26
Sergeant Anthony George BROMLEY

22-Dec-65 WP968 Chipmunk T10 UAS Winter Hill Near Bolton ?

Flew into ground during descent through cloud

05-Jan-66 XR721 Lightning F3 56 Sqn Helmington Suffolk 1

Following a radar failure the pilot decided to do some instrument approaches to base and after completing a GCA, asked for a practice diversion to Bentwaters. However, the No 1 engine flamed out and the pilot could not maintain height and, therefore announced that he would eject. The seat, however, did not fire because the canopy would not detach. The pilot was left with no option but to try to land the aircraft and this he did with little damage. Unfortunately, the aircraft struck a wall as it came to a stop and the impact fired the seat. As it was outside limits it did not provide the pilot with a safe escape and he was killed.

Flying Officer Derek Rollo LAW

02-Feb-66 WT531 Canberra PR7 80 Sqn Berriedale Scotland 2

Flew into high ground 5 miles north west of Berriedale on the slopes of Scaraben (2054 feet) about 1000 feet from the top and within sight of the memorial to the Duke of Kent. The aircraft was on a hi-lo-hi sortie from RAF Bruggen and had passed Lossiemouth at 1025 and was due to return for refuelling about 2 hours later before returning to base. Nothing was heard after about 1030 hours and the wreckage was not discovered for 2 days after an extensive search.

Flying Officer David Lawrence GIRLING Pilot
Flying Officer Rowland Beresford SMITH Navigator

05-Feb-66 XS221 Jet Provost T4 20 Sqn Alor Star Malaya 1

Aircraft was engaged on trials to judge the suitability of using the Jet Provost as an airborne Forward Air Control aircraft. It was overflying the target area when it crashed into the trees and the pilot did not attempt to eject and was killed.

Flight Lieutenant Peter Sydney LOVEDAY

11-Feb-66 XH536 Vulcan B2 12 Sqn North of Swansea 5

Despite very poor weather conditions the crew elected to continue with a low level navigation exercise and flew into high ground.

Flight Lieutenant John Donald MACDONALD 30 Captain
Flying Officer Graham Howard SUTCLIFFE 21 Co-Pilot
Flight Lieutenant Brian WARING 32 Navigator
Flight Lieutenant Roger CLARE 31 Navigator
Flight Lieutenant Geoffrey Edward FULLER 27 Air Electronics Officer

---

17-Feb-66 XJ915 Sycamore HR14 CFS RAF Tern Hill 0

Loss of cyclic pitch control authority with the wind from behind whilst practising hovering out of wind.

28-Feb-66 XL826 Sycamore HR14 CFS RAF Tern Hill 0

Rolled over after loss of cyclic pitch authority because of wind conditions. This accident and another within a few weeks spelt the end of the Sycamore as a training aircraft, a role for which it was not well suited anyway.

Date Serial Aircraft Unit Place Casualties
Brief Circumstances of Accident
Casualty Details (If Applicable)

15-Mar-66 XM190 Lightning F1A 226 OCU RAF Coltishall 0

Abandoned after engine fire by a United States Air Force Exchange Programme officer; Captain Al Peterson

---

04-Apr-66 XK641 Canberra B15 45 Sqn Lake Chini Pahang Malaya 3

Dived into ground after low fly past of jungle camp site where other squadron members were on an expedition training exercise

Flying Officer Martin William (Rufus) REDLEY
Flying Officer Philip Arthur HARRISON
Flying Officer Colin COOKE

04-Apr-66 XH785 Javelin FAW9 60 Sqn Near RAF Tengah Singapore 0

Abandoned after engine explosion

05-Apr-66 XP670 Jet Provost T4 7FTS Near Coxwold Yorks 0

Loss of control whilst spinning

13-Apr-66 XP507 Gnat T1 4FTS RAF Valley 2

Crashed into sea on approach

Flight Lieutenant Bill Edwy Carrad FORSE Instructor
Pilot Officer Peter William STEWART Student Pilot

18-Apr-66 XH556 Vulcan B2 230OCU RAF Finningley 0

Fire on the ground

26-Apr-66 XH717 Javelin FAW9 60 Sqn RAF Butterworth 0

Fire whilst starting

26-Apr-66 WB555 Chipmunk T10 Liverpool UAS RAF Woodvale 0

Crashed following a stall whilst approaching to land.

02-May-66 WT515 Canberra PR7 31 Sqn Ingolstadt Germany 0

Struck tanker whilst taxying and damaged beyond repair

03-May-66 WH857Canberra B2 97 Sqn RAF Watton 2

Stalled following asymetric approach. The Air Electronics Operator, Flight Lieutenant Ken Topas ejected safely and became the first AEO ever to eject from an RAF aircraft. The navigator was flying his last sortie with the RAF before returning to Canada

Flight Lieutenant Roger John Bazley JACKSON Pilot
Flight Lieutenant G R JENKINS RCAF Navigator

03-May-66 WL106 Meteor F8 85 Sqn RAF Binbrook 0

A tyre burst on landing and the aircraft was damaged beyond repair.

04-May-66 TG575 Hastings C1 RAF El Adem 0

Believed to be an undercarriage collapse whilst landing and the aircraft was damaged beyond repair.

Date Serial Aircraft Unit Place Casualties
Brief Circumstances of Accident
Casualty Details (If Applicable)

06-May-66 XM213 Lightning F1A 226 OCU RAF Coltishall 0

Undercarriage retracted during take off. Although the aircraft was damaged beyond repair the pilot; Squadron Leader Paul Hobley, was uninjured

---

07-May-66 XE617 Hunter FGA9 208 Sqn RAF Muharraq (Bahrain) 0

Ran out of fuel and subsequently crashed.

13-May-66 XR539 Gnat T1 4FTS Near Gwynedd 0

Spun into ground

23-May-66 XR570 Gnat T1 4FTS Near Mona 0

Hit high tension cables

26-May-66 XM384 Jet Provost T3 2FTS Woodborough Leics 0

Mid air collison with XP631

26-May-66 XP631 Jet Provost T3 2FTS Woodborough Leics 0

Mid air collison with XM384. The crews, comprising Flight Lieutenant D Henderson, Flying Officer T Thorne and Pilot Officer D Sedman, ejected safely.

02-Jun-66 XP342 Whirlwind 10 CFS Llangollen 0

Hit HT cables in valley. The captain (Flight Lieutenant John Dicken) and the student (Pilot Officer Richard Kingston) escaped with relatively minor injuries. Subsequently, when posted to fly Belvederes on 66 Sqn, Kingston was less than happy to learn that the Squadron training officer was none other than Dicken!

02-Jun-66 XH980 Javelin FAW9 29 Sqn N'dola Zambia 0

Undercarriage collapsed and aircraft declared beyond repair.

05-Jun-66 XM270 Canberra B(I)8 16 Sqn RAF Gutersloh 1

Spun into ground on approach. The pilot; Flying Officer T D Taylor ejected safely

Flying Officer James Victor LANFRANCHI 23 Navigator

14-Jun-66 XH709 Javelin FAW9 64 Sqn Skudai Estate Malaya 0

Cause not known

14-Jun-66 WF334 Varsity T1 BCBS Immingham 1

Forced landing after mid air collison with Cessna 337 aircraft, serial number G-ATJO. Several crew from the Varsity parachuted to safety but one member of the crew did not survive nor did Captain Graham McRae, the pilot of the civil aircraft.

Flight Lieutenant Alfred Lawrence LESLIE-MILLER

15-Jun-66 WZ459 Vampire T11 7FTS RAF Church Fenton 0

Overshot the runway after an abandoned take off and damaged beyond repair

Date Serial Aircraft Unit Place Casualties
Brief Circumstances of Accident
Casualty Details (If Applicable)

16-Jun-66 XG157 Hunter F6 234 Sqn Challacombe Devon 1

Crashed into high ground after emerging from cloud. Flying Officer Kenneth Becker, who was flying in company with the aircraft, stated that he lost contact with it after they had been flying about 400 yards apart in a 'pairs' sortie.

Flight Lieutenant Colin Stuart MATHIESON

19-Jun-66 XJ757 Whirlwind 10 CFS(H) RAF Tern Hill 0

During a forced landing at RAF Tern Hill the rotors cut through the tail boom and the aircraft was declared beyond repair. It was subsequently 'patched up' and for a number of years was taken around the recruiting and display circuit painted in Search and Rescue colours

---

22-Jun-66 WH967Canberra B15 32 Sqn Wheelus Libya 0

Wing root explosion and abandonment

23-Jun-66 WK631 Chipmunk T10 Birmingham UAS Tibberton Grange Shropshire 2

Mid air collison with WP834

Pilot Officer Geoffrey Wallace DOWD 25 Pilot
Pilot Officer Robert Anthony SPOONER 26

23-Jun-66 WP834 Chipmunk T10 UAS Tibberton Grange Shropshire 1

Mid air collison with WK631

Cadet Pilot Michael David FOX 21 Pilot

27-Jun-66 XH847 Javelin FAW9 29 Sqn RAF Khormaksar 0

Damaged beyond repair after swinging off the runway.

29-Jun-66 XM716 Victor SR2 543 Sqn Near Warboys Airfield 4

Broke up in high speed low level turn. The aircraft, the first SR2 to enter service with the squadron, was being demonstrated to the Press. The evidence suggests that it was overstressed in the turn and broke up over the old airfield at Warboys.

Squadron Leader John Anthony HOLLAND Captain
Flying Officer Harry WALSH Co-Pilot
Flight Lieutenant Royston Arthur NORMAN Navigator
Flight Lieutenant Kenneth SMITH Air Electronics Officer

01-Jul-66 XS453 Lightning T5 226 OCU Hapisburgh Norfolk 0

Jammed undercarriage led to aircraft being abandoned by Flying Officer Geoff Fish

---

11-Jul-66 XH445 Javelin FAW9 64 Sqn RAF Tengah 0

Swung off the runway and severely damaged after falling into a drain.

12-Jul-66 XE622 Hunter FGA9 28 Sqn RAF Kai Tak 0

Damaged beyond repair following an engine explosion whilst starting.

15-Jul-66 XL517 Pioneer 209 Sqn Long Pasia Sarawak 0

Flew into trees whilst approaching a jungle airstrip. The pilot, Master Pilot Cheesewright, scrambled from the wreckage and was then asked by a senior Army passenger to return inside the wreck to retrieve his hat. When Cheesewright enquired why, the senior officer retorted 'In case someone wants to salute me when we're rescued'! Cheesewright dined out on the story for sometime.

Date	Serial	Aircraft	Unit	Place	Casualties
Brief Circumstances of Accident Casualty Details (If Applicable)					
27-Jul-66	XP625	Jet Provost T3	CAW	North Frodingham	0
Abandoned after birdstrike					
27-Jul-66	XR714	Lightning F3	111 Sqn	RAF Akrotiri	0
Damaged beyond repair after the undercarriage was retracted on take-off and the aircraft was caught in the slip stream of another.					
24-Aug-66	XP760	Lightning F3	23 Sqn	Near Seahouses Fife	0
Abandoned after engine failure by Flight Lieutenant Al Turley					
24-Aug-66	XH876	Javelin FAW9	64 Sqn	RAF Tengah Singapore	0
Abandoned following engine fire. Flight Lieutenant J J Jackson and Flight Lieutenant P J Hart (for the second time from a Javelin) ejected safely					
14-Sep-66	XP616	Jet Provost T4	1FTS	Near Helmsley	1
Flew into high ground in poor weather Sub Lieutenant Derek BREEN 20 Royal Navy					
28-Sep-66	XM704	Gnat T1	CFS	RAF Kemble	0
Crashed during take off					

04-Oct-66 XR645 Jet Provost T4 7FTS Stellingfleet 1
Dived into the ground
Acting Pilot Officer Richard Edward PASSMAN

11-Oct-66 XH958 Javelin FAW9 228OCU RAF Leuchars 0
Crashed on landing after the undercarriage jammed.

20-Oct-66 XH909 Javelin FAW9 228OCU RAF Leuchars 0
The aircraft was structurally damaged by overstressing in flight and was declared to be beyond economical repair

---

06-Nov-66 XJ412 Whirlwind 10 230 Sqn Tinkers Hill Sarawak Borneo 0
Tail rotor failed and aircraft landed skilfully by the pilot; Flying Officer Paul Shaw. However, the aircraft was landed on a remote spot which was generally inaccessible and would have been difficult to recover. It was, therefore, abandoned and remains there to this day

---

06-Dec-66 WZ864 Chipmunk T10 UAS Hamble 0
Mid air collision with Chipmunk G-ATEA

14-Dec-66 XH848 Javelin FAW9 29 Sqn RAF Akrotiri 0
Abandoned on approach after loss of control having flown through another aircraft's slipstream

---

30-Dec-66 XE646 Hunter FGA9 1 Sqn RAF Leconfield 0
Engine failure on approach. Aircraft crashed into a house injuring a local vicar, who was the chaplain to RAF Leconfield. The pilot, Flight Lieutenant P B Curtin escaped without serious injury.

Date Serial Aircraft Unit Place Casualties
Brief Circumstances of Accident
Casualty Details (If Applicable)

30-Dec-66 XP569 Jet Provost T4 2FTS East Drayton Notts 2

Spun into ground

Squadron Leader David Alan NOON
Pilot Officer Christopher ROBERTS

02-Jan-67 XM971 Lightning T4 226 OCU RAF Coltishall 0

Abandoned after radar fairing came loose and components were ingested into the engines. Squadron Leader Terry Carleton and Flight Lieutenant Lloyd Grose ejected safely

---

18-Jan-67 XH800 Javelin FAW9 29 Sqn RAF Akrotiri Cyprus ?

Crashed on approach

23-Jan-67 WW595 Hunter FR10 4 Sqn Furstenburg Germany 1

Flew into high ground

Master Pilot Thomas Lionel RATCLIFFE

20-Feb-67 XF414 Hunter FGA9 20 Sqn Layang Malaya 0

Abandoned following power loss. The pilot; Flight Lieutenant W D Thomson ejected and was subsequently casevaced to UK for treatment of his injuries. Whilst returning to the Joint Services Medical Rehabilitation Unit at RAF Headley Court, following a weekend break, Dave Thomson was killed in the Hither Green rail crash

20-Feb-67 XF440 Hunter FGA9 8 Sqn Al Ittihad 0
Abandoned following In-Flight Fire

23-Feb-67 WT322 Canberra B(I)6 213 Sqn Wesseke Germany 3
Crashed following loss of control at low level on the Nordhorn Ranges

Flying Officer George William WILKINSON 22 Pilot
Flying Officer Ian Kenneth CHALK 22 Navigator
Flight Lieutenant David William James HARRIS 28 Navigator

01-Mar-67 XT798 Sioux AH1 CFS RAF Tern Hill 0
Crashed and burnt out

03-Mar-67 XP699 Lightning F3 56 Sqn Near Weathersfield Suffolk 0
Abandoned by Flying Officer Stu Pearse after fire warning

23-Mar-67 XF421 Hunter FGA9 8 Sqn RAF Khormaksar Aden 0
Overshot into the sea after an engine off landing

01-Apr-67 XL111 Whirlwind 10 SAR Flight RAF Khormaksar Aden 0
Engine failure, damaged beyond repair in crash landing

06-Apr-67 XL385 Vulcan B2 27 Sqn RAF Scampton 0
Destroyed after port engines exploded during take-off. The crew of five plus an Air Training Corps cadet escaped despite 40 tons of aviation fuel catching fire.

Date Serial Aircraft Unit Place Casualties
Brief Circumstances of Accident
Casualty Details (If Applicable)

17-Apr-67 XM184 Lightning F1A 226 OCU RAF Coltishall 0
Caught fire on landing but the pilot; Flight Lieutenant Gerry Crumbie was uninjured

---

17-Apr-67 WT489 Canberra T4 231OCU Steeple Morden Cambs 3
Crashed on approach to RAF Bassingbourne at night

Flight Lieutenant Brian Wilfred SEAMAN Captain & Instructor
Flying Officer Graham Malcolm BEECH Student Pilot
Flying Officer Brian David MEEHAN Student Navigator

18-Apr-67 XG273 Hunter F6 54 Sqn RAF El Adem Libya 0
Mid air collison on approach with XF446

18-Apr-67 XF446 Hunter F6 54 Sqn RAF El Adem Libya 0
Mid air collision with XG273

27-Apr-67 XJ691 Hunter FGA9 208 Sqn 18m South-east Bahrain 1
Crashed into sea, cause not known

Flying Officer John Dudley HOWICK-BAKER

28-Apr-67 XN321 Twin Pioneer CC1 209 Sqn RAF Butterworth Malaya 0
Engine failed on take off

09-May-67 XH204 Canberra B(I)8 Abandoned after controls jammed	3 Sqn	Near Wesel Germany	0
15-May-67 XG200 Hunter F6 Mid air collision	229 OCU	Tintagel Cornwall	0
15-May-67 XG235 Hunter F6 Mid air collision	229 OCU	Tintagel Cornwall	0
18-May-67 XN588 Jet Provost T3 Dived into ground	1FTS	Wharren Le Street Yorkshire	?
30-May-67 XH708 Javelin FAW9 Mid air collision with XH896 Flying Officer William Brendan KAY Pilot Corporal Kenneth ASHBEE	64 Sqn	RAF Tengah Singapore	2
30-May-67 XH896 Javelin FAW9 Mid air collision	64 Sqn	RAF Tengah Singapore	0
05-Jun-67 VP966 Devon C1 Destroyed on ground by Isreali air attack	Embassy Flt	Amman Jordan	0
09-Jun-67 WD491 Hastings C2 Circumstances of loss not known			

Date	Serial	Aircraft	Unit	Place	Casualties
Brief Circumstances of Accident					
Casualty Details (If Applicable)					
21-Jun-67	XM106	Beverley C1	84 Sqn	Habulaya Aden	0
Struck a mine on runway					
22-Jun-67	XJ414	Whirlwind 10	202 Sqn	off Great Yarmouth	3
Aircraft broke up in the air and crashed into the sea just off the coast but the crew could not be rescued. Archie Gavan was a particularly experienced helicopter pilot who had previously been the flight commander of 1563 Flight in Belize					
Flight Lieutenant Arthur (Archie) GAVAN Flight Lieutenant Gilbert Aubrey (Gil) PINK Master Navigator Henry William Edward CROSSMAN					
28-Jun-67	XN597	Jet Provost T3	2 FTS	not known	?
The circumstances of the loss of this aircraft are not known					
29-Jun-67	WD963	Canberra T4	45 Sqn	2m S RAF Tengah	0
Abandoned after double engine failure. Flying Officers I D Hill and T V Hudson survived. Hill was killed subsequently in a Jaguar in 1987 having ejected from a Canberra.					
30-Jun-67	XM707	Gnat T1	CFS	2 1/2m West-north-west RAF Kemble	0
Abandoned after pitch control failure					
03-Aug-67	XF443	Hunter F6	229 OCU	1m South-east RAF Chivenor	0
Crashed into railway cutting during emergency approach after engine failed					

07-Aug-67 XR478 Whirlwind 10 230 Sqn RAF Odiham 0
Damaged beyond repair in heavy landing during practice engine off approach

---

23-Aug-67 XP512 Gnat T1 4FTS Rhosneigr Anglesey 0
Hydraulic failure

04-Sep-67 XG198 Hunter F6 229 OCU Ferryside Carmarthen 1
Crashed following dive attack on Pembrey Range
Flight Lieutenant Trevor Martin SHARP

07-Sep-67 XR766 Lightning F6 23 Sqn 51m East-north-east Leuchars 0
Abandoned by Squadron Leader Ron Blackburn after failing to recover from spin

---

12-Sep-67 WK610 Chipmunk T10 UAS 2m South-west Portishead Bristol 0
Mid air collision with WP838

12-Sep-67 WP838 Chipmunk T10 UAS 2m South-west Portishead Bristol 0
Mid air collision with WK610

13-Sep-67 XM136 Lightning F1 TFF RAF Coltishall 0
Reheat fire followed by control loss made it inevitable that Flight Lieutenant Jock Sneddon should eject

---

19-Sep-67 XM959 Twin Pioneer C1 152 Sqn Tajibah Oman 0
Crashed on landing

Date	Serial	Aircraft	Unit	Place	Casualties
Brief Circumstances of Accident					
Casualty Details (If Applicable)					

11-Oct-67 XH788 Javelin FAW9 60 Sqn off RAF Tengah Singapore 2

Whilst on a training sortie from RAF Tengah the aircraft was seen to approach two other aircraft at a speed of between 370 and 430 knots and height of about 400 feet. Just after overtaking the pair, XH788 was seen to pull up into a shallow climb and start a tight barrel roll to starboard. The aircraft reached a maximum height of about 1500 feet but then descended to about 300 to 600 feet. After about three quarters of the roll had been completed, the aircraft was seen to explode from the centre of the fuselage and it disintegrated before crashing into the sea. Neither crew member made any attempt to eject and were killed instantly. Although the cause was never firmly established it seems likely to have been caused by either a catastrophic engine failure or structural failure caused by overstressing.

Flying Officer Gerald Charles (Gerry) BARNARD Pilot
Flying Officer Howard John Charles (Gus) GEEVE Navigator

12-Oct-67 XL638 Britannia C1 511 Sqn RAF Khormaksar Aden 0

Overshot into the sea after power applied on landing instead of reverse thrust. The wreck could not be removed easily and so was blown up in-situ

---

27-Oct-67 XK990 Whirlwind 10 202 Sqn RAF Acklington 0

Engine failed during practice forced landing and damaged beyond repair

---

04-Nov-67 WL786 Shackleton MR2 205 Sqn Indian Ocean off En Route To Gan 8

The aircraft was being flown from Gan to Changi at 9000 feet when there was a major component failure of the No 4 (starboard outer) engine which rapidly led to the propeller overspeeding and this could not be feathered, whilst at the same time a major fire began, caused by fuel and oil leaking from fractured pipes. The engine broke off but after a short time the fire re-established itself and a part of the wing detached. The aircraft was then ditched in a reasonably straight and level attitude but after a couple of skips a very heavy impact was felt and the aircraft broke into three sections, with the main crew compartment rapidly filling with water. An air signaller and a passenger escaped from the rear of the aircraft and the flight engineer from the front through the fractured nose. The three survivors spent over 16 hours in a dinghy before being rescued by HMS Ajax and although two bodies were recovered, the remaining six crew were not found.

Flight Lieutenant Hugh BLAKE Captain
Flight Lieutenant Kenneth Michael GREATOREX Navigator
Flight Lieutenant Ivor Benjamin STANLEY 30 Air Electronics Officer
Flying Officer Robert Kenneth BUNGAY 22 Navigator
Flying Officer David LOVE Co-Pilot
Flight Sergeant Roger Neill ADAMS
Flight Sergeant Richard Gwyn REES
Flight Sergeant David Harold MORGAN Air Electronics Operator

Flight Sergeant K R Wordsworth and Flight Sergeant B E Saunders and one other survived.

19-Nov-67 WR976 Shackleton MR3 201 Sqn 200miles off Cornwall 9

Stalled in low level turn and crashed into sea before recovery possible

Squadron Leader Brian Campbell LETCHFORD 34 Pilot
Flight Lieutenant Frank Raymond HOLLINS 37 Pilot
Flight Lieutenant Joseph Dennis FILLION 35 RCAF Navigator
Flight Lieutenant Edward Thomas SPICER 34 Navigator
Flight Lieutenant Peter John STOWELL 23
Flying Officer Keith Robert GORDON 29
Lieutenant Commander C B SCOFIELD 34 RN
Flight Sergeant John Francis GENT 29
Sergeant Arthur BROWN 24

Date Serial Aircraft Unit Place Casualties
Brief Circumstances of Accident
Casualty Details (If Applicable)

20-Nov-67 XE654 Hunter FGA9 8 Sqn Oman 1

Flew into ground during practice low level attack

Flight Lieutenant Roger Howis PATTERSON

07-Dec-67 XR487 Whirlwind HCC12 Queen Flight Brightwalton Berkshire 4

Main rotor head failed and the blades detached. The Whirlwind aircraft fleet was grounded for several weeks whilst inspections were carried out and restrictions were lifted. The accident hastened the replacement of the Whirlwind in the Queens Flight by the Wessex

Squadron Leader Jack Harry LIVERSIDGE DFC AFC Pilot
Air Commodore J H L BLOUNT DFC Captain of The Queens' Flight
Squadron Leader Michael William HERMON Senior Engineering Officer The Queens' Flight
Flight Lieutenant Ronald FISHER Navigator

14-Dec-67 XP509 Gnat T1 4FTS RAF Valley 0

Belly landing

15-Dec-67 XL150 Beverley C1 34 Sqn 60m N RAF Seletar Singapore 6

The crew was briefed for a practice sortie for the B C Bennett Trophy competition for which tactical transport squadrons in the Far East Air Force competed annually. On the morning of the accident the weather was extremely poor with heavy rain and low cloud as well as poor visibility in the rain. At various stages of the flight the Beverley was seen or heard by various other aircraft. Shortly after requesting details of the pressure settings at Singapore the aircraft was descended into cloud and collided with a 1150 foot hill about 150 feet below its summit. The local evidence was that at this stage the cloud base was about 600 feet. It seems likely that the crew were flying below the margins set down when they should have been flying under IMC rules and hence several thousand feet higher than they were.

Squadron Leader Nigel Olney BACON Captain
Flying Officer David Smith BRODIE Co-Pilot
Flying Officer Brain HUDSON Navigator
Sergeant Ernest William TRIGWELL
Sergeant John CURTIS
Sergeant Brian Raymond GEORGE

21-Dec-67 XF702 Shackleton MR3 206 Sqn Near Inverness 11

Dived into the ground in extreme weather conditions of heavy airframe icing and severe turbulence

Squadron Leader Michael Charles MACULLUM 33 Captain
Squadron Leader Harry HARVEY 46
Flight Lieutenant Brian George Wishart MACKIE 33
Flying Officer Terence Charles SWINNEY 25
Flying Officer Ralph Joseph FONSECA 27
Flying Officer David John EVANS 22
Flying Officer John Verner YOUNG 31
Pilot Officer Ian Campbell MACLEAN
Flight Sergeant David John HARIS 30
Sergeant Charles Peter MATTHEWS 33
Sergeant Michael Barry BOWEN 23
Sergeant Kenneth Brown HURRY 26
Sergeant Malcolm Arthur JONES 27

24-Jan-68 XS900 Lightning F6 5 Sqn RAF Lossiemouth 0

Abandoned by Flight Lieutenant Miller after control restriction

30-Jan-68 XM604 Vulcan B2 9 Sqn Cow Close Farm Cottesmore 4

The crew was briefed to fly a high level navigation and bombing exercise training profile and was to carry the squadron Navigation Radar Leader for the purposes of carrying out a categorisation check. Shortly after take-off the bomb bay temperature rose to an unacceptable level and, having closed the engine air valves the aircraft was returned to the local area to carry out continuation training. The aircraft carried out an approach using the aircraft's internal systems and bombing radar and then overshot to an ILS pattern with the intention of carrying out several of these as fuel was burned off to an acceptable landing weight. At about 800 feet and after being warned of a possible conflict of traffic at which time the aircraft was banked to port and the power increased, a number of explosions and reverberating thumps were felt and severe vibration set in. As the aircraft could not be controlled the captain, Flight Lieutenant Peter Tait, ordered the rear crew to abandon the aircraft and because he could not control the aircraft instructed the co-pilot (Flying Officer Mike Gillette) to do likewise. The captain looked around to see how the rear crew were progressing with their own evacuation but because the curtain between the two parts of the cabin was down, he could see nothing and ejected at about 300 feet with the aircraft in a very high rate of descent. Although, theoretically, beyond the seat's operating limits the captain's parachute rigging lines caught in some overhead cables and he was deposited safely on the ground. Unfortunately, the 'G' forces prevented any of the rear crew from escaping from the aircraft and they were killed on impact. The cause of the accident was later attributed to the No: 2 engine low pressure compressor failing with subsequent overspeed and blades separating and severing the control runs where they passed through the bomb bay. From the moment the captain advanced the throttles to climb out after the initial approach he lost control and the crash was inevitable.

Flight Lieutenant Alistair William BENNETT Navigator Radar Instructor
Flight Lieutenant Stephen Roderick SUMPTER Navigator Plotter
Flight Lieutenant Barry Donald GOODMAN Navigator Radar
Flying Officer Michael Joseph WHELAN Air Electronics Officer

01-Feb-68 WT209 Canberra B6 45 Sqn RAF Tengah Singapore 0

Aircraft damaged beyond repair after a wheels up landing following hydraulics failure. The crew of Fg Off I D Hill, Fg Off R Head and Fg Off S Godfrey were uninjured. (Hill was subsequently killed in Jun 87 whilst flying a Jaguar and had already ejected once from a Canberra)

03-Feb-68 XF508 Hunter FGA9 20 Sqn off Johore Malaya 0

Abandoned over the sea

21-Feb-68 XP561 Jet Provost T4 1FTS RAF Linton On Ouse 0

Abandoned after loss of control in cloud. Sub Lieutenant G F Harris RN survived.

26-Feb-68 XP675 Jet Provost T4 CFS Hanling Gloucestershire 0

Mid air collision with XP229

26-Feb-68 XS229 Jet Provost T4 CFS Hanling Gloucestershire 0

Mid Air Collision With XP675. The two pilots, Flight Lieutenant D J Smith and Flying Officer J Tye escaped without serious injury

---

11-Mar-68 WJ770 Canberra B16 6 Sqn Calbria Italy 3

Flew into a mountain. The aircraft was with another when they encountered poor weather and commenced a low level abort procedure. However, instead of climbing straight ahead having entered cloud, this aircaft made a turn to achieve separation from the other aircraft and in doing so struck the hillside

Flying Officer Roger CRAWLEY-CHALLENER Pilot
Flying Officer David CRYER Navigator
Flying Officer Michael John DUNNE Navigator

Date Serial Aircraft Unit Place Casualties
Brief Circumstances of Accident
Casualty Details (If Applicable)

19-Apr-68 WB833 Shackleton MR2 210 Sqn Mull of Kintyre 11

Flew into high ground. The aircraft was exercising with the submarine HMS Onyx in poor weather under a cloud base of 400 feet. It turned over the narrow coastal strip to practice an attack on the submarine and then repeated the exercise. However, on this occasion it flew further inland and collided with the ground near Machrihanish

Squadron Leader Robert Charles Leonard HAGGETT 33 Captain
Flying Officer David Robert BURTON 23 Pilot
Flying Officer Michael CREEDON 24 Pilot
Flight Lieutenant George Craigie FISKEN 26 Navigator
Flight Lieutenant Roger John Duncan DENNY 31 Navigator
Flight Lieutenant Rodney HELLENS 27 Air Electronics Officer
Master Signaller Ronald Cecil STRATTON 44 Air Signaller
Flight Sergeant Thomas Frederick Anglin BUTTIMORE 33 Air Electronics Operators
Sergeant Bruce Robert DIXON 24
Sergeant Nathaniel Michael DUFFY 24
Sergeant John Richard Frank CREAMER 27 Flight Engineer

24-Apr-68 WH971 Canberra B15 6 Sqn RAF Akrotiri 0

Bounced and swung off runway on landing and broke into three parts

---

25-Apr-68 XT677 Wessex HC2 18 Sqn Rheinsehein Camp Germany 0

Flew Into ground whilst Approaching In Fog At Night

29-Apr-68 XS924 Lightning F6 5 Sqn Beelsby Lincs 1

Dived into ground after control loss during air to air refuelling and whilst taking part in the flypast to mark the formation of RAF Strike Command.

Flying Officer Alan John Davey

02-May-68 WZ874 Chipmunk T10 CFS Morton In The Marsh Gloucestershire ?

Spun into ground

03-May-68 VP969 Devon CC1 ? ? ?

Details of this loss are not known

06-May-68 XE532 Hunter FGA9 208 Sqn 3m West-south-west Dubai 0

Abandoned over sea after striking a radio mast in the vacinity of a range

---

07-May-68 XR133 Argosy C1 267 Sqn Got El Afraq Airfield Libya 11

The aircraft was ferrying equipment and personnel between Got El Afraq and RAF El Adem about 80 miles away. Having taken off for the last sortie, the pilot requested permission for a flypast of the Air Traffic Control tower for the purpose of checking the undercarriage. When permission was granted the aircraft was flown around a nearby hill and then descended rapidly towards the airfield. The aircraft struck a 45 gallon oil drum (used as a shower) mounted 10 feet above the ground. The starboard wing struck the ground and broke off the outer section complete with aileron. The aircraft climbed to a height of about 100 feet and then descended, scraping the starboard wing along the ground before cartwheeling onto its back and crashing nose first onto the runway where it exploded.

Flying Officer Richard John Gibbon PROCTER Pilot
Flying Officer Michael John GREENOP Pilot

Date Serial Aircraft Unit Place Casualties
Brief Circumstances of Accident
Casualty Details (If Applicable)

Sergeant Jeffrey James WASS Air Engineer
Sergeant Alan James WISE Air Quartermaster
Flight Lieutenant Alan CRISP Navigator
+ 6 soldiers whose identities are not known

02-Jun-68 XM188 Lightning F1A 226OCU RAF Coltishall 0

Whilst taxying the brakes failed and the aircraft ran into the walls of a squadron office (sucking out the entire contents of the paper trays in the process). The throttles were jammed and hence the engines could not be shut down and the local Rolls Royce representative crawled beneath the aircraft to turn the engines off. The pilot; Squadron Leader Arthur Tyldesley, made good his escape by climbing on to the half roof of the hangar offices!

08-Jun-68 XR999 Gnat T1 4FTS Over Sea off North Wales Coast 0

Abandoned after controls jammed

11-Jun-68 WT363 Canberra B(I)6 14 Sqn Annendal Holland 0

Mid air collision with XM278 which landed safely. The navigator bailed out and the pilot, Flight Lieutenant G N Morris, subsequently ejected

---

18-Jun-68 XS412 Whirlwind 10 230 Sqn Basingstoke 0

Forced landed in a wood following engine failure

19-Jun-68 WH714Canberra T19 85 Sqn RAF Binbrook 0

Brakes failed on landing and the aircraft was damaged beyond repair

---

26-Jun-68 XF388 Hunter FGA9 8 Sqn 50m South-east Dubai 0

Abandoned after engine failure. The pilot was Flight Lieutenant V W Yates who escaped without serious injury

---

15-Jul-68 WV253 Hunter T7 ETPS Lyme Bay Dorset 0

Failed to recover from an intentional spin. The Royal Navy pilot ejected safely

---

22-Jul-68 XJ674 Hunter FGA9 20 Sqn 1m S RAF Tengah Singapore 0

Returning from a high level sortie, the pilot, Chris Pinder, experienced hydraulics failure exacerbated by an asymetric undercarriage leg when first selecting undercarriage down. Having overshot his first approach, the pilot attempted a very tight circuit in manual control but was subsequently unable to prevent the aircraft rolling to port and so, from about 800 feet he ejected and was rescued by a passing Whirlwind helicopter.

31-Jul-68 WJ783 Canberra B16 249 Sqn RAF Akrotiri Cyprus 0

Port undercarriage failed and aircraft went into the barrier and was damaged beyond economical repair

---

19-Aug-68 XH646 Victor K1A 214 Sqn Kelling Heath Norfolk 4

Whilst flying in extremely poor weather conditions which rendered the radar cover inadequate, the Victor was in collision with a Canberra. The crews of both aircraft were killed. Squadron Leader Doyle had assumed his responsibilities as a flight commander on 214 Squadron on the morning of his death.

Squadron Leader Michael Thomas DOYLE Navigator
Flight Lieutenant William Anthony GALLIENE Captain
Flight Lieutenant Kenneth John PEACOCK Navigator
Flight Lieutenant Roger Stanley MORTON Co-Pilot

Date Serial Aircraft Unit Place Casualties
Brief Circumstances of Accident
Casualty Details (If Applicable)

19-Aug-68 WT325 Canberra B(I)6 213 Sqn Kelling Heath Norfolk 3

Mid air collision with XH646 as outlined above

Flying Officer Stuart COWIE 24
Flying Officer Johan SLABBER 25 Navigator
Flying Officer John Henry WOOLNOUGH 25 Navigator

23-Aug-68 WH795Canberra PR7 81 Sqn RAF Kai Tak 0

After a series of frustrations relating to clearances from ATC and having descended to low level early, thereby burning extra fuel, the aircraft was positioned for a downwind landing. Although the approach was both well directed and flown, the aircraft was about 25 knots above the acquaplaning speed when it crossed the threshold. In addition, although a wet runway technique was used it seems that braking began too early and the aircraft burst its starboard tyre and the port tyre suffered scalding. The aircraft began a swing which became much worse as the aircraft ran onto the grass and it ended up running into a sewage drain where it broke into several parts. The crew of Flight Lieutenants Dyer and Philips received minor injuries

---

26-Aug-68 WT369 Canberra B16 249Sqn RAF Luqa 0

Port undercarriage leg collapsed and the aircraft was damaged beyond repair

---

12-Sep-68 XS896 Lightning F6 74 Sqn 4m North-east RAF Tengah Singapore 1

The aircraft was returning to base after a series of high level practice interceptions when near the end of the downwind leg the pilot reported a 'Reheat 2' fire caption and reported that he was closing the engine down. The flight leader broadcast a 'Mayday' and cleared the way for the pilot of XS896 to land. The aircraft pilot then made a normal 'three greens' call but almost immediately the aircraft pitched up sharply, dropped a wing and entered a flat spin. The formation leader called on the pilot to eject and this he did with a very high rate of descent and at a very low height. Although it appears that the ejection sequence operated correctly there was very little height for the parachute to deploy and the pilot was killed on impact. The subsequent examination of the aircraft wreckage indicated many of the symptoms known to exist in Lightning Zone 3 reheat fires and the rear control rods would have been burnt through very quickly.

Flying Officer Peter Francis Thompson

26-Sep-68 WT313 Canberra B(I)6 213Sqn Not known ?

Cause of loss not known

01-Oct-68 WH715Canberra B2 ETPS Near Crewkerne Somerset 1

Cause of loss not known

05-Nov-68 XR456 Whirlwind 10 103 Sqn 7m W Mersing Malaya 0

Whilst flying with a second Whirlwind the engine began to rundown and despite recovery action by the pilot it could not be restarted leaving no alternative but to land in heavy primary jungle where the aircraft was extensively damaged. The engine was recovered and strip examination showed that a seventh stage compressor stator blade had broken off at its root. This caused a compressor stall and many of the power turbine blades were burnt and the free turbine seized. The pilot, Flying Officer Brian Wright, was commended for his skill and coolness in handling this very unpleasant emergency.

14-Nov-68 XP510 Gnat T1 4FTS Nevin North Wales 0

Abandoned after loss of control

Date Serial Aircraft Unit Place Casualties
Brief Circumstances of Accident
Casualty Details (If Applicable)

20-Nov-68 WJ988 Canberra T17 360 Sqn RAF Watton 0

The aircraft suffered a severe birdstrike on take-off and the pilot raised the undercarriage to stop. The aircraft was declared to be beyond economical repair

---

29-Nov-68 XM174 Lightning F1A TTF Bullmullo Quarry Near Leuchars 0

Abandoned following engine fire. This was Flight Lieutenant E C Rawcliffe's second ejection

---

30-Nov-68 WB573 Chipmunk T10 UAS Dunkery Beacon Somerset ?

Flew into high ground in poor weather

20-Dec-68 WH778Canberra PR7 81Sqn RAF Tengah 0

Nosewheel collapsed on landing and the aircraft was declared beyond repair

---

07-Jan-69 XH164 Canberra PR9 13 Sqn RAF Luqa Malta 2

Crashed on approach

Flight Lieutenant Anthony John PROWSE Pilot (Engineer on flying tour)
Flight Lieutenant Peter John GREENAWAY Navigator

15-Jan- 69 XF517 Hunter FGA9 1 Sqn off West Raynhan 1

Aircraft was seen to dive towards the sea with the pilot slumped over the controls and it seems possible that he may have suffered a sudden illness or anoxia

Flight Lieutenant David John PAGE

24-Jan-69 XM360 Jet Provost T3 CFS Brown Clee Hill Abdon Shropshire 2

Flew into ground

Flight Lieutenant John Sims WATSON 31 Instructor
Pilot Officer Ian Scott PRIMROSE 21

31-Jan-69 XV727 Wessex HC2 A&AEE Norway 0

Crashed in white out conditions

18-Mar-69 WT213 Canberra B15 45Sqn RAF Tengah 0

Categorised 'Category 5' but this may have been simply because the aircraft was life expired

---

18-Mar-69 XG453 Belvedere HC1 66 Sqn RAF Seletar 0

Start up fire destroyed the aircraft (Avpin Starter System). The Belvedere was very prone to starter fires because of the volatile nature of the starter fluid. Once a fire gained a hold of the aircraft it was very unlikely to be extinguished because of the magnesium alloy content of some of the components; one reason why the Royal Navy refused to have the Belvedere in RN service.

24-Mar-69 XV180 Hercules C1 30 Sqn Near RAF Fairford 6

The aircraft was undertaking co-pilot training, including roller landings and was climbing away from a roller when the Captain presumably asked the co-pilot (Flying Officer Plumtree) to feather No 4 engine for a three engined climbaway. No 4 engine, however, went into full reverse thrust. The aircraft pitched up and went into a wing over to starboard and immediately crashed and caught fire, although the crew compartment broke off. The squadron commander had been meant to fly the sortie but was called away urgently and Flying Officer Moir flew instead. The crew are buried together at South Cerney churchyard.

Flight Lieutenant John COUTTS Pilot (Training Captain)
Flying Officer Robin Michael PLUMTREE Co-Pilot
Flying Officer Alan George WALSINGHAM Co-Pilot
Flying Officer Gavin Ian MOIR Navigator
Flying Officer Peter Henry MEDHURST Flight Engineer (Deputy Squadron Engineer Leader)
Flight Sergeant Brian Michael McGING Air Loadmaster

25-Mar-69 XH130 Canberra PR9 13 Sqn Near Hal Far Malta 2

Stalled on approach

Flight Lieutenant Anthony Roger THOMAS Pilot
Flying Officer Robert George NEWTON Navigator

26-Mar-69 XR573 Gnat T1 CFS RAF Kemble 1

Hit trees whilst attempting to rejoin formation. This was a Red Arrows training sortie

Flight Lieutenant Jeremy John BOWLER 27

02-Apr-69 XJ673 Hunter FGA9 20Sqn At sea off Manila 0

Flight Lieutenant K R Barley forced to eject, precise reason not known. 20 Sqn used the route Tengah-Labuan (or Manila) - Kai Tak quite frequently during the period following the disbandment of the resident Hong Kong Hunter squadron (No: 28) in January 1967 in order to demonstrate the ability to reinforce the colony and to use the Clearwater Bay ranges

---

13-May-69 XP332 Whirlwind 10 28 Sqn Brothers Island Hong Kong 0

Crashed into sea following an engine failure

21-May-69 XE616 Hunter FGA9 1 Sqn off Norfolk Coast 1

Crashed into sea during combat manouvering, precise cause not determined

Wing Commander James Alec MANSELL

29-May-69 WJ822 Canberra PR7 81 Sqn RAF Tengah Sigapore 0

Aircraft crashed and was damaged beyond repair after take-off abandoned when an engine failed

---

07-Jun-69 XP396 Whirlwind 10 230 Sqn Leicester 0

Tail rotor failure led to forced landing and aircraft damaged beyond repair

---

13-Jun-69 XP501 Gnat T1 CFS RAF Fairford 0

Undershot runway after hydraulics failed

13-Jun-69 XR952 Gnat T1 4FTS Near Conway North Wales 0

Abandoned in a spin

26-Jun-69 XE610 Hunter FGA9

Details of loss not known

09-Jul-69 XV395 Phantom FGR2 6 Sqn Horncastle Lincs 0

Systems failure led to the crew of Flight Lieutenants Forbes M Pearson and John E Rooum ejecting from the aircraft. This was the first loss of its type in RAF service

Date	Serial	Aircraft	Unit	Place	Casualties
Brief Circumstances of Accident					
Casualty Details (If Applicable)					
15-Jul-69	WH956	Canberra B15	45Sqn	RAF Tengah	0
Cause of loss not known but possibly life expired due to the type's impending withdraw from service					
23-Jul-69	WG488	Chipmunk T10	4AEF	6m East Woolacombe Devon	?
Spun into ground					
15-Aug-69	XG204	Hunter F6	4FTS	Rhosneigr	0
Take off crash					
21-Aug-69	WJ895	Varsity T1	5FTS	Oakington	0
Damaged beyond repair after mid air collision with Cessna 150					
04-Sep-69	XN576	Jet Provost T3	CFS	Northleach Gloucester	0
Abandoned after engine failure					
22-Sep-69	XS926	Lightning F6	5 Sqn	North Sea 51 M off Flamborough Head	0
Loss of control and abandoned by Major Charlie B Neel a USAF exchange programme pilot					
30-Sep-69	XN575	Jet Provost T3	3FTS	Leeming	0
Stalled on take off					

30-Oct-69 XR477 Whirlwind 10 28 Sqn Near Fanling New Territories Hong Kong 2

Lost rotor blades after striking HT cables

Flight Lieutenant Ernest Robert TAYLOR
Sergeant James LUCAS

26-Nov-69 XP343 Whirlwind 10 CFS RAF Valley 0

Rotors struck boom and aircraft crashed

16-Dec-69 XR992 Gnat T1 CFS Cirencester Gloucestershire 0

Abandoned following report of engine fire

16-Dec-69 XR995 Gnat T1 CFS Cirencester Gloucestershire 0

Abandoned after erroneous call that engine was on fire

03-Jan-70 XR997 Gnat T1 4FTS Llanfaelog Wales 2

Crashed on take off

Flight Lieutenant Peter Jack PHILLIPS 32
Flying Officer Anthony Trevor CARTER 23

05-Mar-70 XS918 Lightning F6 11 Sqn 9m E RAF Leuchars 1

Abandoned following an in flight fire. Doidge died of exposure, in part because he had cut the boots off the end of his immersion suit and his underclothes sucked in water.

Flight Lieutenant Anthony David DOIDGE

Date	Serial	Aircraft	Unit	Place	Casualties
Brief Circumstances of Accident					
Casualty Details (If Applicable)					
16-Mar-70	XP576	Jet Provost T4	3FTS	RAF Leeming	0
Abandoned on approach. The student pilot: Pilot Officer R W Exler ejected safely					
17-Mar-70	XN556	Jet Provost T3	1FTS	RAF Linton On Ouse	0
Crashed on overshoot					
19-Mar-70	XE596	Hunter FR10	229 OCU	Paderborn Germany	0
Engine failure					
22-Apr-70	XV310	Sioux HT2	CFS	Hinstock Shropshire	0
Mid air collision with XV316					
22-Apr-70	XV316	Sioux T1	CFS	Hinstock Shropshire	0
Mid air collision with XV310. One pilot was very seriously injured and flown to RAF Hospital Cosford whilst the other was taken to sick quarters at RAF Tern Hill					
30-Apr-70	XP566	Jet Provost T4	RAF College	RAF Cranwell	1
Crashed during night approach					
Senior Flight Cadet William Leslie MILLER 21					
01-May-70	WJ632	Canberra TT18	A&AEE	3m South-east Bridport	2

Abandoned whilst engaged on target towing trials, basic cause not known. Although Flight Lieutenant J F Nicol ejected, the other crew members were killed

Flight Lieutenant George William Edward FOSTER
Major G J WEAVER USAF

07-May-70 XP742 Lightning F3 111 Sqn Great Yarmouth 0

Abandoned following engine fire. Flight Lieutenant Stu Tulloch ejected

---

26-May-70 XR767 Lightning F6 74 Sqn 50m North-west Singapore 1

Flew into sea at night

Flight Lieutenant John Charles WEBSTER

04-Jun-70 XP441 Argosy C1 114 Sqn RAF Benson 0

Crashed on approach to land and damaged beyond repair

22-Jun-70 XN469 Jet Provost T3 1FTS East Moor Yorkshire 0

Crashed during emergency landing following engine failure

22-Jun-70 XD183 Whirlwind 10 103 Sqn RAF Changi Singapore 0

Forced landing following engine failure

26-Jun-70 WZ861 Chipmunk T10 UAS 3m South-east Nairn 0

Struck a wall whilst making a forced landing

Date	Serial	Aircraft	Unit	Place	Casualties

Brief Circumstances of Accident

Casualty Details (If Applicable)

04-Jul-70	XW264	Harrier T2	A&AEE	Salisbury Plain	0

Abandoned after technical fault rendered aircraft uncontrollable

---

13-Jul-70	WK575	Chipmunk T10	Wyton	Laxfield Sussex	1

The pilot attempted to loop the aircraft from a very low height and impacted with the ground.

Pilot Officer John Malcolm WOMPHREY 22 Pilot

The passenger; Flying Officer B K Reid 30, an RAF navigator, was critically injured and paralysed with spinal injuries.

27-Jul-70	XS930	Lightning F6	74 Sqn	RAF Tengah Singapore	1

The pilot was the second aircraft in a stream take off. It was planned that he would be photographed undertaking a 'snap rotation' where the aircraft is accelerated as quickly as possible by holding low after take off to build speed and then pulled up sharply into a max rate climb. Unfortunately, it appears that the photographer was positioned too far along the runway and allowing insufficient distance for the aircraft to gain the necessary speed. It is surmised that the pilot decided to pull up nonetheless but in doing so he stalled the aircraft and it fell off into a kampong. The pilot ejected but was only just releasing from his seat when the seat struck the ground and he was killed. Two local civilians were also killed in the accident. Whitehouse, a former RAF College cadet, lies buried in the church in Cranwell village.

Flight Lieutenant Frank WHITEHOUSE 24

27-Jul-70	WH641	Canberra B2	85 Sqn	RAF Wattisham	2

Spun into ground on short finals

Flying Officer Peter John Michael SPINKS 22 Pilot
Flying Officer Harry PITTARD 23 Navigator

12-Aug-70 XS893 Lightning F6 74 Sqn 18m E RAF Changi Singapore 0

Abandoned after undercarriage jammed. Flying Officer Mike Rigg ejected

---

08-Sep-70 XS894 Lightning F6 5 Sqn Flamborough Head 1

The USAF exchange officer pilot managed to ditch the aircraft successfully but despite an extensive search he was never found. The mystery hinges around the fact that the cockpit canopy was still on the aircraft and it is unlikely that the pilot could have got out of the aircraft with it in the position as found.

Major William SCHAFFNER USAF

17-Sep-70 XW297 Jet Provost T5 1 FTS Kiplingcoates East Yorkshire ?

Crashed, circumstances not known

19-Sep-70 XM990 Lightning T4 226 OCU Little Plumstead Norfolk 0

Uncontrolled roll during aerobatic display which caused Flight Lieutenants Brian Fuller and John Sims to eject

---

06-Oct-70 XV796 Harrier GR1 1 Sqn Ouston Co Durham 0

Abandoned after Engine Failure. Flight Lieutenant Neill Wharton, a former Hunter pilot with 20 Squadron and subsequently with the Red Arrows, ejected safely

---

17-Oct-70 XL109 Whirlwind 10 28 Sqn Hong Kong 0

Circumstances of loss not known

Date Serial Aircraft Unit Place Casualties
Brief Circumstances of Accident
Casualty Details (If Applicable)

12-Nov-70 XR510 Wessex HC2 HOCF RAF Odiham 3

Mid air collision on the airfield with XT679

Flight Lieutenant Richard SYMONS
Flight Lieutenant Desmond REES 35
Master Signaller David WILLIAMS 37

12-Nov-70 XT679 Wessex HC2 HOCF RAF Odiham 2

Mid air collision with XR510. Flight Lieutenant Leyden, a particularly experienced helicopter pilot who had been commissioned from Master Pilot a few years previously, had been awarded a Queens Commendation for his handling of a partial engine failure in a Sycamore in 1963 whilst searching for a missing Belvedere

Flight Lieutenant Eric LEYDEN 45
Pilot Officer Donald BELL 22

13-Nov-70 XR994 Gnat T1 CFS RAF Kemble 0

Engine failure during aerobatics practice (Red Arrows)

20-Nov-70 XL112 Whirlwind 10 202 Sqn Patrick Brimpton Yorkshire 4

Broke up in turbulence

Captain John BALSER 34 Pilot Canadian Armed Forces
Master Navigator Brian STERLAND 35 Winch Operator
Flight Sergeant Charles Peter FORD 31 Winchman
Pilot Officer Helen Susan MACLAREN 21 WRAF: Passenger

15-Dec-70 XM267 Canberra B(I)8 3 Sqn RAF Akrotiri Cyprus 2

Crashed into ground during overshoot

Flying Officer Roderick Colin Murray MACMILLAN
Senior Aircraftman Kim Colin PETTY-FITZMAURICE

08-Jan-71 XM610 Vulcan B2 44 Sqn Wingate Notts 0

Major engine fire - abandoned. For his leadership and airmanship during this accident the captain, Flight Lieutenant Alcock, was awarded the Air Force Cross. He was also the captain of a Vulcan which crashed at Luqa. Alcock, his co-pilot: Flying Officer Hoskins and the rest of the crew escaped safely by parachute

---

18-Jan-71 XJ432 Whirlwind 10 28 Sqn Sai Kung Hong Kong 0

Engine failure

20-Jan-71 XR545 Gnat T1 CFS RAF Kemble 2

Mid air collision between syncro pair

Flight Lieutenant John Stuart HADDOCK
Flight Lieutenant Colin ARMSTRONG

20-Jan-71 XR986 Gnat T1 CFS RAF Kemble 2

Mid air collison between red arrows syncro pair. Immediately after the accident, the Leader of the Red Arrows took the remaining pilots for a training sortie

Flight Lieutenant Ewan Robert PERREAUX
Flight Lieutenant John LEWIS

24-Jan-71 XP303 Whirlwind 10 28 Sqn Peak Alpha Hong Kong 0

Struck obstacle during hover and rolled over

Date	Serial	Aircraft	Unit	Place	Casualties

Brief Circumstances of Accident
Casualty Details (If Applicable)

25-Jan-71	XP756	Lightning F3	29 Sqn	Great Yarmouth	0

Engine fire warning and aircraft abandoned safely by Captain Bill Povilus USAF

28-Jan-71	XN772	Lightning F2	92 Sqn	Diepholz Germany	0

Loss of control during a spin forced Flying Officer Peter Hitchcock to eject

---

29-Jan-71	WH874	Canberra T17	360 Sqn	Sutton In Ashfield Nottinghamshire	0

Mid air collision with WJ862

29-Jan-71	WJ862	Canberra T4	360 Sqn	Sutton In Ashfield	0

Mid air collision with WH874. The crews of both aircraft comprising Flying Officers J W Pearson, D Irwin, Alan Threadgold, C R Pitt and P T Jennings escaped

---

24-Feb-71	XN465	Jet Provost T3	3FTS	Easingwold	0

Spun into ground. Flight Lieutenant F Morrison and his student pilot; Pilot Officer Spears ejected

---

02-Mar-71	XW300	Jet Provost T5	1FTS	RAF Church Fenton Yorshire	2

Mid air collision with Royal Navy Sea Prince WP312 flown by Commander David Dunbar-Dempsey RN as solo crew. It seems probable that Commander Dunbar-Dempsey was unable to see the Jet Provost and whilst flying solo in the aircraft had nobody else to assist with the lookout. Elwyn Bell had previously been a helicopter pilot on 110 Squadron. A short history of the squadron which Bell had written was published on the day of his death.

Flight Lieutenant Elwyn David BELL 29 Pilot & Qualified Flying Instructor
Pilot Officer Bruce John Mouberry BLACKETT 20 Student Pilot

19-Mar-71 XG131 Hunter F6 229 OCU Exmoor 1

Flew into high ground

Second Lieutenant SIOW Yang 24 Republic of Singapore Air Force

---

25-Mar-71 XM418 Jet Provost T3 3 FTS RAF Leeming 0

Engine exploded during a ground run causing severe structural damage to the airframe

---

25-Mar-71 XW532 Buccaneer S2 12 Sqn RAF Laarbruch Germany 2

Crashed shortly after take off when, it is believed, the pilot became disorientated when the aircraft entered cloud immediately after take off or was distracted by an in-cockpit task

Wing Commander David John Harrison COLLINS Pilot (Officer Commanding 12 Squadron)
Flight Lieutenant Paul Anthony KELLY Navigator

23-Apr-71 XV798 Harrier GR1 20 Sqn RAF Wildenrath Germany 0

Control lost during vertical approach to landing pad

28-Apr-71 XS938 Lightning F6 23 Sqn 12m East of RAF Leuchars 0

Fuel fire after take off caused the pilot: Flying Officer Scott Mclean, to abandon the aircraft

---

10-May-71 XP744 Lightning F3 29 Sqn 15m W RAF Akrotiri 0

Flight Lieutenant Bob Cole, the pilot, abandoned the aircraft over the sea after a fire warning

Date	Serial	Aircraft	Unit	Place	Casualties
Brief Circumstances of Accident					
Casualty Details (If Applicable)					
17-May-71	XL622	Hunter T7	4FTS	Blanenau Festiniog Wales	2
Flew into high ground during a sortie from RAF Valley					
Flight Lieutenant John Vincent LOFTUS					
Flight Lieutenant John Anthony DUCKWORTH					
20-May-71	XP752	Lightning F3	111 Sqn	Colmar France	0
Mid collision with French Air Force Mirage IIIe and the aircraft was ajudged to be beyond repair					
26-May-71	XS902	Lightning F6	5 Sqn	15m North-east Grimsby	0
Abandoned after engine fires. Flight Lieutenant Ali McKay escaped safely					
05-Jun-71	XN978	Buccaneer S2A	12 Sqn	28m North-east Le Bourget France	0
Control lost whilst low level AAR but the crew of Flight Lieutenants R G Kemp and A W Marrs ejected safely					
29-Jun-71	XN558	Jet Provost T3	3FTS	RAF Dishforth	0
Birds ingested on approach and the pilot: Flight Lieutenant C S Hall, abandoned the aircraft					
08-Jul-71	XP705	Lightning F3	29 Sqn	35m South of RAF Akrotiri	0
Abandoned following engine fire warnings by Flight Lieutenant Graham Cooke					
03-Aug-71	XV803	Harrier GR1	1 Sqn	RAF Wittering	1

Nozzle control problems caused USAF pilot to eject. However, during his pre-flight actions he had failed to remove his ejection seat rocket pack pins and the ejection sequence was not properly completed, although ejection was initiated within the limits of the seat.

Captain Lewis V DISTELWEG USAF (RAF/USAF Exchange Programme Pilot)

12-Aug-71 XL384 Vulcan B2 617 Sqn RAF Scampton 0

Damaged beyond repair in heavy landing, written off and used subsequently as a crew escape trainer. This in turn caused problems in a later abandonment of a Vulcan. Basically, having been used so frequently the door locking mechanism was particularly free and when a crew subsequently attempted to escape from a real emergency the door would not open as expected!

22-Aug-71 XJ426 Whirlwind 10 22 Sqn off Lundy Island Bristol Channel 0

Ditched whilst engaged in live casevac following fire warnings. The pilot: Flight Lieutenant Iaden Hughes, his crew and the casualty were subsequently rescued by another helicopter

---

27-Aug-71 XG229 Hunter F6 229 OCU Merton Devon 0

Flying controls seized and the pilot: Flight Lieutenant Scoffham abandoned the aircraft

---

22-Sep-71 XP736 Lightning F3 29 Sqn 40m North-east Great Yarmouth 1

Dived into the sea cause not determined

Flying Officer Philip Gordon MOTTERSHEAD

30-Sep-71 XR764 Lightning F6 56 Sqn 35m E RAF Akrotiri 0

Abandoned following fire warnings. Flight Lieutenant Richard Bealer ejected safely. Dick Bealer was a mountaineer of some note who could always be relied on during his Cranwell days for some jolly jape or another!

Date Serial Aircraft Unit Place Casualties
Brief Circumstances of Accident
Casualty Details (If Applicable)

05-Oct-71 WT366 Canberra B(I)8 16 Sqn Luttingen Holland 2

Aircraft was seen to pull up into a climb and then to enter a wing over and to dive straight into the ground. Although initially suspected to be a bird strike or an attempt to avoid birds, no damage could be found consistent with the aircraft flying into birds. An experienced squadron pilot subsequently attempted to repeat the flight and to make the aircraft depart from controlled flight but was unable to do so

Flying Officer Keith Roland (Sonny) HOLMES 22 Pilot
Flight Lieutenant Christopher William KING 27 Navigator

06-Oct-71 WH973Canberra B15 98 Sqn 3m S RAF Cottesmore 0

Loss of control on approach led to Flying Officer K Woolford and Flight Lieutenant W Woolley ejecting from the aircraft

---

09-Oct-71 XG156 Hunter FGA9 229 OCU RAF North Front Gibraltar 1

The undercarriage failed to lower and despite being advised to fly out to sea and eject, the pilot attempted a landing. However, in doing so he struck a sea wall and was killed on impact. It subsequently transpired that the pilot was unhappy at the prospect of ejecting over the sea because he was not a good swimmer.

Flight Lieutenant David Clement MARSHALL

12-Oct-71 XV479 Phantom FGR2 54 Sqn Karup Denmark 0

Abandoned after engine failure. Although the crew: Flight Lieutenant Dick Northcote and Flight Lieutenant Steve Cox escaped by parachute a woman and her child on the ground were killed.

15-Oct-71 XT904 Phantom FGR2 228OCU RAF Coningsby 0

Abandoned near Cromer following loss of control during spin. Squadron Leader John Armstrong and Flight Lieutenant Miles ejected

---

29-Oct-71 XR711 Lightning F3 111 Sqn RAF Wattisham 0

Stalled at take off following premature rotation. The pilot; Flight Lieutenant Eric Steenson was uninjured

---

08-Nov-71 XL575 Hunter T7 4FTS Devil's Bridge Dyfed Wales 2

Flew Into The ground

Flight Lieutenant John METCALFE 31 Pilot Instructor
Lieutenant Bertram YONG 26 Student Republic of Singapore Defence Force

---

09-Nov-71 XV216 Hercules C1 24 Sqn 17 Miles East of Pisa off Lelonia Rocks 52

Flew into sea during low level trail with three other Hercules transport aircraft. Forty six Italian military parachutists killed

Flight Lieutenant Colin George HARRISON Captain
Flight Lieutenant Meurig SWANN-PRICE 25 Co-Pilot
Flying Officer Michael Fred FAWCETT Navigator
Flight Sergeant Brian David KING Flight Engineer
Sergeant Brian Paul FULFORD 28 Air Quartermaster
Sergeant Ralph Russell LEE Parachute Jumping Instructor, No 1 Parachute Training School
1st Lieutenant Pier Maria MAGNAGHI Italian Army Parachutists
1st Lieutenant Ernesto BORGHESAN
Warrant Officer 2nd Class Giuseppe AUGELLO
Staff Sergeant Carmine CELOZZI

Corporal Carlo COLOMBINI
Lance Corporal Maurizio BENERICETTI
Lance Corporal Silvano BOLZONI
Lance Corporal Antonio FIUMARA
Lance Corporal Giuseppe IANNI
Lance Corporal Paolo INTERRANTE
Lance Corporal Sandro LOCORI
Lance Corporal Franco VANTAGGIATO
Parachutist Leonardo ANGELINI
Parachutist Michele CARASI
Parachutist Ettore CARTA
Parachutist Arcangelo CIAPPELLANO
Parachutist Arturo DELANA
Parachutist Vincenzo DE MARCO
Parachutist Luciano DALLAGO
Parachutist Ubaldo DE MITRI
Parachutist Pietro DESSI
Parachutist Paolo DONNARUMMA
Parachutist Danilo DAL ZOTTO
Parachutist Angelo DE VITO
Parachutist Giuseppe D'ALESSANDRO
Parachutist Antonio D'ALESSANDRO
Parachutist Guglielmo DINATALE
Parachutist Fulvio DALL'ASTA

Parachutist Micro FARRARI
Parachutist Giuseppe FACCHETTI
Parachutist Carlo FRASSON
Parachutist Salvatore FUMUSA
Parachutist William FUGERI
Parachutist Renato FRACASSETTI
Parachutist Rocco GIANNATTASIO
Parachutist Giovanni GIANNINI
Parachutist Bruno GUIDOZZI
Parachutist Giuseppe GUARNIERI
Parachutist Andrea GINEX
Parachutist Alberto GIGIOLI
Parachutist Roberto LIUZZI
Parachutist Danele MATELLI
Parachutist Roberto MORGANTI
Parachutist Elia QUARTI
Parachutist Silvano SABATINI
Parachutist Leonardo TORSELLO

09-Dec-71 XV347 Buccaneer S2 — 12 Sqn — RAF Lossiemouth — 0
Ground fire

13-Dec-71 XR567 Gnat T1 — CFS — RAF Upper Heyford — 2
Crashed on approach
Flight Lieutenant David Clem LONGDEN AFC 28 Pilot
Flight Lieutenant Richard Michael STORR 26 Pilot

Date Serial Aircraft Unit Place Casualties
Brief Circumstances of Accident
Casualty Details (If Applicable)

05-Jan-72 XW539 Buccaneer S2 12 Irish Sea 2

Flew into sea

Squadron Leader Thomas Gordon GILROY 35 Pilot
Flight Lieutenant Thomas William WILLBOURNE 26 Navigator

12-Jan-72 XW918 Harrier GR1 3 Sqn RAF Wildenrath 1

The pilot took off to demonostrate the handling characteristics of the Harrier to a party of Swiss officials. Immediately after take off he entered cloud and, presumably having decided to execute a wing over, he emerged from the cloud in a very steep dive. although he ejected, the seat was carried into the side of a building and the pilot did not survive. Shortly before his death, the pilot whose first tour had been flying Hunters with 20 Squadron in the Far East, had been a background figure when a publicity and flight safety film featuring the actor Richard O'Sullivan, had been made at RAF Wildenrath.

Flight Lieutenant Christopher Maunder HUMPHREY

19-Jan-72 XR001 Gnat T1 CFS Pershore 0

Abandoned following engine compressor failure

09-Feb-72 WB552 Chipmunk T10 6AEF RAF Bicester 1

Loss of control during a spin

Flying Officer Barry Robert McCLURE 23 Pilot

The passenger; Sergeant Technician Apprentice Alan Choat 20 was seriously injured

14-Feb-72 XT913 Phantom FGR2 228OCU North Sea 0

Abandoned after suffering hydraulic failure. Flying Officer Jack Stone and Flight Lieutenant P Lee Preston ejected

---

16-Feb-72 XP698 Lightning F3 29 Sqn 60m E Harwich 0

Mid air collision with XP747 but Flight Lieutenant Paul Reynolds survived

---

16-Feb-72 XP747 Lightning F3 29 Sqn 60m E Harwich 1

Mid air collision with XP698

Flight Lieutenant Paul Anthony COOPER

14-Mar-72 XR948 Gnat T1 4FTS Llanbedr Wales 0

Abandoned after engine failed

21-Mar-72 XV802 Harrier GR1 20 Sqn Near Hanover Germany 1

Flew Into ground

Flight Lieutenant Peter Anthony Donald WILLIAMS

08-Apr-72 XS609 Andover C1 46 Sqn Sienna Italy 4

Engine failure on take off, wing hit ground and cartwheeled (Falcons Display Team)

Squadron Leader Frederick William LAST No 1 Parachute Training School
Sergeant Royston Charles BULLEN No 1 Parachute Training School

other crew casualties not known

Date Serial Aircraft Unit Place Casualties
Brief Circumstances of Accident
Casualty Details (If Applicable)

26-Apr-72 XV749 Harrier GR1 1 Sqn Theddlethorpe 0
Abandoned after a birdstrike

01-May-72 XV777 Harrier GR1 1 Sqn RAF Wittering 0
Abandoned when control lost

04-May-72 XV794 Harrier GR1 4 Sqn RAF Wildenrath 0
Abandoned after engine problems but after ejection engine picked up and a/c flew on for some time before crashing

---

13-Jun-72 XV162 Buccaneer S2 12 Sqn off Bridlington 2
Flew into sea in formation in poor visibility

Captain Thomas VIPOND USAF Pilot
Flying Officer James Derek WALMSLEY Navigator

20-Jun-72 XW920 Harrier GR1A 3 Sqn Deccimomannu Sardinia 0
Fuel system failure led to Flight Lieutenant James Downey ejecting from the aircraft

---

26-Jun-72 WJ610 Canberra B2 85 Sqn RAF West Raynham 2
Crashed into trees at Rougham Norfolk whilst approaching to land

Flight Lieutenant Nicholas Charles WHITLOCK Pilot
Flight Lieutenant John Duncan SHERAN Navigator

27-Jun-72 XV780 Harrier GR1A 4 Sqn RAF Wildenrath 0
Abandoned following bird strike

07-Aug-72 XP700 Lightning F3 29 Sqn RAF Wattisham 0
Tail bumper and ventral tank damaged on take off and aircraft subsequently abandoned by Flight Lieutenant Ian Fenton

---

10-Aug-72 XF387 Hunter F6 4FTS RAF Valley 1
Mid air collision with XF384

Flight Lieutenant Charles Francis ASHE

a female on the ground was killed by debris when the aircraft crashed

---

10-Aug-72 XF384 Hunter F6 4FTS RAF Valley 1
Mid air collision with XF387

06-Sep-72 XS455 Lightning T5 5 Sqn off Spurn Head 0
Hydraulic failure, aircraft abandoned by Squadron Leader Tim Gauvain and his passenger 1st Lieutenant R Verbist of the Belgian Air Force.

12-Sep-72 XV799 Harrier GR1 233 OCU Scotland 1
Flew into high ground (pilot was Stn Cdr Wittering Designate)

Group Captain Jeremy Thorndike HALL

12-Sep-72 XW356 Jet Provost T5A RAF College Cranwell Tupton Derbys 0
Loss of control in cloud

Date	Serial	Aircraft	Unit	Place	Casualties

Brief Circumstances of Accident

Casualty Details (If Applicable)

19-Sep-72	XV194	Hercules	C1	Lyneham Wing Norway	0

Ran off the side of the runway and extensively damaged during landing run

---

27-Sep-72	XW218	Puma HC1	230 Sqn	Thetford Norfolk	0

Tail rotor struck ground and aircraft damaged beyond repair

06-Oct-72	XH172	Canberra PR9	13 Sqn	RAF Akrotiri Cyprus	2

Loss Of Control. The aircraft was one of a formation taking part in a flypast to mark the end of a detachment to Cyprus. It was seen to make a turn to fly over the airfield but immediately pitched down and crashed into the ground. It seems possible that the aircraft flew through the wake of another in the formation and one wing may have stalled. The pilot was unable to take corrective action in time.

Flight Lieutenant Anthony WADE Pilot
Flight Lieutenant Edward Peter CONSTANT Navigator

17-Nov-72	?????	Hunter F6	228 OCU	Lundy Island Bristol Channel	0

Abandoned after engine failure

21-Nov-72	XV477	Phantom FGR2	6 Sqn	9m E Penrith	2

The aircraft was one of a pair returning to base after a sortie. Near Penrith, the visibility deteriorated and the aircraft carried out the 'low level abort' procedure. This basically requires the aircraft to be climebed as quickly as possible to the safe height for Instrument Maintained Conditions (IMC), having been flown thus far in Visually Maintained Conditions (VMC). For whatever reason the crew of XV477 did not do this and the aircraft crashed into rising ground.

Flight Lieutenant Christopher Maurice HAYNES Pilot
Flight Lieutenant Martin SMITH Navigator

13-Dec-72 XP349 Whirlwind 10 22 Sqn Holyhead Harbour 0
Engine failure over the harbour and aircraft ditched

14-Dec-72 XM974 Lightning T4 226 OCU Happisburgh Northumberland 0
Abandoned after engine and both reheats caught fire. The crew; Squadron Leader John Spencer and Flying Officer Evans ejected successfully

---

24-Jan-73 XW535 Buccaneer S2 16 Sqn Lubeck Germany 0
Loss of control

06-Feb-73 XL110 Whirlwind 10 84 Sqn RAF Nicosia Cyprus 0
Main rotor failure during ground running

07-Feb-73 XW214 Puma HC1 33 Sqn RAF Aldergrove 0
Damaged beyond repair after rotors struck hangar wall

11-Mar-73 XW331 Jet Provost T5 3FTS RAF Leeming 0
Damaged beyond repair in heavy landing

27-Mar-73 XG256 Hunter FGA9 229 OCU Bodmin Moor Cornwall 0
Struck wires supporting a TV mast and subsequently abandoned

03-Apr-73 XS934 Lightning F6 56 Sqn 20 miles east north east of Akrotiri Cyprus 0
Abandoned after engine fire by Flight Lieutenant Al Greer

Date Serial Aircraft Unit Place Casualties
Brief Circumstances of Accident
Casualty Details (If Applicable)

06-Apr-73 XG135 Hunter FGA9 45 Sqn RAF Wittering 0

At the conclusion of a training sortie, the aircraft was leading a pair for landing when the pilot of the second Hunter; Flight Lieutenant R W Hyde, advised the lead pilot; Flight Lieutenant Grant Macleod, that the aircraft appeared to be on fire. At such a late stage in the approach with low altitude and speed, there was little option but to eject and this MacLeod did successfully with the Hunter crashing about two miles from the airfield

---

15-Apr-73 XN237 Kirby Cadet TX3 618GS West Malling 2

Crashed from stall, cause unknown

Wing Commander Kenneth Alfred HUTCHINGS 48
Cadet Corporal Douglas NEWLING 17 Air Training Corps

Wing Commander Hutchings was an experienced pilot who flew both gliders and powered aircraft in his spare time. At the time of the accident he was based at the Ministry of Defence London and instructed at the Gliding School at weekends.

23-Apr-73 XJ781 Vulcan B2 9 Sqn Shiraz Iran 0

damaged beyond repair in landing accident. The pilot; Flight Lieutenant Eddie Baker was compelled to force land. The rear crew members were trapped by the navigators table and the AEO; Flight Lieutenant Steff Episkopi used his considerable strength to release them. The aircraft could not be recovered realistically from so remote a location and hence it was abandoned as a total loss.

07-May-73 XR647 Jet Provost T4 6FTS Norton Le Clay Yorkshire 0

Mid air collision with XS216 which landed safely. Two farm workers on the ground were killed by falling wreckage

---

10-May-73 XL230 Victor SR2 543 Sqn RAF Wyton 6

Loss of control during unauthorised asymetric night approach and rolled over. It appears that the pilot may have allowed the speed to decay too much and that he lost control authority and was unable to prevent the aircraft rolling onto its back. As a co-pilot, Stevenson had been amongst a crew taking part in a transatlantic race held in 1969 to mark the anniversary of the Alcock and Browne crossing.

Flight Lieutenant Stuart Hawthorne STEVENSON Captain
Flight Lieutenant John Weir PHILIPS 27 Co-Pilot
Flight Lieutenant Keith Robert QUINNEY 29 Navigator
Squadron Leader John Philip MUSSON 38 Navigator (Flight Commander)
Flight Lieutenant Richard John SWAIN 33 Navigator
Flight Lieutenant John Henry GIBBS 42 Air Electronics Officer

---

01-Jun-73 XV397 Phantom FGR2 17 Sqn Germany 0

Instrument (ADI) failure. The crew decided to abandon the aircraft and as the navigator's seat began to leave the aircraft, the pilot, Squadron Leader George Roberts, ejected. Unfortunately, the pilot's canopy struck the navigator and he was killed. Subsequently, it became practice for the pilot to eject and for the navigator to follow.

Flight Lieutenant David Nicholas BAKER 27 Navigator

05-Jun-73 XG169 Hunter FGA9 229 OCU Holsworthy 0

Abandoned after engine failure

05-Jun-73 XM988 Lightning T4 226 OCU off Great Yarmouth 0

Entered spin from Mach 1.1 spiral descent. Wing Commander Chris Bruce the pilot ejected safely

Date Serial Aircraft Unit Place Casualties
Brief Circumstances of Accident
Casualty Details (If Applicable)

05-Jun-73 XR719 Lightning F3 56 Sqn RAF Coltishall 0

Damaged beyond repair in heavy landing

25-Jun-73 XV440 Phantom FGR2 31 Sqn Vliebos Holland 2

Flew into sea at night

Flight Lieutenant Hugh Peter Calday KENNEDY Pilot
Squadron Leader David Noel HODGES Navigator

28-Jun-73 XW919 Harrier GR3 1 Sqn RAF Lyneham 0

Loss of power

05-Jul-73 XS783 Basset CC1 26 Sqn 4 miles from RAF Valley 1

Incorrect fuel caused power loss and forced landing. The Bassett used Avgas fuel but it was refilled with Avtur which caused the engines to fail and it crashed.

Flight Lieutenant Peter LANE Navigator

09-Jul-73 XV791 Harrier GR3 20 Sqn RAF Wildenrath 0

Abandoned after birdstrike by Squadron Leader Peter Sturt

27-Jul-73 XF420 Hunter F6 229 OCU Chawleigh Devon 0

Engine failure, pilot; Group Captain Ian Pedder station commander RAF Chivenor, ejected

28-Jul-73 XR993 Gnat T1 4FTS Lee On Solent 0

Forced landing after birdstrike damaged beyond repair

30-Jul-73 XV805 Harrier GR1A 20 Sqn Coesfeld Germany 0

The aircraft suffered severe birdstrike damage and the USAF pilot; Major J Gibson abandoned it

---

02-Aug-73 WJ674 Canberra B2 231OCU near South Witham by RAF Cottesmore 1

Control lost during attempted overshoot. Both crew ejected and the navigator; Flight Lieutenant Maxwell Riley Murray aged 38 survived. However, the pilot suffered severe injuries because his parachute had not deployed and he died at the scene of the crash

Flight Lieutenant David John DENNIS 26 Pilot

22-Aug-73 XV427 Phantom FGR2 17 Sqn West Germany 2

Flew into high ground attempting a rejoin after losing formation. The aircraft was at the rear of a formation of 4 aircraft and it lost its position during a turn. The pilot attempted to rejoin by 'cutting a corner' but in doing so the aircraft crashed

Flight Lieutenant Keith Alan SPAWTON Pilot
Flight Lieutenant Michael Austin HARRIS Navigator

06-Sep-73 XP508 Gnat T1 4FTS RAF Valley 0

Loss of power, pilot ejected

06-Sep-73 XV750 Harrier GR3 20 Sqn RAF Wildenrath 0

Engine failure from an unknown cause forced the pilot; Squadron Leader Edmondston to eject

Date Serial Aircraft Unit Place Casualties
Brief Circumstances of Accident
Casualty Details (If Applicable)

10-Sep-73 XV198 Hercules C1 48 Sqn RAF Colerne 5

The aircraft was carrying out an overshoot with a simulated engine failure when the other engine on that side failed. At the height and speed involved, the asymetric forces proved too much for the crew to control and the Hercules dived into the ground. There were certain similiarities between this accident and the March 1969 crash at RAF Fairford

Squadron Leader Anthony Victor BARRETT 36 Captain
Flight Lieutenant Douglas Gerald MILLS 26 Co-Pilot
Flight Lieutenant Stewart Alexander FRASER 25 Navigator
Sergeant Peter Robert COATE 27 Flight Engineer
Master Air Loadmaster Walter Charles NATT 36 Air Loadmaster

24-Sep-73 XV739 Harrier GR1A 1 Sqn Cyprus 0

Control was lost near Kings Field and the pilot; Flight Lieutenant Geoff Hulley ejected. Photographs of the ejection were widely circulated afterwards and clearly show the sequence of events

---

12-Oct-73 XR537 Gnat T1 4FTS RAF Leeming 0

Forced landing after birdstrike damage sustained

02-Nov-73 XL596 Hunter T7 4FTS RAF Shawbury 2

Flew into trees on approach at Besford Wood whilst practising circuit training.

Squadron Leader Ronald Clive ETHERIDGE 41 Instructor
Officer Cadet ABDULLA Kasem Nusierat 20 Royal Jordanian Air Force Student Pilot

27-Nov-73 WF411 Varsity T1 CFS RAF Little Rissington 0

Damaged beyond repair after control lost during a roller landing

---

10-Dec-73 XP738 Lightning F3 111 Sqn RAF Wattisham 0

Undercarriage failed on landing and aircraft was damaged beyond repair

---

23-Jan-74 XV797 Harrier GR3 4 Sqn Vreedepeel Holland 1

Flap drive failure, pilot ejected but parachute rigging lines damaged by koch fasteners which did not release properly and the parachute failed to deploy correctly. It appears that the airbrake was not selected in correctly and this contributed to loss of control.

Flight Lieutenant Gorden REVELL

13-Feb-74 XR715 Lightning F3 29 Sqn Blyford Green Southwold Suffolk 0

Abandoned following engine fires. The pilot; Flight Lieutenant Terry Butcher ejected

---

14-Feb-74 XG161 Hunter F6 229 OCU Near Boscastle Cornwall 1

Crashed into sea during formation flying practice

Lieutenant CHOIN Kwang Eng 21 Singapore Defence Force

26-Mar-74 XV785 Harrier GR3 4 Sqn RAF Wildenrath 1

Crashed after flapless landing technique caused control to be lost. The aircraft was approaching for a flapless landing and the pilot attempted to use nozzle braking. This technique caused the aircraft to pitch upwards and the application of further vectored thrust only made matters worse. With the aircraft stalled in a near vertical position, the pilot ejected but was outside the seat limits and the ejection sequence did not complete before the pilot struck the ground.

Flight Lieutenant Andrew Roby BLOXHAM

Date Serial Aircraft Unit Place Casualties
Brief Circumstances of Accident
Casualty Details (If Applicable)

03-May-74 XM991 Lightning T4 19 Sqn RAF Gutersloh 0

Damaged at RAF Gutersloh and declared beyond economical repair

---

16-May-74 XV800 Harrier GR3 4 Sqn RAF Wildenrath 0

Abandoned following birdstrike

29-May-74 XN788 Lightning F2A 19/92Sqn RAF Gutersloh 0

The undercarriage collapsed aftre the brake chute failed during a landing and the aircraft was damaged beyond repair and became a ground instructional airframe and decoy target

---

07-Jun-74 XG130 Hunter FGA9 45 Sqn Melton Mowbray 0

The aircraft had been detached to RAF Cottesmore during a Royal College of Defence Studies visit to its home base of Wittering. The pilot; Flight Lieutenant I C Firth, who was nominally a 58 Squadron pilot, became disorientated in cloud and so ejected from the aircraft which crashed near a railway tunnel entrance at Melton Mowbray. Since the aircraft had been the squadron commander's favourite, he was not at all happy about the loss

---

24-Jun-74 XR748 Lightning F3 29 Sqn Near RAF Coltishall 0

A double hydraulics failure left Flying Officer Kevin Mason no option but to eject

---

09-Aug-74 XV493 Phantom FGR2 41 Sqn Bexwell Norfolk 2

Mid air collision with crop spraying aircraft. The subsequent investigation was able to show that it was probable that the Phantom crew could not see the crop spraying aircraft because of the relative angles of approach kept the crop sprayer in a blind spot caused by the windscreen arch. Group Captain Blucke was the son of a very distinguished wartime station commander; Air Commodore R S Blucke. The pilot of the civilian Pawnee aircraft G-ASVK; Mr Paul Hickmott was also killed.

Group Captain David Robert Kidgell BLUCKE 43 Pilot : Officer Commanding RAF Coningsby
Flight Lieutenant Terence Wesley KIRKLAND 28 Navigator

09-Sep-74 XX144 Jaguar T2 226 OCU RAF Lossiemouth 0

Despite being very heavily damaged in a crashed landing after the undercarriage failed, the aircraft was declared 'Category 4' and repaired by contractors before returning to RAF service

---

11-Oct-74 XV431 Phantom FGR2 31 Sqn RAF Bruggen 0

Aircraft took off with wings unlocked! Flight Lieutenants Ray Pilley and Kevin Toal ejected

---

11-Oct-74 XV758 Harrier GR3 3 Sqn RAF Wildenrath 0

Loss of power on take off

29-Oct-74 XR768 Lightning F6 5 Sqn 13m E Saltfleet Lincs 0

A double reheat fire forced Flight Lieutenant T W Jones to eject. During its service life, the Lightning was the subject of a number of fire integrity programmes aimed at reducing the incidence of fires caused by leaks of fuel and hydraulic fluids into the the very confined areas around the engines and in close proximity to the control runs in the spine. The problem was never completely cured

---

01-Nov-74 XX477 Jetstream T1 CFS RAF Little Rissington 0

Double engine failure after a roller landing caused the aircraft to crash and to be damaged beyond repair

Date Serial Aircraft Unit Place Casualties
Brief Circumstances of Accident
Casualty Details (If Applicable)

15-Nov-74 XW203 Puma HC1 33 Sqn North Whitchurch 0

Damaged beyond repair after crash landing following control loss

---

21-Nov-74 XV441 Phantom FGR2 31 Sqn RAF Bruggen 0

Engine fire on take off. Flight Lieutenants Ian D Vacha and Mike Keene ejected

---

22-Nov-74 XX136 Jaguar T2 A&AEE Wimborne St Giles Dorset 0

Crashed following engine fire. The air force flight test crew of Wing Commander C C Rustin and Flight Lieutenant C J Cruikshank ejected

---

16-Dec-74 XV779 Harrier GR3 3 Sqn RAF Wildenrath 0

Hydraulic failure caused belly landing

27-Jan-75 XR454 Whirlwind 10 84 Sqn RAF Akrotiri 0

Destroyed after blade failure whilst being hover taxyed.

15-Feb-75 XF274 Meteor T7 RAE RAE Farnborough 2

Crashed near the Control Tower shortly after an asymetric overshoot at Farnborough and loss of control during the climb out

Flight Lieutenant John Michael O'DWYER Pilot
Squadron Leader Gordon Lamont SMITH Flight Medical Officer

03-Mar-75 XV416 Phantom FGR2 111 Sqn River Witham 0

Abandoned after engine failure. Flight Lieutenants Phil Tolman and P Trotter ejected

---

24-Mar-75 XH618 Victor K1A 57 Sqn off Sunderland 4

Mid air collision with Buccaneer XV156. The Victor was taking part in simulated refuelling when the Buccaneer struck the tailplane rendering the Victor immediately uncontrollable. It bunted over and the 'g' forces made it impossible for the crew to escape; the captain, Flight Lieutenant Keith Handscomb managed to reach the ejection handle with the fingers of one hand and although injured was subsequently rescued by a merchant ship. The aircraft exploded as it reached the cloud tops. The Buccaneer was undamaged and returned to base.

Flight Lieutenant David Hallam CROWTHER
Flight Lieutenant Peter Joseph Leo SLATTER
Flying Officer Terence Patrick EVANS
Flying Officer John Arthur PRICE

07-Apr-75 XR762 Lightning F6 11 Sqn off Akrotiri 1

Crashed into sea during a tail chase

Flight Lieutenant David Leslie HAMPTON

09-Apr-75 XV776 Harrier GR3 1 Sqn RAF Wittering 0

Abandoned after engine flamed out. Flight Lieutenant J Buckler ejected safely

---

30-Apr-75 XX831 Jaguar T2 226 OCU RAF Lossiemouth 0

The aircraft was being used by Flight Lieutenant Whitney Griffiths, an OCU instructor, to practice his air display sequence. In accordance with the normal arrangements, the rear seat straps were tied with thin string. Having taken off and done some flying nearby he began his display sequence which went normally until he began an inverted run at 1000 feet and 380 knots. The pilot began to roll out by applying full right spoiler and when he attempted to stop the roll just prior to reaching wings level he found that he could not move the control column. Despite using both hands he could not free the column and the aircraft continued to roll and its nose dropped. Being unable to control the aircraft, the pilot ejected at about 500 feet with 60 degrees of bank on. Although he was injured during the sequence, he landed safely and the aircraft crashed just outside the airfield.

22-May-75 XW212 Puma HC1 33 Sqn RAF Aldergrove 0

Damaged beyond repair After Gearbox Cowling Detached

16-Jun-75 XW536 Buccaneer S2B 15 Sqn North Sea off Denmark 0

Mid air collision with XW528 which returned safely to base. The crew of Flight Lieutenants R G Haynes and A Shaw ejected

---

29-Jul-75 XV360 Buccaneer S2A 237OCU off Southwold 0

Flew into sea after loss of control but fortunately the two crew escaped by ejection seat

---

29-Jul-75 WB562 Chipmunk T10 7AEF Near Winthorpe 2

Whilst en route between RAF Waddington and RAF Newton the aircraft carried out some aerobatics at Winthorpe airfield but crashed when control was lost

Flight Lieutenant Thomas Owen LEWIS 32 Pilot (seconded from RAF Kinloss for Air Training Corps camps)

Flight Lieutenant Gwyn Elfred RICHARDS 50 RAFVR(T) Officer Commanding Bovingdon Squadron Air Training Corps

---

03-Sep-75 XS103 Gnat T1 CFS Leck Germany 0

Mid air collision with Italian Air Force F104S

11-Sep-75 XX557 Bulldog T1 UAS Near Glasgow 0

Hit trees during low level flight

18-Sep-75 XV580 Phantom FG1 43 Sqn Near Kirriemuir 0

Abandoned after control lost during aerobatic practice. The crew of Flying Officer Wright and Flight Lieutenant Jack Hammil ejected

---

29-Sep-75 XN780 Lightning F2A 92Sqn RAF Gutersloh 0

Damaged beyond repair in a ground fire

14-Oct-75 XM645 Vulcan B2 9 Sqn Malta 6

Broke up in the air after overshoot from heavy landing which damaged fuel tanks. The wreckage fell on civilian houses and caused several deaths on the ground. The rear crew members, including two crew chiefs, were unable to escape given the available time. Flight Lieutenant Alcock, the captain had been awarded an AFC for his handling of a major incident some years previously. Both Alcock and his co-pilot; Flight Lieutenant E C Alexander ejected safely

Squadron Leader David Leslie BEEDON Navigator
Flight Lieutenant Ernest Stanley LAMBERT Navigator
Flight Lieutenant Gordon Anthony PULMAN Air Electronics Officer
Chief Technician Thomas Gordon BARROW Crew Chief
Sergeant Peter John ATKINS Crew Chief

Date	Serial	Aircraft	Unit	Place	Casualties

Brief Circumstances of Accident

Casualty Details (If Applicable)

16-Oct-75	XS106	Gnat T1	4FTS	Llanwrst Wales	0

Loss of control in a spin

24-Nov-75	XV405	Phantom FGR2	228OCU	RAF Coningsby	0

Loss of control led to the crew of Flight Lieutenants Smith and Rob Lunn ejecting

01-Dec-75	XV788	Harrier GR3	1 Sqn	Belize	0

Engine problems caused abandonment

17-Dec-75	XV463	Phantom FGR2	41 Sqn	Mawbury In Solway Firth Region	2

Loss of control and flew into sea

Flight Lieutenant Brian Alan JELLICOE
Flight Lieutenant Henry Keith TENNET BEng

19-Jan-76	XV745	Harrier GR3	1 Sqn	Near Crewe Cheshire	1

Mid air collision with XV754

Flight Lieutenant James Edward DOWNEY BSc

19-Jan-76	XV754	Harrier GR3	1 Sqn	Near Crewe	1

Mid air collision with XV745. The aircraft were part of a four ship to attack a target from different directions. They failed to maintain separation and crashed as they crossed over. Downey had led a charmed life until then, ejecting from another Harrier and also handling several other emergencies extremely well.

Flight Lieutenant John Keith ROBERTS

22-Jan-76 XL579 Hunter T7 ETPS Winterborne Gunner 0

Crashed approaching Boscombe Down. The naval crew of Commander Kemp and Lieutenant Commander W Honour escaped by ejection seat

---

05-Feb-76 XX137 Jaguar T2 226 OCU Milltown Scotland 0

The aircraft was being flown by an instructor and a student and had been undertaking an instrument flying sortie. On approaching base a series of indications led to the diagnosis of serious fuel problems which could not be rectified and the aircraft was abandoned. The cause was found to be a filure of an HP turbine blade in the No 1 engine which set up a high frequency vibration causing fatigue failure to the fuel pipe connecting the LP cock to the backing pump and thereby producing a massive fuel leak. Unfortunately, the crew did not correctly react to the fuel leak symptoms and did not carry out the necessary drills. However, the emergency procedures were confusing and subsequently rewritten with additional training provided in the OCU syllabus. Fortunately the instructor and student; Flight Lieutenants A I Aitkin and R K Jackson ejected safely

---

13-Feb-76 XS211 Jet Provost T4 SRF RAF Leeming 0

Aircraft undershot suffering from loss of power due to fuel starvation

---

16-Feb-76 XP531 Gnat T1 4FTS

Details of loss not known

03-Mar-76 XV166 Buccaneer S2B 15 Sqn RAF Honington 0

Crashed on approach having stalled and control lost but the crew of Flying Officer G Bowerman and Flight Lieutenant C Davies ejected

Date Serial Aircraft Unit Place Casualties
Brief Circumstances of Accident
Casualty Details (If Applicable)

12-Mar-76 XV746 Harrier GR3 233 OCU Norway 1

Flew into mountain. It is thought probable that the pilot suffered 'white out'

Flight Lieutenant Stephen David WAKELY

19-Mar-76 XS678 Wessex HC2 ETPS Salisbury Plain 0

Damaged beyond repair in heavy landing

21-Apr-76 XG185 Hunter F6 4FTS Maltreath Sands Wales 0

Abandoned by the pilot; Flight Lieutenant W R Lewis, following engine failure

---

27-Apr-76 XR105 Argosy C1 ETPS RAF Boscombe Down 2

Wing dropped on asymetric approach and struck building. Although two crew were killed a third officer survived

Flight Lieutenant Terence John COLGAN
Captain Giuseppe PUGLISI Italian Air Force

30-Apr-76 XP536 Gnat T1 4FTS Near Dolgellau 2

Mid air collision with XR983

Flight Lieutenant Kenneth Graham IVELL
Flight Lieutenant David James MATHER

30-Apr-76 XR983 Gnat T1 4FTS Near Dolgellau 2

Mid air collision with XP536. The two aircraft were being flown by experienced instructors as part of a larger formation to mark the retirement of the squadron commander. It is understood that the formation was flying tactically and that one crew reported a Phantom aircraft nearby. It is supposed that another crew looking out for the Phantom flew into the underside of the first aircraft and they crashed into the ground locked together.

Flight Lieutenant Ian James SANDFORD
Captain David KIEFER United States Air Force

04-May-76 XJ635 Hunter FGA9 TWU Near Aberystwyth 1
Loss of control

Flying Officer Winton Gilbert IRVINE

03-Jun-76 XX703 Bulldog T1 UAS Glenrothes Airfield 0
Damaged beyond repair in forced landing after engine failure

13-Jun-76 XP357 Whirlwind 10 202 Sqn Newgate Beach Near Brawdy 0
Damaged beyond repair in forced landing

24-Jun-76 XS111 Gnat T1 CFS RAF Kemble 0
Damaged beyond repair after undercarriage raised to stop aircraft after brakes failed on landing

---

02-Jul-76 XX822 Jaguar GR1 14 Sqn 5 miles North West Cloppenburg Germany 1
Flew into ground whilst taking part in a Salmond Trophy work-up exercise. The pilot was very experienced and it can only be assumed that he was distracted whiclst carrying out some in-cockpit task and did not realise the proximity of the ground. There were also reports of another aircraft in the vicinity and it may be that the pilot lost control when taking avoiding action

Flight Lieutenant Terence Michael BUSHNELL

Date Serial Aircraft Unit Place Casualties
Brief Circumstances of Accident
Casualty Details (If Applicable)

06-Jul-76 XW770 Harrier GR3 3 Sqn Borken Germany 0

Abandoned after engine failure

22-Jul-76 XX618 Bulldog T1 UAS Southport 0

Loss of control in a spin and abandoned by its crew. Another Bulldog then landed on a beach to investigate and turned over in the soft sand and was damaged. Both crews, comprising Squadron Leader George Dunn, Flight Lieutenant David Sergeant and Officer Cadets Martin Brown and Tony Atkinson were not badly injured.

23-Jul-76 XV417 Phantom FGR2 29 Sqn Mablethorpe 0

Structural failure of the starboard wing forced the ejection of Flight Lieutenant Jim W Jackson and Captain B A 'Dave' Newberry Canadian Armed Forces

---

30-Jul-76 XS937 Lightning F6 11 Sqn off Spurn Head 0

Abandoned out to sea after undercarriage failed to lower. Flying Officer Simon Manning ejected

---

16-Aug-76 XG191 Hunter F6 1TWU 30m South-west RAF Brawdy 1

Crashed into the sea cause not known

Flight Lieutenant Richard SUTCLIFFE

27-Aug-76 XW230 Puma HC1 1563 Flt Toledo Belize 3

destroyed in forced landing after engine failure

Flight Lieutenant Anthony Peter George LONG Pilot
Flight Lieutenant Roger Julian Lacy WHITELEY Pilot
Master Aircrew Christopher Anthony BOLAM Air Loadmaster

04-Sep-76 XN786 Lightning F2A 19Sqn RAF Gutersloh 0

Damaged beyond repair in a ground fire

15-Sep-76 XX735 Jaguar GR1 6 Sqn Eggebeck Germany 1

The aircraft was No 2 in a pair briefed for an airfield attack at low level; the plan being to run-in on a south westerly heading and carry out a 'toss' attack before departing to the north. The spacing between the aircraft was to be 2000 yards and the leader was to recover to the south and then turn right and the No 2 would make a right hand turn and rejoin the leader. On the rin in the No 2 was only about 1000 yards from his leader and pulled up from the attack more steeply than planned. When the pilot began to make a hard right hand turn whilst regaining low level the aircraft pitched up rapidly and departed from controlled flight and crashed. The pilot did not attempt to eject. The aircraft was found with slats closed and airbrake partially open. This suggested a mis-selection of airbrakes for slats prior to the attack. In this configuration the speed would have decayed very rapidly in the turn and the safe angle of attack reduced. If the reheat was then used this would have aggravated the pitch up and the head up AOA would not have been visible because the 'Nav' mode was selected and hence the pilot's otherwise normal control movements would have pitched the aircraft beyond its limits.

Flight Lieutenant Patrick Christopher CARROLL

17-Sep-76 XX120 Jaguar GR1 54 Sqn Near Samsoe Germany 1

The sortie, although originally planned as a four ship was reduced to a pair with the aircraft being No 2. It appears that the weather was fairly marginal with cloud bases between 1200 and 2000 feet with a low pressure air mass and considerable rain and reduced visibility. Outside the rain, there was a forecast of good visibility. The flight made an Instrument Flight Rules (IFR) departure to 2000 feet and was then able to continue Visual Flight Rules (VFR) for some time. To avoid poor weather, the leader made a climbing turn to port with the No 2 in close echelon starboard but lost mutual contact and agreed to meet about 5 miles to the north. Shortly thereafter the No 2 aircraft was seen in a 20 to 30 degree dive and banked some 45 to 90 degrees to the left and in a constant attitude. Without changing its position the aircraft crashed into the sea and the pilot made no attempt to eject. The most likely cause of the accident was loss of control in cloud and failure to recover in time in the prevailing poor weather conditions.

Flight Lieutenant Paul Samuel WEST

28-Sep-76 XL513 Victor K2 55 Sqn RAF Marham 0

Crashed into the overshoot following birdstrike whilst taking off

---

08-Oct-76 XR996 Gnat T1 4FTS RAF Shawbury 2

Crashed on approach very close to the site of an accident involving a Hunter about 3 years previosly

Flight Lieutenant John Leszek GRZYBOWSKI 27 Pilot Instructor
Flying Officer Ashley William SMART 21 Student

25-Oct-76 XJ636 Hunter FGA9 1TWU Mathry Wales 0

Engine failed on take off and Flight Lieutenant E Hunkin ejected

---

29-Oct-76 XW531 Buccaneer S2B 12 Sqn Bodo Norway 0

Crashed following loss of control but Flight Lieutenants Parkinson and Easterbrook ejected

---

14-Dec-76 XZ102 Jaguar GR1 | 2 Sqn | Near RAF Laarbruch Germany | 0

The aircraft took off for an air test following a problem with the No 2 engine. Almost immediately it rolled rapidly to the left and the pilot managed to retain some measure of control with the aircraft banked about 20 or 30 degrees to port and was able to climb to about 800 feet. At this point the aircraft's nose dropped and it rolled and yawed uncontrollably. After a couple of rolls, the pilot calmly timed his ejection to coincide with erect flight and then escaped. The aircraft crashed and exploded immediately afterwards. The cause was thought to be failure to connect the tailplane powered flying control units properly. The pilot; Flight Lieutenant Bill Langworthy ejected - something of a regular event for him!

17-Jan-77 XM600 Vulcan B2 | 101 Sqn | Near Spilsby Lincs | 0

Abandoned after serious engine fire but the pilots; Flight Lieutenant R M Aspinall, Flight Lieutenant A Ryder, the co-pilot, and the three rear crew members all escaped safely

---

03-Feb-77 XW548 Buccaneer S2B | 16 Sqn | Near Vokel Germany | 0

Engine fire at low level. Flight Lieutenants M W Brown and R P Kemp ejected

---

24-Feb-77 XM968 Lightning T4 | 92 Sqn | RAF Gutersloh Germany | 0

Hydraulics failure. Squadron Leaders Mike Lawrence and Granville-White ejected to safety

---

25-Feb-77 XZ120 Jaguar GR1 | 2 Sqn | 2 miles south Nordhorn Range | 1

The aircraft was No 2 in a four aircraft formation on a bombing sortie to the Nordhorn Range. After the attack the No 2 was flying on the wing of the No 4 when they flew through a patch of cloud and lost contact with each other. It was supposed that the No 2 then made a steep diving turn to link up with the No 3 who was low and to the left of the No2 but in doing so he had entered a near maximum rate left hand turn from which he could not recover in the height available.

Flight Lieutenant Douglas Graham STEIN

Date Serial Aircraft Unit Place Casualties
Brief Circumstances of Accident
Casualty Details (If Applicable)

03-Apr-77 XW424 Jet Provost T5A 1FTS RAF Linton On Ouse 0

Crashed during aerobatic practice

04-Apr-77 XW525 Buccaneer S2B 208 Sqn Claerwen Reservoir 0

Crashed whilst avoiding 2 Hunters. The aircraft, which had been fully instrumented for trials purposes, was flying on a normal training sortie when it encountered the other aircraft. In attempting to avoid a collision, the aircraft departed controlled flight and the crew of Flight Lieutenant Summers and Hill ejected

---

03-May-77 XH137 Canberra PR9 39 Sqn Oxmore Housing Estate Near RAF Wyton 2

Loss of control during asymetric overshoot (3 Civilian Fatalities)

Flight Lieutenant Lawrence Andrew DAVIES Pilot
Flight Lieutenant John Philip ARMITAGE Navigator

13-May-77 XE651 Hunter FGA9 1TWU 40m S Brawdy 0

Abandoned after engine fire over the sea. The student pilot; Flying Officer Ruddock ejected

---

14-Jun-77 XX978 Jaguar GR1 31 Sqn 20m South-east Bremen Germany 1

The aircraft was on a low level navigation sortie and was seen to make a 270 degree turn to rejoin its planned track. It entered a shallow dive until shortly before impact when the wings were levelled and the nose pulled up abruptly to an incidence of 20-30 degrees and the aircraft passed through some power cables and struck the ground in tail down attitude with the wreckage being thrown forward into a built up area but without causing serious casualties to those on the ground. The cause was not postively determined but it appears that the pilot may have been unaware that he was descending until just before impact and he may have been distracted by some task in the cockpit or attempting to retrieve a loose article

Flight Lieutenant Timothy Valentine PENN

29-Jul-77 XX148 Jaguar T2 226 OCU Whittingham Northumberland 2

The aircraft was flying a simulated attack sortie with an along track 'tip in'. The aircraft pulled up correctly and rolled inverted but insttead of a gentle 8 degree dive attack the nose came down very sharply into 30-40 degrees. The aircraft then rolled upright and the crew ejected about half way between the pull up point and the target. Only one ejection seat had cleared the aircraft at impact and its parachute had no time to open. It appears that the aircraft was being pulled down at about 5g when inverted and no reason for this could be established

Flight Lieutenant John Stephen (Taff) HINCHCLIFF Pilot and Instructor
Flying Officer Russell Ferguson GRAHAM Pilot Student

15-Aug-77 WH948Canberra B6 100 Sqn RAF Coltishall 0

Crashed after engine fire but Squadron Leader Gordon and Flight Lieutenant Smith ejected

---

18-Aug-77 XX890 Buccaneer S2B 15 Sqn Near RAF Laarbruch 0

Loss of control on approach. The crew of Flight Lieutenants K I Mackenzie and R A Pittaway ejected

---

08-Sep-77 XL571 Hunter T7 1TWU Strumble Head 0

Abandoned after engine failure. Flight Lieutenants H E Spirit and S Parfitt ejected

---

31-Oct-77 XV348 Buccaneer S2 237OCU Glomfjord Norway 1

Crashed after flying into power cables. Flight Lieutenant P D Locke ejected but the identity of the casualty is not known

Date Serial Aircraft Unit Place Casualties
Brief Circumstances of Accident
Casualty Details (If Applicable)

23-Jan-78 XW426 Jet Provost T5A 1FTS Pickering North Yorkshire 0

Failed to recover from a dive

23-Jan-78 XW205 Puma HC1 33 Sqn Voss Norway 3

Cabin door detached and struck tail rotor leading to loss of control

Squadron Leader Maurice James BENNEE Pilot
Flight Lieutenant Brian TOMLINS Co-Pilot
Master Aircrew Allen GASKELL Air Loadmaster

03-Mar-78 XR981 Gnat T1 CFS RAF Kemble 2

Struck ground whilst practising aerobatics. Wing Commander Hazell was a former leader of the Red Arrows and was visiting them to keep abreast of their work and current techniques

Flight Lieutenant Stephen Edward NOBLE Pilot
Wing Commander Dennis George HAZELL AFC

05-Mar-78 WZ875 Chipmunk T10 12AEF Loch Glow 1

Flew into ground during aerobatics

21-Mar-78 XX971 Jaguar GR1 31 Sqn Lahr Germany 0

The aircraft took off normally but almost immediately the No 2 engine failed. The pilot raised the undercarriage and jettisoned he external stores, reaching about 150 feet with a high angle of attack. Trading height for reduced angle of attack it became possible to accelerate the aircraft and to set up for a single engined approach. Unfortunately, the pilot then became distracted and allowed the angle of attack to increase and the aircraft to descend below the glide path. Believing he had insufficient height and speed to reach the runway, the pilot; Flight Lieutenant P A New, then ejected

---

26-Apr-78 XR544 Gnat T1 4FTS RAF Valley 0

Crashed during approach

27-Apr-78 XX149 Jaguar T2 226 OCU Cullin Scotland 2

The sortie was an Instrument Rating Test with an experienced OCU instructor in the front seat and a student in the rear seat. They executed a practice low level abort and reported levelling at 10000 feet. The aircraft was next seen emerging from cloud in a very steep inverted dive and although the crew had initiated ejection neither sequence completed and they were killed. No positive cause was established and it can only be assumed that they became distracted and lost control

Flight Lieutenant Christopher John EVERITT
Flight Lieutenant John Arthur RIGBY

25-May-78 XH176 Canberra PR9 A&AEE RAF Chilmark Wiltshire 0

Control lost during test flying

01-Jun-78 XN598 Jet Provost T3A 1FTS Gouthwaite Reservoir Yorkshire 1

Wing tip struck water whilst low flying

Flight Lieutenant John Hutton FOX

06-Jun-78 XX761 Jaguar GR1 226OCU RAF Lossiemouth 0

Destroyed by a ground fire whilst having engine runs conducted on the Attenuator. The Engine Fitter operating the controls had a particularly lucky escape by climbing over the front windscreen and sliding down the nose!

Date Serial Aircraft Unit Place Casualties
Brief Circumstances of Accident
Casualty Details (If Applicable)

14-Jun-78 XN975 Buccaneer S2 RAE Not known (Germany) 0

Control lost whilst taking avoiding action with a helicopter

19-Jun-78 WJ753 Canberra B2 100 Sqn RAF Marham 0

Wing tip struck ground and aircraft cartwheeled. The crew escaped and were extremely fortunate to do so as photographs of the accident clearly show!

24-Jul-78 XV483 Phantom FGR2 92 Sqn Drenke Germany 2

Flew into ground during practice interception

Squadron Leader Christopher Ian Cunningham ROUNCE
Flight Lieutenant Christopher John MEADE

25-Jul-78 XX823 Jaguar GR1 17 Sqn off Sardinia 1

Whilst carrying out an unauthorised low level aerobatics over a beach in Sardinia, the pilot lost control and crashed

Flight Lieutenant Roger John WEST

04-Aug-78 XV403 Phantom FGR2 111 Sqn 58 miles east of Aberdeen 2

Flew into sea during practice interception

Captain Josh TALLENTYRE 35 United States Marine Corps Pilot
Flight Lieutenant Christopher Charles FERRIS 33 Navigator

11-Aug-78 XL390 Vulcan B2 617 Sqn Glenview Naval Air Station 4

Crashed during flying display practice. The squadron commander; Wing Commander Stephenson-Oliver, who was a navigator, did not fly on this sortie and survived. Flight Lieutenant Jamie Hamilton had survived a Shackleton crash on Cullodon Moor some years previously

Flight Lieutenant Christopher Michael EDWARDS 31 Pilot Captain
Flight Lieutenant Simon Peter FARLOW 31 Co-Pilot
Flight Lieutenant James Andrew MacDonald HAMILTON 36 Air Electronics Officer
Flight Lieutenant Nigel Hayden THOMAS 29 Navigator

21-Sep-78 XX530 Bulldog T1 RNEFTS Stokesley North Yorkshire 2

Aircraft crashed into the ground

Flight Lieutenant John David (Jack) PIERCY 30 Pilot and Instructor
Midshipman Mark SIMON RN 19 Student Pilot

01-Nov-78 XX759 Jaguar GR1 226 OCU Selkirk 1

The student pilot was undertaking a low level navigation exercise with an OCU instructor acting as chase. Having encountered poor weather the pair pulled up. The student was seen to enter cloud in a gentle climb but without having engaged reheat. He acknowledged an instruction to call 'VMC on top' but about 20 seconds later was seen in a near vertical dive from which he did not recover. (Ecuadorian Student)

23-Nov-78 XV598 Phantom FG1 111 Sqn off RAF Leuchars 2

Flew into sea during approach

Flight Lieutenant Christopher John JONES
Flight Lieutenant Michael Hardy STEPHENSON

Date Serial Aircraft Unit Place Casualties
Brief Circumstances of Accident
Casualty Details (If Applicable)

Flight Lieutenant Jones' brother was a Jaguar pilot who subsequently ejected from a Jaguar following a mid-air collision with a Tornado and who then managed to land a badly damaged Jaguar after a second mid-air collision.

07-Dec-78 WT530 Canberra PR7 13 Sqn RAF Luqa Malta 0

Loss of power on take off caused by fuel contamination resulted in the crew of Flight Lieutenant G Morgan and Flight Lieutenant V A Mee ejecting

---

15-Dec-78 XV801 Harrier GR3 3 Sqn Eniegedoch Germany 0

Abandoned after loss of control

28-Feb-79 XV578 Phantom FG1 111 Sqn off Scottish Coast 0

Abandoned after engine failure. Squadron Leader Mal Gleave and his fellow crew member Flying Officer Al Lewry ejected

---

14-Mar-79 XJ637 Hunter F6 1TWU Talfarn Wales 0

Abandoned after engine failure by the appropriately named Flight Lieutenant I M Hunter

---

26-Mar-79 XX147 Jaguar T2 17 Sqn Sudlohn Germany 0

The aircraft was flying at 250 feet above ground level and 420 knots when a bird struck the front canopy, continued into the cockpit to damage the partitioning visor and the headup display glass. The noise level rose dramatically but it appeared that the aircraft was flying normally. Having taken stock of the situation and recovered from their immediate shock the crew noticed the aircraft slowing down and saw that the No 2 engine TGT was extremely high and so they throttled back the engine but the temperature changed little. Power was increased on the No 1 engine but the TGT temperature was also high; reheat on this engine was not selected. Believing both engines to be damaged the crew of Flight Lieutenants M Brooks and W Kirkpatrick decided to eject. It was subsequently found that the airbrakes had been extended to 30 degrees and that although the No 1 engine had overheated for a brief period, had reheat been selected it might have been possible to recover the aircraft.

28-Mar-79 XN585 Jet Provost T3 1FTS RAF Linton On Ouse 0

Fire warning on take off and so the instructor; Flight Lieutenant J M Doggart and his student; Pilot Officer C D Tingay ejected

---

19-Apr-79 XR500 Wessex HC2 28 Sqn Hong Kong 0

Flew into sea whilst engaged on winching practice in poor visibility

---

22-May-79 XP539 Gnat T1 CFS RAF Leeming 0

Fuel blockage caused engine problems and aircraft abandoned

25-May-79 XS931 Lightning F6 5 Sqn off Flamborough Head 0

Control restriction after take off, aircraft abandoned over the sea by Flying Officer Pete Coker

---

12-Jun-79 XV781 Harrier GR3 3 Sqn RAF Gutersloh 0

Abandoned by Flight Lieutenant T R Watts coming into hover following a fire warning

Date Serial Aircraft Unit Place Casualties
Brief Circumstances of Accident
Casualty Details (If Applicable)

12-Jun-79 XX950 MRCA (Tornado) BAe Irish Sea 2

The aircraft, one of the MRCA development batch crashed into the sea whilst engaged on a training development and test flight with BAe. The crew were killed. The pilot; Russ Pengelly, had served in the RAF and was a Lightning fighter pilot before becoming a test pilot and subsequently joining British Aerospace. The navigator was a serving RAF officer

Squadron Leader John Smillie GRAY Navigator

22-Jun-79 XX142 Jaguar T2 226 OCU off RAF Lossiemouth 2

On signing for the aircraft the captain was told that it would be necessary for him to undertake inverted flight to check for a loose article. Once airborne and over the sea at 1500 feet and 420 knots the aircraft was rolled inverted for about 5 seconds and then rolled upright again. Shortly afterwards this was repeated for a period of about 10 seconds and the aircraft descended to about 1000 feet. The aircraft then yawed sharply, its nose dropped steeply and it crashed into the sea. Although both crew attempted ejection neither survived. The aircraft departed from controlled flight through the application of postive 'g', spoiler and rudder but, importantly, the laid down minimum height for a loose article check of this sort was 5000 feet

Flight Lieutenant John Michael SKINNER
Overseas student Royal Danish Air Force

03-Jul-79 XK140 Hunter FGA9 2TWU Lochives 0

Abandoned over the sea after control lost

03-Jul-79 XW371 Jet Provost T5A 7FTS Near Lancaster 1

Crashed in poor weather whilst engaged on a navigation exercise

Flight Lieutenant Thomas Durk BAYLIFF

06-Jul-79 XG197 Hunter F6 1TWU Near Tintagel Cornwall 0

Abandoned over the sea after engine failure

12-Jul-79 XW526 Buccaneer S2 16 Sqn Near Osnabruck Germany 2

Crashed after failure of the wing

Flight Lieutenant Alan COLVIN
Squadron Leader David Richard COUPLAND

18-Jul-79 XZ137 Harrier GR3 4 Sqn Wissmar Germany 1

Crashed into houses

Captain Thomas PASQUALE US Marine Corps

18-Jul-79 XX960 Jaguar GR1 14 Sqn Iserlohn Germany 0

The aircraft was No 4 in a four aircraft formation. Approaching the target area the pilot realised he was out of position in the formation and and adjusted by making a turn followed by a reversal back on to the track. He identified the rest of the formation and crossed a river valley and approached a steep wooded area beyond with rising ground to about 1000 feet. On top of the hill was a TV mast about 90 feet high. The aircraft pulled up but struck the mast with its port air intake and immediately catching fire. The aircraft continued to climb and near the top of its trajectory the pilot ejected. It is probable that the pilot became distracted whilst trying to identify his position and was unaware of the proximity of the rising ground.

17-Aug-79 XP737 Lightning F3 5 Sqn Near RAF Valley 0

Undercarriage failed and aircraft abandoned over the sea by the pilot; Flight Lieutenant Ray Knowles

Date Serial Aircraft Unit Place Casualties
Brief Circumstances of Accident
Casualty Details (If Applicable)

18-Sep-79 XR723 Lightning F6 5 Sqn 15m S RAF Akrotiri Cyprus 0

Abandoned over the sea following engine failure. The pilot; Group Captain Peter Carter ejected safely

---

21-Sep-79 XV757 Harrier GR3 1 Sqn Wisbech Cambridgeshire 0

Mid air collision (3 civilians killed on the ground). Officer Commanding 1 Squadron; Wing Commander R B (Dickie) Duckett ejected as did the other pilot; Flight Lieutenant C J Gowers

---

21-Sep-79 XZ128 Harrier GR3 1 Sqn Wisbech 0

Mid air collision With XV757

04-Oct-79 XW766 Harrier GR3 3 Sqn Ravensberg Germany 0

Abandoned after loss of power. Pilot; Flight Lieutenant C C N Burwell

---

08-Nov-79 XV756 Harrier GR3 1 Sqn Holbeach Range 0

Crashed after ricochet from own cannon although Flight Lieutenant Boyens ejected successfully

---

23-Nov-79 XX762 Jaguar GR1 226 OCU Near RAF Lossiemouth 1

The aircraft was being flown as a chase to another aircraft when the sortie encountered bad weather and began the low level abort procedure. At some stage in the pull up the pilot ejected and was killed by a severe blow to the head, possibly on landing in strong winds. It is thought most probable that the pilot experienced contradictory cues from his radar altimeter showing the steep side of a hill and his other instruments which were indicating a substantial rate of climb and he thus became alarmed and confused and decided to eject lest he was about to fly into the ground.

Flight Lieutenant Alan Graham PROCTER

10-Dec-79 XX749 Jaguar GR1 226 OCU Near Lumsden 1

In clear weather and at heights of 500 to 1000 feet above ground level a formation of four Jaguar aircraft were practising formation flying. The particular manouevre required the formation to change direction 90 degrees starboard in card formation. To do this the aircraft on the left side of the formation changed position in the turn by passing behind those on the right hand side so that they swopped relative positions on completion of the turn. This is accomplished by the aircraft on the outside of the turn banking more steeply than those on the inside. During the turn the leading aircraft in the left hand pair turned more sharply and collided with the second aircraft in the right hand pair

Flight Lieutenant Nicholas James BROWN AFC

10-Dec-79 XX755 Jaguar GR1 226 OCU Lumsden 0

Mid air collision with XX749 as described above

27-Dec-79 XW228 Puma HC1 33 Sqn Mtoko Rhodesia (Zimbabwe) 3

Struck telegraph pole whilst being flown at extremely low level and was destroyed completely in the subsequent crash

Flight Lieutenant Michael George Fenwick SMITH Pilot
Flying Officer Archibald COOK Co-Pilot
Master Aircrew Robert Thomas HODGES Air Loadmaster

07-Feb-80 XV345 Buccaneer S2A 15 Sqn Near Nellis Air Force Base Nevada USA 2

Wing failed due to fatigue during low level sortie on Red Flag exercise and was seen to break away as the aircraft dived into the ground. This accident resulted in the grounding of the Buccaneer fleet and

Date Serial Aircraft Unit Place Casualties
Brief Circumstances of Accident
Casualty Details (If Applicable)

---

subsequent checks revealed that many aircraft were suffering from severe fatigue damage because of their role. Although some aircraft were returned to service a number of Buccaneers could not be repaired economically and they were withdrawn from service. This decision led to the disbandment of one squadron of the type, No: 216

Squadron Leader Kenneth Johnstone TAIT 36
Flight Lieutenant Charles Robert RUSTON 30

12-Feb-80 XK151 Hunter FGA9 2TWU Blaven Headland Isle of Skye 1

Crashed into high ground on low level training sortie

Flight Lieutenant Robin David GREEN

05-Mar-80 XV436 Phantom FGR2 29 Sqn RAF Coningsby 0

Crashed after missing cable during flapless landing. Flight Lieutenants Andy Cairncross and Nig Randall ejected

---

12-Mar-80 XW765 Harrier GR3 3 Sqn Lampeter North Wales 0

Abandoned after birdstrike. The pilot; Flight Lieutenant Paul Barton ejected. He subsequently served with distinction during the Falklands conflict

---

08-May-80 XW314 Jet Provost T5A RAF College Near Cranwell 0

Abandoned on approach following los of control. Flight Lieutenants C Massey and P Jones ejected safely

08-May-80 XN127 Whirlwind 10 CFS RAF Shawbury 0

Rolled into dive and crashed. Although most of the crew escaped with relatively minor injuries, the crewman; Master Air Loadmaster Michael Edwards was very seriously injured

---

16-May-80 XL953 Pembroke C1 60 Sqn RAF Wildenrath 0

Destroyed in fire on ground. Only prompt action by groundcrew personnel prevented a major fire in a hangar at the base from getting out of control

---

17-May-80 XX262 Hawk T1 CFS Brighton 0

Struck a yacht mast during an aerobatic display and Squadron Leader Steve Johnson was compelled to eject. The boat had sailed into the display area unknown to the Red Arrows

---

28-May-80 XG261 Hunter FGA9 2TWU Near Dufftown 0

Abandoned after loss of control during low level combat training but the pilot; Flying Officer M C Longstaffe ejected

---

28-May-80 XX961 Jaguar GR1 17 Sqn RAF Bruggen 1

On returning to base, a formation of four aircraft were in arrow formation for a visual break to land at 410 knots and 600 feet. The No 1 broke normally but the No 2 broke early and turned into the No 1, causing both aircraft to crash. It was assumed that the No 2 missed seeing the leader break and thus began his own break too soon.

Flying Officer John Lander CATHIE

28-May-80 XX964 Jaguar GR1 17 Sqn RAF Bruggen 0

Mid air collision with XX961 although the pilot; Flight Lieutenant W Kirkpatrick ejected (for the second time on the Jaguar force) safely

Date	Serial	Aircraft	Unit	Place	Casualties

Brief Circumstances of Accident

Casualty Details (If Applicable)

29-May-80	XL597	Hunter T7	216 Sqn	Near Little Saxham	0

Engine exploded and aircraft abandoned by Squadron Leaders J R McEvoy and B F Mahaffey. The Hunter was used to provide dual training and check rides on Buccaneer squadrons where there was no dual controlled aircraft

---

03-Jun-80	XV589	Phantom FG1	111 Sqn	RAF Alconbury	0

Abandoned after control lost when nose randome opened in flight and forcing Flight Lieutenants Pat R Watling and Steve L James to eject

---

11-Jul-80	XV418	Phantom FGR2	92 Sqn	Near Diepholz Germany	2

Aircraft dived into the ground during filming sortie. The crew of this aircraft were asked to fly the filming sortie after various things led to other crews withdrawing. Unfortunately, they were probably not best prepared for the task and whilst formating on the camera aircraft, control was lost but neither crew member was able to escape

Flight Lieutenant Richard Andrew John MOTT
Flight Lieutenant Ian Michael JOHNSON

17-Jul-80	XX817	Jaguar GR1	17 Sqn	RAF Bruggen	0

About 20 minutes after take off the pilot selected full dry power and noted that the port engine instruments showed 92-94% RPM with a TGT 40 degrees lower and fuel flow slightly less than the starboard engine. He diagnosed this as TGT amplifier failure and elected to return to base and turned off the TGT amplifier but obtained no change in the engine indications. When establihed on the GCA and as speed reduced through 230 knots, the pilot selected undercarriage down and compensated by increasing the power. Both reheat fire warning lights came on and when he throttled back slightly the starboard light went out but the port backing pump warning light illuminated. On teating the CWP the starboard reheat fire warning light failed to illuminate. At this stage, the pilot; Flight Lieutenant J Wittingham, noticed a bright flickering orange glow reflected off the starboard outboard pylon and so, after making a radio call he ejected and the aircraft crashed adjacent to some houses at the edge of a wood and was totally destroyed. The fire was caused by leakage in the LP fuel system which allowed fuel to migrate into the reheat zones where it was ignited by coming into contact with hot components.

31-Jul-80 XN590 Jet Provost T3A RAF College RAF Elvington 0

Birdstrike when taking off

18-Sep-80 XX545 Bulldog T1 London UAS RAF Abingdon 0

Abandoned after simulated engine failure

14-Oct-80 XV792 Harrier GR3 3 Sqn RAF Gutersloh 0

Uncontrolled roll developed when coming into a hover approach

---

28-Oct-80 XV761 Harrier GR3 4 Sqn Near Bitburg Germany 0

07-Nov-80 WH667Canberra B2 100 Sqn RAF Akrotiri 2

Crashed following engine explosion on take off and subsequent loss of control

Squadron Leader George William THOMPSON Pilot
Flying Officer Mark WRAY Navigator

12-Nov-80 XV413 Phantom FGR2 29 Sqn 50m off Cromer 2

Crashed into the sea at night

Date Serial Aircraft Unit Place Casualties
Brief Circumstances of Accident
Casualty Details (If Applicable)

Squadron Leader Stephen GLENCORSE Pilot
Flight Lieutenant Graham Edward FINCH BSc Navigator

17-Nov-80 XV256 Nimrod MR2 Kinloss Wing off End of RAF Kinloss runway 2

Crashed following massive bird ingestion to engines when all but one engine was severely damaged on take off and the pilot crash landed in a forest off the end of the runway. The escape of 18 crew members was little short of a miracle and it is particularly tragic that the captain and co-pilot should not have survived the accident since it was their skill which put the aircraft on the ground intact.

Flight Lieutenant Neol ANTHONY Royal Australian Air Force (posthumous Air Force Cross) Pilot and Captain
Flying Officer Stephen Paul BELCHER (posthumous Queen's Commendation for Brave Conduct) Co-Pilot

---

18-Nov-80 ZA801 Gazelle HT3 CFS Chetwynd Airfield Shropshire 0

Loss of control in a turn

09-Dec-80 XV414 Phantom FGR2 23 Sqn 10miles off Lowestoft 0

Abandoned over sea following engine fire. The crew of Flight Lieutenants Steve J Martin and Nick Morgan ejected

---

28-Jan-81 XW308 Jet Provost T5A 1FTS Kilmarny Fifshire 1

Crashed during solo navigation exercise. The aircraft had been detached to RAF Leuchars from RAF Linton on Ouse because of a period of bad weather in the Vale of York. The pilot was briefed to fly a low level sortie to another base, refuel and then return to Leuchars at high level later in the day. The weather was 2/8ths cloud at 700 feet, complete cover by 1000 feet and a cloud ceiling between about 2500 and 5000 feet. The visibility was about 7 miles. After take off the aircraft enetered cloud and the pilot requested clearance to turn on to heading and acknowledged the response and the details of the region pressure setting. The aircraft was subsequently seen diving steeply out of cloud and a little later in level flight but banked to the right. The aircraft crashed into a field and the pilot made no attempt to eject. Although it is possible that the pilot became disorientated whilst in cloud and making changes to radio frequencies necessitating changing hands on the controls, the cause of the accident could be satisfactorily determined.

Flight Lieutenant Paul John BISHOP BSc

12-Feb-81 XX827 Jaguar GR1 17 Sqn Nellis Ranges Navada 1

The aircraft was deployed on Red Flag and was taking part in a stafe attack as the No 2 of a pair. The aircraft was acquired by a ground radar and was seen to pull up sharply and roll to starboard until inverted. At this point it stopped climbing and continued to roll but at a slower rate before descending and striking the ground with about 100 degrees of left bank and with both engines in reheat. It seems possible that the pilot mishandled the controls during the manoeuvre and could not recover in the height available.

Flight Lieutenant David PLUMBE

23-Feb-81 XE552 Hunter FGA9 2TWU Near RAF Lossiemouth 1

Crashed into sea

Flight Lieutenant Lawrence WARNER

03-Apr-81 XG151 Hunter FGA9 2TWU RAF Lossiemouth 0

Abandoned on finals after engine flamed out but Wing Commander Dougie Marr ejected safely

Date Serial Aircraft Unit Place Casualties
Brief Circumstances of Accident
Casualty Details (If Applicable)

14-Apr-81 XX973 Jaguar GR1 31 Sqn RAF Gutersloh 0

During two versus one air combat training and at 16000 feet and 280 knots, the pilot; Squadron Leader David Milne-Smith, selected 5 degrees of flap and increased the angle of attack at which point he encountered slip stream. The aircraft rolled away from the applied spoiler and entered a flat spin from which the pilot could not effect a recovery. At 7500 feet the pilot ejected. The Release to Service allowed 14 Alpha to be used in the configuration of the aircraft but the pilot is believed to have gone to 16 Alpha. However, this particular aircraft was limited by its modification state to only 12 Alpha.

26-May-81 XW923 Harrier GR3A 1417 Flt Belize 0

Loss of control during short take off . Flight Lieutenant Jack Mardon ejected.

01-Jun-81 XX828 Jaguar T2 226 OCU Near Forfar 0

Having been struck by a single bird both engines were running erratically and the crew; Flight Lieutenants I P Kenvyn and D Webb ejected. The examination of the wreckage showed that both engines had been severely damaged by the ingestion of perspex fragmants from the front canopy which had been shattered by the bird. Subsequently a modification was introduced to provide a stronger front canopy to resist bird strike damage and to protect the front seat pilot

---

03-Jun-81 XP347 Whirlwind 10 RAF Germany Koksijde Belgium 0

Tail rotor failed and crashed on landing en route to RAF Gutersloh to be a gate guardian aircraft

---

16-Jun-81 XW329 Jet Provost T5A 3FTS RAF Leeming 0

Stalled during practice ‘turn back’

30-Jun-81 XX396 Gazelle HT3 2FTS RAF Shawbury 0

Damaged beyond repair after tail struck ground in heavy landing

---

09-Jul-81 XT866 Phantom FG1 43 Sqn RAF Leuchars 0

Abandoned on finals at night after ADI failed. Squadron Leader Ray Dixon and Flying Officer Matt Syndercombe ejected safely

---

14-Jul-81 XV807 Harrier GR3 1417Flt Georgeville Belize 0

Tailplane linkage disconnected and control lost

17-Jul-81 XX113 Jaguar GR1 226 OCU (RAF Abingdon) Near Great Malvern 0

Whilst engaged on a post-Major maintenance airtest, the pilot suffered a severe control restriction which he was unable to clear nor was he able to keep control of the aircraft. After it had rolled several times he ejected and was injured on landing. It was discovered that a loose article had jammed a powered flying control unit (PFCU) feedback mechanism and the resulatant forces could not be overcome by the pilot.

23-Jul-81 XR765 Lightning F6 5 Sqn 50 Miles North north east RAF Binbrook 0

Abandoned at sea following engine fire. The pilot; Flight Lieutenant Jim Wild ejected safely

---

24-Jul-81 XX916 Jaguar T2 ETPS Bristol Channel 1

The aircraft was carrying out a NAVWASS assessment exercise as part of the Empire Test Pilots' Course when it suffered a single birdstrike which shattered the canopy. Subsequently the engines began to behave very erratically and the crew was forced to eject. Although both were recovered from the sea about 40 minutes after ejection and the pilot; Squadron Leader Barnett survived, the navigator was found to have drowned

Flight Lieutenant Sean SPARKS Navigator

30-Jul-81 XN643 Jet Provost T3 1FTS Snainton North Yorkshire 0

Engine flamed out during aerobatics

06-Aug-81 XX972 Jaguar GR1 31 Sqn Barnards Castle Northumberland 1

The pilot was flying No 4 in a four aircraft formation and climbed out from low level in deteriorating weather. When marshalling the formation, the No 4 was seen to complete a tight 180 degree turn and then to dive into the ground. The cause was not determined but may have been pilot distraction, instrument failure or a combination of the two.

Squadron Leader Roger Martin MATTHEWS

25-Aug-81 XZ139 Harrier GR3 3 Sqn Near Alhorn Germany 0

Tail plane linkage failed. However, Flight Lieutenant M D Beech survived by ejecting

---

23-Sep-81 XW537 Buccaneer S2 237OCU RAF Wattisham 0

Stalled on approach to land

21-Oct-81 XX957 Jaguar GR1 20 Sqn RAF Bruggen 0

Several minutes after take off the aircraft was struck by lightning and the left hand engine TGT rose to 900 degrees centigrade, so the pilot completed the shut down drills but did not select the LP cock to OFF. The pilot then dumped fuel and prepared for a single engine recovery but as it began its descent the right hand engine flamed out and so the pilot ejected. Examination of the wreckage showed the right hand LP fuel cock to be in the OFF position and although the pilot had no recollection of doing so, it seems possible that he selected the right hand engine LP cock to OFF during a period of high workload in error for completing the closure of the left hand LP cock.

21-Oct-81 XL619 Hunter T7 1TWU 50miles South RAF Brawdy 0

Loss of control in inverted spin

22-Oct-81 XM366 Jet Provost T3 7FTS Holme On Spalding Moor 0

Crashed following an engine flame out which could not be corrected in time

---

13-Nov-81 XL361 Vulcan B2 9 Sqn Goose Bay 0

Damaged beyond repair and subsequently used as a ground display exhibit

---

18-Nov-81 XX758 Jaguar GR1 226 OCU Near Dingwall 1

The aircraft was being flown by a student pilot on a simulated attack sortie when it encountered bad weather and shortly thereafter crashed. Although there is no clear evidence it seems possible that the pilot continued at low level in the poor weather conditions and was not aware of the proximity of the ground.

01-Dec-81 XL583 Hunter T7 1TWU RAF Brawdy 0

Engine failed on finals forcing the crew of Flight Lieutenants Dave Wakefield and Dick Lotinga to eject

Date Serial Aircraft Unit Place Casualties
Brief Circumstances of Accident
Casualty Details (If Applicable)

12-Feb-82 XZ973 Harrier GR3 233 OCU Berwy Hill Northwales 1

Flew into high ground killing the US Navy pilot who was about half way through his Harrier conversion training

Lieutenant John MACBETH 28 US Navy

20-Feb-82 XX662 Bulldog T1 UAS Neacham 0

Loss of control in a spin

22-Feb-82 KF314 Harvard T2B A&AEE Near RAF Chilmark Wilts 2

The aircraft was being flown to renew a pilot's currency on type and after take off climbed to 8000 feet and called ATC to say that it would be commencing spinning. Nothing more was heard from the aircraft but it was established that it had completed one spin sequence followed by another and was then seen in a turn at 500 feet before descending still further. It began a right hand turn and subsequently the nose was seen to go up, it climbed steeply and then a wing dropped and it dived into the ground. Despite an exhaustive investigation the cause of the accident was never satisfactorily explained.

Squadron Leader Thomas Edwards Banks CHAMBERS 51 Pilot
Flight Lieutenant Raymond Curt Harry BEYER 28 Pilot

25-Feb-82 WK116 Canberra B2 100 Sqn RAF Akrotiri 0

Double engine flame out on take off forced Flight Lieutenants M S McGeown and T J B Tucker to eject

---

08-Mar-82 XN977 Buccaneer S2B 15 Sqn RAF Laarbruch 0

Damaged beyond repair after an engine explosion and fire when on a sortie to the Nordhorn bombing range

17-Mar-82 XE531 Hunter T12 RAE RAE Farnborough 0

The crew of Flight Lieutenant R Sears and Mr T Leng ejected after the engine failed when taking off

---

02-Apr-82 XX122 Jaguar GR1 54 Sqn The Wash 1

The aircraft was No 3 in a formation of three Jaguars awaiting the arrival of a fourth before commencing a range sortie. For various reasons it was decided that the No 4 would proceed to the range as a singleton to check the weather whilst the other three aircraft maintained their holding formation. As the No 4 passed beneath the others he noticed the No 3 peel off and head towards No 4 whom the No 3 called to say he was in visual contact with. The No 4 carried on through the range area but the No 3 did not and was found to have crashed. It appears most likely that the pilot of the No 3 aircraft was spatially disorientated in the hazy conditions whilst trying to join the No 4. (Norwegian Pilot)

14-Apr-82 XT912 Phantom FGR2 228OCU Walcot Lincolnshire 0

Mid air collision with another Phantom, which landed safely, shortly after take-off. The crew of Squadron Leaders Dick George and Guy Slocum ejected safely

---

22-Apr-82 XP564 Jet Provost T4 1TWU Nant-Y-Moch Reservoir 0

Throttle linkage failed and aircraft abandoned. Flight Lieutenant D M McIntyre and his passenger; Commander A Prakash ejected

---

13-May-82 XE649 Hunter FGA9 1TWU Near Aberyswyth 0

Abandoned After Engine Fire

17-May-82 XW288 Jet Provost T5A 1FTS Near RAF Linton On Ouse 1

Crashed during aerobatics practice

Flight Lieutenant Robert Arthur ROGERS BSc

Date	Serial	Aircraft	Unit	Place	Casualties

Brief Circumstances of Accident

Casualty Details (If Applicable)

21-May-82	XZ972	Harrier GR3	1 Sqn	Port Howard West Falkland	0

Shot down during air operations against Argentinians. Flight Lieutenant Jeff Glover, the pilot, ejected and was rescued from the water by Argentinian troops. Subsequently, Glover returned to flying duties and a tour with the Red Arrows

---

23-May-82	WP979	Chipmunk T10	5AEF	Near Cambridge Airport	0

Pilot incapacitation led to the aircraft being badly damaged on landing

---

25-May-82	XX963	Jaguar GR1	14 Sqn	Near Wesel Germany	0

The aircraft was No 2 of a pair and on climbing out of the low level area the pilot; Flight Lieutenant Steve Griggs, was concentrating on his forward look out because of anticipated traffic when he felt an explosion and his aircraft became uncontrollable. He received a call from his leader to eject and because he was unable to control the aircraft or read his instruments, he did so. The aircraft had been struck by a live Sidewinder missile fired from a Phantom!!! Subsequently, Steve Griggs ejected from another Jaguar and more recently (circa 1993-95) commanded 41 Squadron at RAF Coltishall.

25-May-82	ZA719	Chinook HC1	18 Sqn	South Atlantic	0

During operations to recover possession of the Falkland Islands a number of newly acquired Chinook helicopters were sent to the area aboard the Atlantic Conveyor. Although one aircraft was flown off the vessel, three other Chinooks were amongst the massive stocks of aircraft and supplies destroyed when the ship was struck by an Exocet missile

25-May-82 ZA706 Chinook HC1 18 Sqn South Atlantic 0

Lost in Atlantic Conveyer as above

25-May-82 ZA716 Chinook HC1 18 Sqn South Atlantic 0

Lost in Atlantic Conveyer as above

27-May-82 XZ988 Harrier GR3 1 Sqn Goose Green Falklands 0

Shot down by enemy AA fire whilst attacking Argentinian positions. The pilot; Squadron Leader Bob Iveson ejected successfully and was rescued by British forces

---

30-May-82 XZ963 Harrier GR3 1 Sqn off Stanley Airport 0

Shot down by enemy AA fire off the coast and Squadron Leader Jerry Pook ejected safely to spend some uncomfortable hours in his life raft

---

08-Jun-82 XZ989 Harrier GR3 1 Sqn Port San Carlos 0

Emergency landing following power loss damaged beyond repair

08-Jun-82 XV744 Harrier GR3 233 OCU RAF Wittering 0

Crashed following loss of power and struck off charge because of the substantial damage suffered

---

11-Jun-82 XX820 Jaguar GR1 31 Sqn RAF Bruggen 0

At the end of a sortie the aircraft was overshot into a second circuit when the pilot heard a rapid banging and felt the aircraft begin to sink rapidly. He levelled his wings, turned the aircraft away from some buildings and then ejected. The right hand engine had ingested a bolt and had surged and flamed out.

Date Serial Aircraft Unit Place Casualties
Brief Circumstances of Accident
Casualty Details (If Applicable)

17-Jun-82 XX898 Buccaneer S2B 12 Sqn Near RAF Lossiemouth 0

Loss of control on approach. The pilot; Flight Lieutenant Jolly and his navigator; Flight Lieutenant Nigel Maddox ejected

---

29-Jun-82 XW272 Harrier T4A 4 Sqn Hohne Range Germany 1

Failed to take off due to incorrect flap setting

Wing Commander Keith Graham HOLLAND AFC (Officer Commanding 4 Squadron)

07-Jul-82 XV491 Phantom FGR2 29 Sqn 35 miles off Cromer 2

The aircraft was one of three Phantoms which took off from RAF Valley to carry out practice interceptions before returning to their base at RAF Coningsby. One aircraft returned early to base but the others continued with the exercise. The weather over the sea was misty with fog banks up to 200 feet in patches, although there was a clear horizon and visibility of about 7 miles. The aircraft, acting as the fighter, completed the interception and passed the target aircraft at a height of about 250 feet before making a left hand turn as instructed by the ground controller. However, radar contact was lost and the aircraft crashed into the sea. It was subsequently determined that the aircraft had struck the sea in an upright and slightly nose up attitude and that it had been under power at the time. Although several possible causes for the crash were postulated, none was conclusive.

Flight Lieutenant Alan Stewart RILEY Pilot
Flight Lieutenant Marcus Robert HANTON Navigator

28-Jul-82 XX305 Hawk T1 4FTS RAF Valley 1

Stalled during emergency landing and although Flight Lieutenant Demery; the instructor, ejected safely his student did not survive

Flight Lieutenant Paul Christian GAY BSc

05-Aug-82 XL593 Hunter T7 1TWU 5m North-east Carmarthen 0

Engine failure caused the crew of Group Captain Peter Oulten and Flight Lieutenant Martin Stoner to eject

---

13-Sep-82 XX760 Jaguar GR1 14 Sqn Near Brora Germany 0

The aircraft was leading a mixed formation of Jaguars and Buccaneers at low level when the CWS alarm sounded and the No 2 engine fire light illuminated. The pilot shut down the engine and called to say that he had a fire warning. The presence of a real fire was confirmed by others in the formation and although the No 2 engine fire warning had extinguished, all the other captions had illuminated!! The pilot ejected and the aircraft made a shallow descent onto open moorland where it crashed. The accident was caused by a fatigue failure of a combustion chamber outer casing which allowed hot gases to burn through the engine bay and into the F4 fuel tank. This was Steve Griggs second ejection from the Jaguar, as it will be recalled, he had been shot down earlier that year by a Phantom

---

20-Sep-82 XV160 Buccaneer S2B 16 Sqn Capo Frasca Range Sardinia 0

The aircraft was practising weapon deliveries on the Capo Frasca Range whilst based at Decimomannu. After three successful attack profiles were flown, the fourth was planned to be a computer directed attack with automatic weapon release after a steep pull up from low level. The pilot pulled up following the directions from his computer and suddenly heard the stall warning sound and the aircraft rolled sharply right and then left, before descending flatly and slowly. Despite the application of spin recovery techniques the aircraft could not be controlled and the crew ejected at about 4000 feet. It seems probable that the pilot pulled up more sharply than is usual and that the speed decayed so that at weapon release the aircraft stalled. The margin of error was very small and the pilot then had insufficient altitude to recover. Flight Lieutenants Braithwaite and Major ejected

---

29-Sep-82 XX768 Jaguar GR1 17 Sqn Near Heinsberg-Randerath Germany 0

Whilst on a target run as the No 2 in a four aircraft formation the pilot heard a bang and saw that the No 2 engine TGT had risen through 700 degrees centigrade. He diagnosed a 'pop' surge and proved the engine in accordance with the Flight Reference Cards but, as a precaution returned to base and left the engine set between 70 and 80% power. Subsequently, various other bangs and severe vibrations occured and the pilot was forced to eject. The cause of the accident was a fatigue failure of an LP compressor stator blade, the frequencies set up by this resulted in the rupture of a number of fuel system components. The squadron commander; Wing Commander Lovett ejected.

15-Oct-82 XL232 Victor K2 55 Sqn RAF Marham 0

Engine explosion and major fire when taking off. The aircraft was brought to a stop and quickly evacuated by its crew and despite prompt attention from the fire crew, the aircraft was engulfed by flames from its heavy fuel load and completely destroyed

---

20-Oct-82 XX300 Hawk T1 2TWU RAF Chivenor 0

After a birdstrike at night, when on finals to land, the pilot; Flight Lieutenant Graham Rawles had no other option but to eject

---

06-Nov-82 XW767 Harrier GR3 1 Sqn off RAF Stanley 0

Crashed into sea following engine failure. The squadron commander; Wing Commander Peter Squire DFC AFC ejected

---

09-Dec-82 XW417 Jet Provost T5A 7FTS Lake Thirlmere Cumbria 1

Flew into high ground in poor visibility. The pilot was engaged on a 'co-pilot enrichment sortie', a scheme to allow V force co-pilots the opportunity to undertake some additional flying and to 'spread their wings' after the restrictive nature of flying in V force aircraft.

Flight Lieutenant Michael Gene O'NEILL 26

23-Feb-83 XV795 Harrier GR3 233 OCU Near Peterborough 0

Mid air collision with XW926

23-Feb-83 XW926 Harrier T4 233 OCU Near Peterborough 2

Mid air collision with XV795. Neither crew member was able to escape. Flight Lieutenant Leeming had served with distinction during the Falklands conflict during the previous year

Flight Lieutenant John Roger LEEMING Pilot and Instructor
Flying Officer David John HAIGH Student Pilot

07-Mar-83 XZ376 Jaguar GR1 17 Sqn off Tain Range 0

During a toss bombing sortie on the Tain Range the pilot did not complete a full recovery in IMC. The aircraft exited cloud in inverted 20 degree dive, exceeding the rolling limits during pull out. The aircraft departed controlled flight and the pilot ejected at about 400 feet

---

22-Mar-83 XV787 Harrier GR3 1453 Flt Near RAF Stanley Falklands 0

Engine failure

Date Serial Aircraft Unit Place Casualties
Brief Circumstances of Accident
Casualty Details (If Applicable)

30-Mar-83 XN495 Jet Provost T3A 7FTS RAF Elvington 0

Damaged beyond repair following belly landing after engine failure. On climbing away from a roller landing, a malfunction with the engine starting system gave thrust variations and unusual noises. Although the instructor turned the aircraft back, he realised that he could not reach the runway and so attempted to land on a taxiway. Unfortunately whilst trying to lower the undercarriage a wing struck the ground and broke off. The aircraft slid along the ground for several hundred yards and the crew sustained serious back injuries. The engine malfunction was caused by fatigue failure of the ground start switch which in turn caused fluctuations in engine power.

17-Apr-83 WT895 Kirby Cadet Mk3 614GS Wethersfield 2

Broke Up In Air During Aerobatics

Air Cadet Ian SUTTON 17

It is believed that Flight Lieutenant John KNOCK RAFVR(T) died subsequently from his injuries

---

19-Apr-83 XX742 Jaguar XX742 6 Sqn off Norfolk Coast 0

The pilot rolled the aircraft into a descending right hand turn but when he attempted to stop the roll the aircraft did not respond and continued to descend and roll. When he saw the altimeter reach 7700 feet and at an airspeed of 360 knots, the pilot ejected. The cause of the uncontrolled roll was never determined. Flight Lieutenant J L Jackson ejected successfully

---

20-Apr-83 XX374 Gazelle HT3 2FTS Mount Snowden 2

Unauthorised aerobatics led to crash into mountain side. The sortie was a medium and low level navigation exercise followed by mountain flying. The aircraft was seen near the summit of Snowden and subsequently flying alongside a miners' track with the crew waving to walkers. It hovered for about 10 seconds in front of a party of school children before turning and diving away into the valley and then pulling up into a wing over and reversing direction. It flew back towards the school children in a gentle descending turn but at high speed before passing them very closely and striking the ground not far beyond them. It slid along on its side and then fell into a valley. Although there was no fire, the aircraft was destroyed and the crew killed

Flight Lieutenant Roy CITRINE 35 Pilot Instructor
Lieutenant MOHAMMUD Ali Bin Awang 25 Royal Brunei Malay Regiment Student Pilot

---

24-Apr-83 XA306 Kirby Cadet TX3 618GS West Malling 0

This accident took place almost exactly 10 years after another Kirby Cadet crashed at West Malling killing the RAF instructor and the student pilot

---

03-May-83 XZ134 Harrier GR3 3 Sqn Lippstadt Germany 0

Abandoned after engine failure whilst taking off. The pilot; Flight Lieutenant S K Brown survived

---

16-Jun-83 XZ105 Jaguar GR1 2 Sqn Near Goose Bay Canada 0

Mid air collision with XZ110

16-Jun-83 XZ110 Jaguar GR1 2 Sqn Near Goose Bay Canada 0

A three aircraft formation was returning to Goose Bay for a visual rejoin into the circuit but they were instructed by ATC to fly a right hand circuit although they had previously understood that they would operate left hand. The leader called for the formation to move from tactical to close echelon port but whilst doing so the No 2 and No 3 aircraft collided and both were destroyed. The prime cause was the

No 3 losing sight of the No 2, at which point the No 3 should have pulled up from the formation and established visual contact. The two pilots; Flight Lieutenants Robinson and Dalton ejected safely

---

22-Jun-83 XX721 Jaguar GR1 54 Sqn Near Hahn Germany 0

The aircraft took off normally but at about 500 feet the audio alarm sounded and warning captions illuminated showing that contents of the N1 and N2 engine fuel feeder tanks were falling. The pilot checked the switches controlling fuel supply were correctly selected but both engines flamed out and the pilot had no option to eject from about 800 feet. Having established that the fuel switches had been set correctly, the investigation could not determine why the fuel supply had been interrupted so seriously and it was concluded that a series of failures had taken place simultaneously to cause the accident. The Norwegian Air Force pilot; Captain Nils Halvgaard ejected safely

---

24-Jun-83 XX166 Hawk T1 4FTS Isle of Man 2

Flew into high ground during navigation exercise

Flight Lieutenant Roger Francis LANE
Flight Lieutenant Julian Mark Baden LEWIS

08-Jul-83 XX195 Hawk T1 2TWU Dyfed Wales 0

Damaged beyond repair after wirestrike and emergency landing

29-Jul-83 XX229 Hawk T1 1TWU Into Irish Sea 0

Abandoned after low level engine flame out

29-Jul-83 XX336 Hawk T1 2TWU Bristol Channel 0

Mid air collision with XX353

29-Jul-83 XX353 Hawk T1 2TWU Bristol Channel 0

Mid air collision with XX336

03-Aug-83 WJ625 Canberra T17 360 Sqn off Gibraltar 3

The aircraft took off as one of a stream returning to UK. Shortly after take off it flew into a fog bank and subsequently crashed into the sea. It seems most likely that the pilot became disorientated in the cloud and failed to establish a positive rate of climb

Flying Officer William Hunter EDWARD Pilot Captain
Flight Lieutenant Peter FORD Navigator
Flying Officer Andrew Guy BENYON Air Electronics Officer

11-Aug-83 XX891 Buccaneer S2B 16 Sqn RAF Laarbruch 1

Aircraft crashed approaching to land. The pilot ejected but the navigator was killed

Flight Lieutenant Anthony Stewart DAKIN Navigator

26-Aug-83 XP753 Lightning F3 Lightning TF Scarborough sea front 1

A pair of Lightnings were to pre-position at a civil airport in preparation for an air display. Before take-off a request was made to fly past a recruiting exhibition at Scarborough but this was refused by the Authorising Officer. As the other aircraft was not ready at take-off time the pilot of XP753 was allowed to continue as a singleton and he became airborne on time. Several minutes late he was seen to approach the Scarborough sea front and to fly past the recruiting display at between 100 and 200 feet before carrying out a wing over at the end of the bay and returning southbound in the landing configuration.

Date Serial Aircraft Unit Place Casualties
Brief Circumstances of Accident
Casualty Details (If Applicable)

Towards the end of this run he engaged reheat, raised the undercarriage and made a climbing turn to port reaching about 1500 feet. He then reversed his turn and headed back towards the headland at the southern end of the bay which had cliffs rising to about 250 feet. He made a tight descending turn to starboard at a high angle of attack and narrowly cleared the headland before heading out to sea at a very low level. As the pilot attempted to roll the wings level, the aircraft pitched up, before yawing and rolling to starboard and then diving into the sea.

Flight Lieutenant Michael Leslie THOMPSON 37

09-Sep-83 XS457 Lightning T5 5Sqn RAF Binbrook 0

The aircraft was written off from damage caused when the undercarriage collapsed

---

19-Sep-83 XX114 Jaguar GR1 226 OCU RAF Lossiemouth 0

Whilst on finals to land the aircraft suffered a multiple bird strike and both engines lost power forcing the pilot; Flight Lieutenant Iain McLean to eject

---

27-Sep-83 ZA586 Tornado GR1 9 Sqn Near Kings Lynn Norfolk 1

Abandoned following major electrical systems failure. Although the navigator; Flight Lieutenant Nick Nickles escaped, the pilot did not although he was conscious up to the time of the navigator's ejection. It is supposed that he he may have been disabled by some debris as the navigator ejected or unable to eject for some other reason

Squadron Leader Michael Donald STEPHENS

17-Oct-83 XV484 Phantom FGR2 23 Sqn Mount Usborne East Falkland 2

Flew into high ground in cloud due to failure to ascertain correct position whilst engaged on a practice interceptions sortie

Flight Lieutenant John Richard GOSTICK BSc Pilot
Flight Lieutenant John Kenneth BELL BSc Navigator

28-Oct-83 ZA558 Tornado GR1 617 Sqn off Sheringham Norfolk 1

A crew who flew regularly together were returning to base when the navigator was unable to communicate with the pilot, despite repeated attempts to do so. The aircraft began a gentle tight hand descending turn and the navigator became alarmed at the proximity of the sea. As the aircraft passed 90 feet the navigator used the Command Ejection System to eject both himself and the pilot from the aircraft. The navigator spent over three hours in the water before rescue but the pilot was never found, although his ejection seat was recovered from the seabed. There seemed to be no external reasons for the pilot's incapacitation and it could only be assumed that some unforeseen medical condition rendered him unconscious.

Flight Lieutenant Ian Charles DIXON

28-Oct-83 XV742 Harrier GR3 233 OCU Holbeach Range 1

Whilst undertaking a practice attack on the range the aircraft crashed. It is thought possible that it was struck by a ricochet.

Flying Officer John Richard SEWELL 24

14-Nov-83 ZA597 Tornado GR1 9 Sqn RAF Honington 0

Damaged beyond repair after heavy landing

Date Serial Aircraft Unit Place Casualties
Brief Circumstances of Accident
Casualty Details (If Applicable)

19-Nov-83 XV762 Harrier GR3 1453 Flt Near Goose Green East Falkland 1

Flew into high ground

Flight Lieutenant Byron Stewart CLEW BSc

21-Nov-83 XM453 Jet Provost T3 3FTS Near Ingleton North Yorkshire 0

The aircraft was being flown on a low level exercise when it struck several birds. The instructor took control and started a climbing turn towards the base airfield. Unfortunately, the engine lost power and despite taking remedial action to clear the engine surge, there was insufficient height available and the instructor ordered an abandonment. The instructor, Flight Lieutenants Larry Betts sustained serious back injuries but the student G O Riddett ejected without injury.

17-Jan-84 XX915 Jaguar T2 ETPS Near Porton Down Wiltshire 0

Crashed on approach to Boscombe Down after initial indications of hydraulics failure followed by evidence of an in-flight fire. The pilot Squadron Leader Tim Allen escaped

06-Feb-84 ZA451 Tornado GR1 15 Sqn Near Jever Germany 0

Abandoned after being struck by lightning. Squadron Leader Ian Travers-Smith and his pilot; Flight Lieutenant F P Smith ejected

07-Feb-84 XX750 Jaguar GR1 14 Sqn 90 M North-west Nellis Ranges 1

During Red Flag the aircraft was operating as No 2 of a pair of Jaguars operating with another pair and two F5s. Whilst take avoiding action from a ground radar threat the No 2 flew into the ground inverted and the pilot was killed. Jackson had previously ejected from a Jaguar in February 1983

Flying Officer Joseph Laurie JACKSON

21-Mar-84 XX251 Hawk T1 CFS RAF Akrotiri Cyprus 0

During the work up training at Akrotiri the aircraft was designated Synchro 2 which meant that it was one of the Synschro pair. Part of their display is a cross over at 100 feet, a loop where they cross again inverted at the top and a third cross at the bottom as the pilots then made for their 'exit gate'. As he was rather high, the pilot pulled more tightly and then relaxed his pull but the aircraft which subsequently impacted the ground despite the pilot's attempt to pull up. The ground impact forced the ejection seat up the rails and a subsequent impact pushed the seat down again and rendered it useless. However, the subsequent impacts initiaited the man/seat separation and the main parachute deployed to pull the pilot from the aircraft. The pilot; Flight Lieutenant Chris Hurst, was exceptionally fortunate to survive

---

20-May-84 XZ430 Buccaneer S2B 208 Sqn Moray Firth off Lossiemouth 2

The aircraft was leading a five ship formation and began a sustained pitch up from low level which results in weapon release in a moderate climbing attitude. The aircraft was seen to enter cloud during the manoeuvre but was not sighted thereafter. From the subsequent investigation the reason for the loss of control could not be established satisfactorily although pilot disorientation coupled with instrument failure might have contributed to the accident.

Squadron Leader William Robertson GRAHAM BSc
Flight Lieutenant Anthony John WHITE

03-Jun-84 XV257 Nimrod MR2 42 Sqn off Lands End 0

The aircraft was airborne from RAF St Mawgan. It had an SAR equipment pack which included a load of 5 inch reconnaissance flares, the release units of which were were switched to 'live' shortly after take-off. Immediately afterwards the crew were warned of a bomb bay fire and the captain set course for base and a Mayday call was broadcast. Although the aircraft was landed safely and the crew evacuated it successfully, the aircraft was badly damaged by the fire. The blaze was caused by a 5 inch flare becoming detached and igniting but the reason for this happening could not be determined.

Date	Serial	Aircraft	Unit	Place	Casualties

Brief Circumstances of Accident

Casualty Details (If Applicable)

03-Jun-84	XZ135	Harrier GR3	4 Sqn	Aschaffenburg Germany	0

Abandoned during air display after engine fire and emergency landing

---

12-Jul-84	ZA408	Tornado GR1	TWCU	Near Sheringham Norfolk	0

Mid air collision with Jaguar XZ393. Squadron Leader Al Boxall-Hunt and Flight Lieutenant T S Cave survived

---

12-Jul-84	XZ393	Jaguar GR1	54 Sqn	Near Sheringham Norfolk	0

Mid air collision with Tornado ZA408 TWCU (45 Sqn). The Jaguar was the lead aircraft of a formation shortly after take off from RAF Coltishall, whilst the Honington based Tornado was acting a singleton on a navigation exercise, including dive bombing on Wainfleet Range. Air Traffic Control at RAF Coltishall warned the Jaguar formation of the presence of the Tornado and although this was acquired by the No 2 in the formation, his warning was not received by the other aircraft. The aircraft collided and both were destroyed. The Jaguar pilot ejected with his aircraft almost inverted, in a steep dive and at low altitude. The Tornado crew also ejected successfully. Squadron Leader D M 'Dim' Jones ejected safely and was rescued. Dim Jones subsequently had a second mid air collision with a Tornado but was able to bring his aircraft back safely despite losing a substantial part of the wing

---

13-Jul-84	XS920	Lightning F6	5 Sqn	Henslingen Germany	1

Crashed after flying into wires during practice interception of an USAF A10 Thunderbolt II

Flight Lieutenant David William FROST BA

18-Jul-84 ZA494 Tornado GR1 27 Sqn Goose Bay 0

Abandoned after control lost during approach to land. The squadron commander; Wing Commander J B Grogan and Flight Lieutenant J Plumb ejected to safety

---

15-Aug-84 XN473 Jet Provost T3A 7FTS RAF Cranwell 0

The aircraft took off and immediately encountered a flock of birds in front of the aircraft. The instructor attempted to fly over the birds but when this was not successful, he abandoned the take off and decided to land back on the runway. In doing so the aircraft struck the ground heavily and was damaged beyond repair.

22-Aug-84 XZ395 Jaguar GR1 54 Sqn 20m E Cromer 0

The aircraft was one of a pair engaged in air combat training, with each acting as leader in a series of tail chases. Having completed one sequence, the pilot of XZ395 took the lead and descended 2000 feet and turned through 120 degrees before levelling his wiings at about 420 knots. He pulled up into a wing over to the right and reached 13000 feet and reduced speed to 280 knots. As he began to descend he saw the other aircraft to his right at close range and closing and so he rolled wings level to assist the other Jaguar to maintain separation. After levelling out the pilot felt a heavy thump run through the airframe and immediately thereafter a sudden yaw to starboard which the pilot could not correct. The nose dropped and the aircraft rolled through 360 degrees to the right and although it returned to the wings level position it continued to slice to the right. At about 10000 feet the pilot ejected. It seems likely that two reasons exist for the very severe yaw experienced; either a disconnected control linkage or an uncommanded rudder movement. However, despite recovering substantial parts of the wreckage, no positive evidence to substantiate these possibilities was found. Squadron Leader John Froud, a Jaguar pilot of many years experience, ejected safely.

Date Serial Aircraft Unit Place Casualties
Brief Circumstances of Accident
Casualty Details (If Applicable)

31-Aug-84 XX257 Hawk T1 CFS Sidmouth 0

Abandoned after engine failure at low level during air display. The aircraft was being flown in the No 8 position and as it approached the top of the 'Vixen' loop the engine appeared to surge and despite attempts by the pilot; Flight Lieutenant Pete Lees the engine could not be relit and he was forced to eject. The failure was subsequently traced to a blade in the low pressure compressor.

01-Oct-84 XN817 Argosy C1 A&AEE West Freugh 0

Damaged beyond repair in a heavy landing - This aircraft had been selected for preservation!

25-Oct-84 XX298 Hawk T1 4FTS Tremadoc Bay 0

Abandoned after control lost

07-Nov-84 XX180 Hawk T1 4FTS RAF Mona 0

Abandoned following birdstrike. The instructor and student; Flight Lieutenant N W Willey and Pilot Officer M G Ball ejected

---

08-Nov-84 ZA603 Tornado GR1 27 Sqn Near Schweinfurt Germany 0

The pilot took avoiding action to provide separation from another aircraft. However, the navigator, who had been looking down into the cockpit, noticed the unusual attitude and proximity of the ground and thought the aircraft was about to crash. He, therefore, ejected both crew using the Command Ejection System.

08-Nov-84 XR761 Lightning F6 5 Sqn 21m North-east RAF Binbrook 0

Abandoned at sea following engine fire

14-Nov-84 ZA676 Chinook HC1 240OCU Near Basingstoke 0

Damaged beyond repair after emergency landing following engine failure on take off

---

29-Nov-84 XZ992 Harrier GR3 1453 Flt RAF Stanley East Falkland 0

The aircraft was being flown as No 2 of a pair practising an attack on Port Stanley airport. As it approached the airfield at 250 feet and 480 knots, the pilot heard a loud band and felt a heavy jolt. His forward vision was obscured by a red mass over the windscreen and side panels and the buffeting was so severe that he had difficulty in reading his instruments. Although he was able to see very briefly out of the canopy he soon lost all visual reference and became disorientated and so, being close to the ground, ejected. The ejection was at very low level and although the sequence worked properly, there was insufficient time for the parachute to slow the pilot down and he suffered serious injuries which incapacitated him. He was saved from drowning by two airmen who were working nearby and came to his aid in a Gemini dinghy. The accident was caused by the aircraft striking a large sea bird, probably a Southern Giant Petrel.

30-Jan-85 XX279 Hawk T1 2TWU Bristol Channel 1

Loss of control

Flight Lieutenant Guy Benedict WARD

18-Feb-85 XW933 Harrier T4 3 Sqn Near RAF Gutersloh 1

Abandoned after mid air collision with German Navy F104S. Although Flying Officer K B McCann ejected safely, it is thought the other pilot, a very experienced instructor was killed on impact

Squadron Leader Albert Bruce COGRAM

Date Serial Aircraft Unit Place Casualties
Brief Circumstances of Accident
Casualty Details (If Applicable)

06-Mar-85 XR772 Lightning F6 5 Sqn Near Spurn Head 1

Control lost and aircraft abandoned but the pilot did not survive

Flying Officer Martin Alan RAMSEY

25-Mar-85 XX660 Bulldog T1 UAS Near Yeldon Oxfordshire 1

Abandoned following loss of control in spin, instructor fell out of harness and was killed but the student survived and parachuted safely

Flight Lieutenant Ian Maurice REDWOOD BSc ARCS

01-Apr-85 XZ388 Jaguar GR1 14 Sqn Near Hapsburg Germany 0

Loss of control when pilot made head down radio frequency change at low level

---

17-Apr-85 XX293 Hawk T1 4FTS RAF Wattisham 0

Canopy came off during take off and pilot lost control

14-Jun-85 XV341 Buccaneer S2B 12 Sqn RAF Lossiemouth 1

Tailplane linkage failed on approach and the navigator abandoned aircraft safely but the pilot did not and was killed in the subsequent crash

Flight Lieutenant William STEELE BSc(Eng)

09-Jul-85 XZ365 Jaguar GR1A 2 Sqn Near Mohne See Germany 0

Flying at 500 feet in hazy conditions the pilot entered cloud and climbed VMC on top of the stratus and expected the weather to clear as forecast. The pilot then experienced apparent conflicts between his HUD and his head down instruments and so initiated full after burner and pulled the aircraft nose up but at that stage he struck trees on top of a 2500 feet high hill and ejected

---

08-Aug-85 WK162 Canberra B2 100 Sqn RAF Alconbury 0

Aborted take off after ASI failed and aircraft damaged beyond repair

---

19-Sep-85 XS921 Lightning F6 11 Sqn 50m North-east Withamsea 0

Abandoned after control failure. The pilot; Flight Lieutenant Craig Penrice ejected safely

---

26-Sep-85 XX333 Hawk T1 2TWU Deccimomannu Range Sardinia 0

Abandoned after mid air collision

26-Sep-85 XX340 Hawk T1 2TWU Deccimomannu Range Sardinia 0

Abandoned after mid air collision

07-Oct-85 XX728 Jaguar GR1A 6 Sqn Near Alston Cumbria 1

Mid air collision with XX731

Flight Lieutenant Leonard STOVIN

07-Oct-85 XX731 Jaguar GR1A 6 Sqn Near Alston Cumbria 0

At 500 feet and 470 knots the No 2 aircraft was slightly behind and starboard of the leader. The leader commenced a right turn which meant his crossing the No 2, however, during the turn the two aircraft collided and although he missed his ejection handle at the first attempt the No 2 pilot ejected.

Date	Serial	Aircraft	Unit	Place	Casualties
Brief Circumstances of Accident					
Casualty Details (If Applicable)					
25-Oct-85	XT669	Wessex HC2	72 Sqn	Forkhill County Armagh	1
Struck radio mast during take off and crashed					
19-Nov-85	XW922	Harrier GR3	1 Sqn	RAF Wittering	0
Rolled over on landing					
02-Dec-85	ZA610	Tornado GR1	617 Sqn	Near Flamborough Head	2
Crashed into sea during night refuelling exercise					
Flight Lieutenant John SHEEN 36					
Flight Lieutenant Michael BARNARD 32					
07-Jan-86	XV434	Phantom FGR2	29 Sqn	20miles North of Harrogate	0
Loss of control at low level resulted in Flight Lieutenants Ian Ferguson and S C Williams ejecting					
02-Apr-86	XV784	Harrier GR3A	233OCU	RAF Wittering	0
Aircraft severely damaged and not repaired following a flight line fire					
13-May-86	ZA715	Chinook HC1	1310 Flt	Mount Young Falkland	3
Flew into ground in whiteout conditions					
Flying Officer David Vincent BROWNING 23 Co-Pilot					
Sergeant Wayne John HOPSON 27 Air Loadmaster					
Unidentified Gurka Soldier 7th Battalion Gurka Rifles					

25-May-86 XH304 Vampire T11 CFS RAF Mildenhall 0

Mid air collision with Meteor T7 WA669 whilst flying in formation at the annual air show. The Meteor and Vampire were attempting a line astern barrel roll to the left but because it could not match the Meteor's rate of roll, the Vampire became displaced. The Vampire moved forward and collided with the Meteor. The pilot; Squadron Leader David Marchant and a member of the ground maintenance crew who was flying as a passenger; Sergeant A Ball, were able to eject.

25-May-86 WA669 Meteor T7 CFS RAF Mildenhall 2

Mid air collision with Vampire XH304

Flight Lieutenant Andrew James POTTER 38 Pilot
Corporal Kevin TURNER 24 Ground support tradesman

06-Jun-86 XW407 Jet Provost T5A 7FTS Helmsley North Yorkshire 0

Mid air collision during tail chase

06-Jun-86 XW411 Jet Provost T5A 7FTS Helmsley North Yorkshire 0

Mid Air Collision In Tail Chase. The three crew members from the aircraft; Squadron Leader R Lindo, Flight Lieutenant B Iddon and Flying Officer D Bryson were all able to escape from the aircraft

---

17-Jun-86 XW916 Harrier GR3 233 OCU Yeovilton 0

Abandoned by Flight Lieutenant Gerry Humphries after fuel leak and electrical failure whilst approaching RNAS Yeovilton

---

17-Jun-86 43+24 Tornado GR1 TTTE North Wales 2

Flew into ground at night despite repeated warnings from the navigator to the pilot to watch the height being flown

Squadron Leader John Philip TOWL 37 Navigator
Luftwaffe pilot also killed

19-Jun-86 XL191 Victor K2 55 Sqn Hamilton Canada 0

Crashed into the undershoot during approach to land. The detailed circumstances of this accident are taught within the RAF flight safety training environment as an example of how not to do things. In essence there was a breakdown in crew cooperation which, when taken with other factors led to the loss of the aircraft

---

28-Jun-86 XW769 Harrier GR3 4 Sqn Chievres Belgium 1

Loss of control in hover at an air display and pilot fatally injured in subsequent ejection

Flight Lieutenant Brian Desmond WEATHERLEY

03-Jul-86 XV471 Phantom FGR2 19 Sqn RAF Wildenrath 0

Major systems failure on approach left Flying Officer Russ Walters-Morgan and Flight Lieutenant Chris Heames no option but to abandon the aircraft

---

07-Jul-86 XX223 Hawk T1 4FTS RAF Valley 0

Abandoned after tyre burst when landing

15-Jul-86 XR760 Lightning F6 11 Sqn 15m North-east Whitby 0

Abandoned by Flight Lieutenant Bob Bees following engine fire

---

03-Nov-86 XX297 Hawk T1 CFS RAF Scampton 0

Abandoned on approach after engine flamed out and the pilot; Flight Lieutenant Dan Findlay, failed to appreciate how much height he had lost.

04-Nov-86 XS518 Wessex HU5 84 Sqn Limassol Bay Cyprus 3

Flew into sea on night casevac

Flight Lieutenant Fiona JOHNSTONE RM PMRAFNS Nursing Officer
Master Aircrew Peter David BARWELL AFC
Corporal Martin COOK PMRAFNS

27-Nov-86 XX732 Jaguar GR1A 226 OCU Near Hawick 1

The aircraft was engaged on a low level training sortie when it flew into the ground just beyond a ridge line in Eskdalemuir. The ground was slopping away and the aircraft was travelling at over 400 knots with 12 degrees nose down angle and wings level. As far as can be ascertained the aircraft was under control at the time and there is no evidence of any unserviceability.

Captain BUHTO USAF

02-Dec-86 ZA555 Tornado GR1 TWCU 45(R) Sqn Near Diss Norfolk 0

A major systems failure caused Squadron Leader E J Wyer and Flight Lieutenant J Magowan to abandon the aircraft

---

10-Dec-86 ZA605 Tornado GR1 617 Sqn Thorney Cambridgeshire 0

Mid air collision with ZA611

Date Serial Aircraft Unit Place Casualties
Brief Circumstances of Accident
Casualty Details (If Applicable)

10-Dec-86 ZA611 Tornado GR1 617 Sqn Thorney Cambridgeshire 0

Mid air collision with ZA605 and not subsequently repaired

01-Feb-87 XT674 Wessex HC2 22 Sqn Mount Ben More Perthshire 1

Crashed taking off in snow storm on rescue sortie - civilian police officer killed

Sergeant Harry LAWRIE Leader, Killin Mountain Rescue Team

27-Feb-87 ZA721 Chinook HC1 78 Sqn Near RAF Mount Pleasant East Falkland 7

Dived into ground on a test flight. The test flight seemed to be proceding normally when the aircraft pitched up and dived into the ground. Although a garbled radio message was received it did not reveal any indication as to the cause of the accident

Flight Lieutenant Stephen John NEWMAN BSc 28 Captain
Flight Lieutenant Anthony Donald MOFFAT 26 Co-Pilot
Sergeant Andrew John JOHNS 30 Air Loadmaster
Chief Technician David John CHITTY 31: Maintenance Technicians
Corporal Jeremy Charles MARSHALL 26
Corporal Karl Mark MINSHULL 25
Corporal Peter Jason WHITWELL 25

19-Mar-87 XP707 Lightning F3 LTF Near RAF Binbrook 0

Crashed during aerobatic practice but Flight Lieutenant Barry Lennon ejected safely

29-Mar-87 ZA412 Tornado GR1 20 Sqn RAF Wildenrath 0

Crashed on landing when undercarriage hit the barrier

30-Mar-87 ZD894 Tornado GR1

Circumstances not known

22-Apr-87 XW540 Buccaneer S2 12 Sqn Near Wick 2

Crashed into sea at night

Flight Lieutenant John Julian COOKE Pilot
Flying Officer Adrian Francis FAHY Navigator

03-Jun-87 ZA366 Tornado GR1 TWCU Near Manby Lincolnshire 0

Abandoned after major systems failure. The two crew of Wing Commanders: A V B (Tony) Hawken AFC - the commanding officer of the TWCU (45(R) Sqn) and Niall Irving - a student on No 53 Course, ejected safely

---

17-Jun-87 ZA493 Tornado GR1 20 Sqn 6m S Keswick Cumbria 0

Mid air collision with Jaguar XZ116. Flight Lieutenants Campion and Head escaped safely

---

17-Jun-87 XZ116 Jaguar GR1A 41 Sqn 6m S Keswick Cumbria 1

Whilst engaged on his combat ready work-up as a squadron pilot, he was involved in a mid air collision with Tornado ZA493. The subsequent enquiry was able to establish that from the relative routes of each aircraft and terrain masking, it would have been very unlikely that either crew would have seen each other before the accident and in time to take avoiding action.

Flight Lieutenant Andrew Simon MANNHEIM BSc

Date Serial Aircraft Unit Place Casualties
Brief Circumstances of Accident
Casualty Details (If Applicable)

24-Jun-87 XZ386 Jaguar GR1A 226 OCU Near Builth Wells 1

Whilst as acting as the 'bounce' aircraft against two other Jaguars, the pilot lost control at very low level. Although he attempted an ejection, this was not successful and he was killed. The pilot had been a very experienced instructor and had previously ejected from a Canberra at RAF Tengah. He was also an accomplished aerobatic pilot and had represented his unit when instructing at Flying Training School

Flight Lieutenant Ian David HILL

01-Jul-87 XR763 Lightning F6 5 Sqn RAF Akrotiri 0

Double engine failure on approach

27-Jul-87 ZD738 Tornado GR1 31 Sqn Sadmoor Yorkshire 0

Controls locked at low level and aircraft abandoned

26-Aug-87 ZE358 Phantom F4J(UK) 74 Sqn Trefenter 10m South-west Aberystwyth 2

Flew into ground during low level training flight

Flight Lieutenant Euan Holm MURDOCH BSc Pilot
Flying Officer Jeremy Lindsey OGG Navigator

07-Sep-87 XT861 Phantom FG1 43 Sqn North Sea 0

Mid air collision in five ship formation. Flying Officer John Hancock and Squadron Leader Tommy Riddell ejected safely

---

02-Nov-87 XV790 Harrier GR3 3 Sqn Otterburn Training Area 1

Mid air collision during low level practice attack. The circumstances of this accident are not entirely dissimilar to one near Nantwich in 1976. The formation of six aircraft from RAF Gutersloh were to attack a target at Otterburn with even numbered aircraft flying direct to the target whilst odd numbered aircraft were to take a less direct route to achieve the necessary separation. The number 2 aircraft passed over the target and after a few seconds separation the No 1 did likewise but the Numbers 3 and 4 aircraft collided with each other almost on top of the target and the two pilots were killed instantly

Lieutenant John CARVER US Navy

02-Nov-87 XZ136 Harrier GR3 3 Sqn Otterburn Training Area 1

Mid air collision with XV790

Flight Lieutenant David Robin SUNDERLAND

11-Nov-87 XV747 Harrier GR3 233 OCU RAF Wittering 0

Abandoned on landing, cause not known

16-Nov-87 XX241 Hawk T1 CFS Melton Lincolnshire 0

Mid air collision. Squadron Leader Tim Miller (the leader of the Red Arrows) and Flight Lieutenant M J 'Spike' Newberry were flying in a routine practice formation training exercise when Newberry, flying at No 2, selected airbrakes but nothing happened! Although he immediately retarded power the rear aircraft collided with the leader and both crashed

---

16-Nov-87 XX259 Hawk T1A CFS Melton Lincolnshire 0

Mid air collision

Date	Serial	Aircraft	Unit	Place	Casualties
Brief Circumstances of Accident					
Casualty Details (If Applicable)					
13-Jan-88	XT607	Wessex HC2	72 Sqn	Crawfordsburn Northern Ireland	0
Forced landing					
22-Jan-88	XX243	Hawk T1A	CFS	RAF Scampton	1
Crashed on to airfield during practice Red Arrows sortie					
Flight Lieutenant Neil Duncan MACLACHLAN BSc					
02-Mar-88	XX712	Bulldog T1	UAS	Southport	1
Crashed onto beach					
Acting Pilot Officer Mark Francis DAVIES					
29-Mar-88	ZA448	Tornado GR1	15 Sqn	Nellis AFB Navada	0
Crashed during Green Flag training although Flight Lieutenants T D Robinson and S P Townsend escaped					
11-Apr-88	XR769	Lightning F6	11 Sqn	5m E Easington Lincolnshire	0
Abandoned following engine failure. The pilot was flying as No 2 in a formation when, after deselecting reheat and retarding the throttles he heard and felt a series of loud bangs. The pilot advanced the throttles to clear the problem but he was subsequently advised by his leader that he was on fire. After turning the aircraft out to sea and completing his pre ejection drills he abandoned the aircraft.					
20-Apr-88	XT860	Phantom FG1	43 Sqn	28m E RAF Leuchars	2

Flew into sea during Exercise Elder Forest. Kev Poysden was engaged to the widow of an officer killed in an earlier Phantom accident

Flight Lieutenant Philip Donald CLARKE Pilot
Flight Lieutenant Kevin John POYSDEN Navigator

06-May-88 ZA672 Chinook HC1 18 Sqn Hannover Airport 2

Taxied into gangway pier whilst hovering

Flying Officer Philip Anthony BREWER
Flying Officer James Stewart MCMENEMY

10-May-88 ZD808 Tornado GR1 17 Sqn Near Osnabruch Germany 2

Crashed during low level sortie

Flight Lieutenant John Patrick O'SHEA
Flight Lieutenant Steven Mark WRIGHT

13-May-88 XX197 Hawk T1A 1TWU RAF Brawdy 0

Abandoned following engine failure on take off. Flight Lieutenant Passfield and Squadron Leader Alan Threadgold - for the second time, ejected

---

20-May-88 XV809 Harrier GR3 3 Sqn RAF Gutersloh 1

Crashed after take off

Flight Lieutenant Paul ADAMS

30-May-88 WF791 Meteor T7 CFS Near Baginton Airport Coventry 1

Loss of control following incorrect selection of airbrakes at the wrong speed/flap setting. The aircraft dived into the ground and the pilot had insufficient height to effect a recovery or to abandon the aircraft without an ejection seat.

Flight Lieutenant Peter Wilson STACEY

24-Jun-88 XX304 Hawk T1A CFS RAF Scampton 0

The aircraft was being flown as Red 4 for a formation take off of the Red Arrows. It was positioned about 750 feet behind the leading echelon and brakes were released about 1.5 seconds after them. On take off at about 140 knots the flpas and undercarriage were selected up but because he was already gaining on the lead section, airbrake was selected out as it was normal practice to work airbrakes against throttle to achieve rapid response. However, Red 4 struck the ground having sunk back and slid off to the side rupturing the smoke pod and subsequently catching fire. The pilot ejected.

02-Aug-88 XV501 Phantom FGR2 56 Sqn Mayenne France 0

Systems failure and aircraft abandoned. Flight Lieutenants D Johnson and Joe Hacke ejected

---

09-Aug-88 ZA329 Tornado GR1 TTTE Near Milburn Cumbria 2

Mid Air Collision With 617 Sqn Aircraft

Flight Lieutenant John Nigel Shaun WATTS 32 Instructor Pilot
Lieutenant Ulrich SAYER 23 Luftwaffe Federal Republic of Germany Student Pilot

---

09-Aug-88 ZA593 Tornado GR1 617 Sqn Near Milburn 2

Mid air collision during evening with TTTE Aircraft

Flight Lieutenant Colin Douglas OLIVER 30 Pilot
Flight Lieutenant Anthony Donald COOK 29 Navigator

18-Aug-88 XW921 Harrier GR3 3 Sqn RAF Gutersloh 0

Abandoned on approach

07-Sep-88 XX834 Jaguar T2A 6 Sqn Near Wildbad Kreuth Germany 1

Whilst on detachment from home base, the pilot was authorised to give air experience to a USAF officer; 1st Lieutenant J O Black. Unfortunately, the aircraft was flown into power cables and although both crew attempted ejection, only the passenger survived.

Flight Lieutenant Sheridan Paul NELSON MA BA

23-Sep-88 XV428 Phantom FGR2 228OCU RAF Abingdon 2

The aircraft had been positioned at Lyneham and in the late afternoon flew to Abingdon to practice its display before the following day's air show. Probably due to various factors, such as wind speed, the aircraft was not very well set up for the display and entered into the loop at a height which did not allow it to recover. It crashed onto the airfield in a very high nose up attitude and with substantial downwards acceleration. It exploded on impact and both crew, who had made no attempt to eject, were killed. The air show was abandoned for that year.

Flight Lieutenant Christopher Charles Maurice LACKMAN Pilot
Flight Lieutenant William John (Jack) THOMPSON Navigator

18-Oct-88 XV437 Phantom FGR2 92 Sqn Near Holzminden Germany 0

The aircraft was engaged on a practice interception against ground attack aircraft as part of the Tactical Leadership Programme. The weather was 8/8ths starto cumulus with tops at 3000 feet and good visibility above this height. After completing several interceptions, the crew commenced a rejoin with another Phantom but whilst turning to starboard at a height of about 3500 feet and a speed of 280 knots they experienced noise, vibration and rumbling. The pilot rolled level and began a climb whilst retarding the engines slightly to about 85% rpm. He diagnosed a right engine surge but subsequently believed that he had lost both engines. With the height and speed available the aircraft could not be recovered and the crew of Flight Lieutenant Pete Lines and Flight Lieutenant Colin Fryer ejected as the aircraft descended through 2000 feet.

09-Jan-89 XT908 Phantom FGR2 228OCU 50m E Dundee 1

During a practice interception sortie and at a height of about 10000 feet, some 80 miles from base, the pilot told the navigator he did not feel well and that they would return to base. After transmitting a radio call to base, the pilot told the navigator that he was feeling numb and losing his vision. The pilot's condition rapidly deteriorated and although he responded to some of the instructions given to him by the navigator; Flight Lieutenant Gordon Moulds, he appears to have lost consciousness and the aircraft departed from controlled flight and dived into the sea

Squadron Leader John David NELSON BSc

13-Jan-89 ZD891 Tornado GR1 14 Sqn Near Wiesmoor Germany 2

Mid air collision with German Alpha Jet during practice attack on airfield

Flight Lieutenant Alan George GRIEVE BSc
Flight Lieutenant Martin Peter Stavely SMITH BSc

08-Mar-89 XN547 Jet Provost T3A 1FTS Near Great Habton North Yorkshire 0

Abandoned after control lost whilst spinning inverted. The student pilot, Flying Officer W K Owen, was undertaking a general handling sortie including aerobatics at a height of 9000 feet. He entered a stall turn to the left with the starboard wing slightly low in the vertical and the aircraft would not yaw to the left despite right rudder being applied. The pilot centralised controls but the aircraft pitched over the vertical and began to yaw. The student, who was relatively inexperienced, applied corrective action but could not recover the aircraft and as it passed 5000 feet he ejected.

28-Mar-89 XZ999 Harrier GR3A 4 Sqn RAF Bruggen 0

Crashed and badly damaged after nosewheel failed during a roller landing

---

13-Apr-89 XZ359 Jaguar GR1A 54 Sqn 2.25 miles west north west St Abbs Head 1

Flew into cliff for reason never satisfatorily explained. It can only be assumed that the pilot was distracted by a NAVWASS management task and entered cloud during the coast in and then flew into the cliff which he did not appreciate was there. The pilot was a very experienced former Royal Naval officer, a profile of him had appeared in a Daily Telegraph magazine article published sometime before the accident.

Squadron Leader Paul Victor LLOYD

24-Apr-89 XT893 Phantom FGR2 56 Sqn 48m E Flamborough Head 0

Systems failure. Squadron Leader Chris Bagnall and Flight Lieutenant Rich A H Watson ejected

---

25-Apr-89 XX517 Bulldog T1 1FTS Near RAF Catterick 0

Disorientated during aerobatic training

Date	Serial	Aircraft	Unit	Place	Casualties

Brief Circumstances of Accident

Casualty Details (If Applicable)

14-Jun-89	XX182	Hawk T1	4FTS	Borth Wales	0

Mid air collision between this aircraft, flown by Lieutenant M H Seymour, and XX291

14-Jun-89	XX291	Hawk T1	4FTS	Borth Wales	1

Mid air collision

Pilot Officer Simon Mark TOMPKINS

20-Jun-89	XW925	Harrier T4A	4 Sqn	RAF Gutersloh	1

Crashed on approach to land

believed to be: Squadron Leader Paul Dennis STONE

20-Jul-89	ZA468	Tornado GR1	15 Sqn	RAF Laarbruch	0

Abandoned after take off

21-Jul-89	ZE833	Tornado F3	23 Sqn	off Sunderland	1

The aircraft was engaged on a low level interceptions exercise with evasion. The aircraft was climbed to 4000 feet on a notherly heading and began to run out from the engagement. The pilot selected wings level and dived at about 20 degrees and as he approached 1000 feet he selected the wings to 67 degrees sweep and began to pitch up the nose slowly. The navigator noticed that the aircraft was descending through 3-400 feet and shouted a warning to the pilot. The navigator; Flight Lieutenant Dave Sully, ejected shortly before the aircraft struck the water and received minor burns from the fireball which ignited as the aircraft struck the water. The pilot, however, received incapacitating injuries and made no attempt to carry out his survival drills and was drowned before he could be rescued.

Flight Lieutenant Stephen William MOIR

25-Jul-89 ZA717 Chinook HC1 78 Sqn Mount Pleasant Falkland Island 0

Gearbox failure

14-Sep-89 ZD710 Tornado GR1 14 Sqn Near Drayton Abingdon Oxfordshire 0

The aircraft struck a flock of birds on take off and was abandoned by its crew

---

20-Sep-89 XX192 Hawk T1A 1TWU RAF Brawdy 2

Engine failed after take off

Flying Officer John Patrick DUGGAN
Flying Officer Alan William George TAYLOR

09-Jan-90 ZA394 Tornado GR1 2 Sqn Spadeadam Range 0

Mid air collision with Jaguar XZ108 (54 Sqn) flown by the squadron commander; Wing Commander D M 'Dim' Jones who landed his aircraft safely despite serious damage to the wing

---

27-Apr-90 XV719 Wessex HC2 72 Sqn RAF Bishops Court 0

Impacted tail first with ground after 'wing over' at low level

---

30-Apr-90 WR965 Shackleton AEW2 8 Sqn Isle of Harris 10

Flew into high ground in mist whilst engaged in maritime training exercise. There are some similarities between this accident and that involving WB533 but it has never been satisfactorily explained how an experienced crew flew into a mountainside with such tragic results

Date Serial Aircraft Unit Place Casualties
Brief Circumstances of Accident
Casualty Details (If Applicable)

Wing Commander Stephen John RONCORONI 44 Captain (Officer Commanding 8 Squadron)
Wing Commander Charles Francis WRIGHTON 42 (Officer Commanding Operations Wing RAF Lossiemouth)
Flying Officer Colin Hudson BURNS 23 Co-Pilot
Flight Lieutenant Alan Duncan CAMPBELL 36 Navigator
Flight Lieutenant Keith Stuart FORBES 26 Fighter Controller
Squadron Leader Jeremy Alan LANE 53 Navigator
Master Air Electronics Operator Roger Anthony SCUTT 45 Air Electronics Operator
Flight Sergeant Kieren Paul RICKETTS 39 Air Electronics Operator
Sergeant Graham Anthony Robert MILLER 23 Flight Engineer
Corporal Stuart James BOULTON 23 Passenger

30-Apr-90 ZA454 Tornado GR1 15 Sqn Goose Bay 0
Abandoned after engine fire

09-May-90 XX347 Hawk T1 4FTS Over Anglesey 0
Abandoned during training flight cause not known

27-Jun-90 WH972Canberra E15 100 Sqn 3m S RAF Kinloss 1
Crashed during approach to land at Kinloss in poor weather. The navigator; Flying Officer G Jackson survived but the pilot did not

Flight Lieutenant Cameron Maxwell LOCKE BSc Pilot

14-Aug-90 ZA464 Tornado GR1 20 Sqn 12m E Spurn Head 1

Mid air collision. The pilot; Wing Commander Buckler (OC 20 Squadron) survived with serious injuries, having been ejected by the navigator in a command ejection

Squadron Leader Gordon Carnie GRAHAM Navigator

14-Aug-90 ZA545 Tornado GR1 TWCU 12m east Spurn Head 2

Mid air collision.

Major Dennis WISE USAF Pilot
Flight Lieutenant John Frederick BOWLES BSc Navigator

16-Aug-90 ZA561 Tornado GR1 27 Sqn 10m E Spurn Head 2

Flew into sea during mishandled recovery from practice toss bombing

Group Captain William Laurence GREEN 43 Pilot Officer Commanding 27 Squadron
Squadron Leader Neil ANDERSON Navigator

12-Sep-90 XZ387 Jaguar GR1A 54 Sqn Solway Firth 1

Flew into sea in 'glassy' conditions whilst avoiding 'bounce' aircraft. The formation were involved in work up training for Operation GRANBY when the accident happened

Flight Lieutenant John Mark MARSDEN BSc(Eng) ACGI

17-Oct-90 ZD355 Harrier GR5 1 Sqn 32m N Karup Denmark 0

The aircraft was taking part in a Danish Air Force air defence exercise and took off in good weather. On passing 23500 feet, the pilot heard a very loud bang and immediately felt the loss of thrust. He immediately noticed all the symptoms of engine failure and after trying to relight the engine several times and as the height passed about 3000 feet he ejected. The accident was caused by the fatigue failure of a second stage LP compressor blade.

Date Serial Aircraft Unit Place Casualties
Brief Circumstances of Accident
Casualty Details (If Applicable)

19-Oct-90 ZA466 Tornado GR1 16 Sqn Tabuk Saudi Arabia 0

Struck crash barrier at approach end of runway which had been raised

---

12-Nov-90 XX754 Jaguar GR1A 54 Sqn Saudia Desert Region Near Bahrain Border 1

Flew into rising ground because of optical illusion depriving pilot of visual cues. Furthermore, the radar altimeter would have given the pilot very little time to react once it was triggered. A Tornado aircraft following and photographing the identical route the following day almost repeated the accident

Flight Lieutenant Keith COLLISTER

08-Jan-91 XV462 Phantom FGR2 19 Sqn off Cyprus 0

Abandoned after loss of control. Flight Lieutenant Graham Williams and Flying officer Gary Winwright ejected safely

---

13-Jan-91 ZD718 Tornado GR1 14 Sqn 140m W Masirah 2

Flew into ground due to poor standards of flying discipline. The aircraft was being flown at extremely low level with the crew firing flares at herds of camels and photographing the terrain. They attempted a turn at low level and a wing tip struck the ground

Flight Lieutenant Keiron James DUFFY
Flight Lieutenant Norman Thomas DENT

17-Jan-91 ZA392 Tornado GR1 27 Sqn Near Shaibah Iraq 2

Flew into ground after JP233 attack on airfield

Wing Commander Timothy Nigel Charles ELSDON 39 Pilot and OC 27 Squadron (in succession to Group Captain Green)
Flight Lieutenant Robert Maxwell (Max) COLLIER 42 Navigator

17-Jan-91 ZD791 Tornado GR1 15 Sqn Southern Iraq 0

Shot down by flak which exploded sidewinder missile. Flight Lieutenant John Peters and John Nichol ejected

---

20-Jan-91 ZA396 Tornado GR1 20 Sqn Near Al Tallil Airfield Iraq 0

Shot down by Roland Missile, although Flight Lieutenants David Waddington and Robbie Stewart ejected safely and were made prisoners by the Iraqis

---

20-Jan-91 ZD893 Tornado GR1 9 Sqn Tabuk Saudi Arabia 0

Major systems failure after take off for operations. The squadon commander; Wing Commander Mike Heath and his pilot Squadron Leader Pete Batson ejected safely although they were injured

---

22-Jan-91 ZA467 Tornado GR1 16 Sqn Near Al Rutbah Airfield 2

Flew into ground during attack

Squadron Leader Gary LENNOX 34
Squadron Leader Kevin Paul WEEKS 37

24-Jan-91 ZA403 Tornado GR1 17 Sqn Over Southern Iraq 0

Premature explosion of 1000lb bomb forced Flying Officer Simon Burgess and his navigator; Squadron Leader Bob Ankerson to eject

Date Serial Aircraft Unit Place Casualties
Brief Circumstances of Accident
Casualty Details (If Applicable)

14-Feb-91 ZD717 Tornado GR1 17 Sqn Near Al Taqaddum Airfield Iraq 1

Shot down by SA2 missile during attack. Although Flight Lieutenant Rupert Clark the pilot ejected safely, his navigator did not and was killed

Flight Lieutenant Stephen Michael HICKS 26 Navigator

18-Mar-91 WJ877 Canberra T4 360 Sqn RAF Wyton 3

Mishandled practice engine failure on take off

Group Captain Reginald MCKENDRICK MPhil MBIM Pilot Officer Commanding Royal Air Force Wyton
Flight Lieutenant David Laird Ferguson ADAM Pilot & Qualified Flying Instructor
Flight Lieutenant Stephen WILKINSON Navigator

10-May-91 ZA376 Tornado GR1 20 Sqn Lubberstadt Germany 0

This is the loss of a Tornado about which Squadron Leader Pablo Mason writes in his second book. He and Flight Lieutenant Woods escaped by ejecting as the aircraft went out of control

---

29-May-91 ZG473 Harrier GR7 4 Sqn 6m S RAF Gutersloh 0

During an air combat sortie the aircraft suffered an electrical problem and started a return to base. Unfortunately, the generator would not reset and the emergency power supplies also failed. As the aircraft passed through about 2000 feet the engine rpm began to decrease and the pilot was compelled to eject. The initial problem was caused by electrical arching in the kapton wiring of the main electrical looms and this in turn led to the loss of electrical supply to the automatic engine control system.

08-Aug-91 ZA941 Puma HC1

29-Aug-91 XX843 Jaguar T2A 41 Sqn Carno North Wales 1

The aircraft was being flown by the squadron commander and the Officer Commanding Operations Wing RAF Coltishall when it struck a civilian light aircraft (Cessna 152 : G-BMHI) which had been taking photographs of houses in the Carno area for several hours. The Jaguar wing failed in overload and both crew ejected within a fraction of a second of each other. Unfortunately, the difference was sufficient to lead to Wing Commander Mardon not surviving although the squadron commander, Wing Commander Bill Pixton DFC AFC did. John Mardon had undergone a heart and lung transplant operation and had been declared fit to fly again, although not solo; he had returned to full service duties and the circumstances of his death are exceptionally tragic

Wing Commander John Stirling MARDON MBE Officer Commanding Operations Wing RAF Coltishall

---

12-Sep-91 ZA540 Tornado GR1 27 Sqn Bristol Channel 0

Flew into Bristol Channel after being abandoned by Flight Lieutenant J Edwards and Wing Commander J Ball

---

25-Sep-91 XZ147 Harrier T4 233 OCU Yorkshire 0

Pilot hit in face by a bird and was stunned and lost control Being concerned about the proximity of the ground he ejected followed immediately by the passenger. Both Squadron Leader A D Stevenson and his University Air Squadron passenger; Officer Cadet Kate Saunders survived. Saunders suffered serious burns after landing amongst blazing wreckage and was rescued by Stevenson who received both a commendation and the Royal Humane Society medal

---

30-Sep-91 ZD412 Harrier GR5 3 Sqn RAF Gutersloh 0

Left the runway whilst taking off and crashed into the Ems Canal

Date Serial Aircraft Unit Place Casualties
Brief Circumstances of Accident
Casualty Details (If Applicable)

30-Oct-91 XV421 Phantom FGR2 1453 Flt off Falkland Islands 2

The aircraft was engaged on air combat training when it crashed into the sea. As little wreckage or evidence could be found the true cause of the accident was never determined

Flight Lieutenant Christopher James WEIGHTMAN Pilot
Flying Officer Ian Michael HALDEN Navigator

07-Feb-92 XW929 Harrier T4 Gutersloh SF RAF Gutersloh 0

Written off after heavy damage sustained whilst landing

12-May-92 ZF316 Tucano T1 CFS Near RAF Lossiemouth 0

Failed to recover from spin

14-May-92 XW543 Buccaneer S2B 12 Sqn 0

Damaged and not repaired because of type's impending withdrawal from RAF service

---

14-May-92 XZ990 Harrier GR3 233 OCU RAF Wittering 0

Engine failure

09-Jul-92 XN972 Buccaneer S2B 12 Sqn off Scotland 2

The aircraft was flying as No 3 in a four aircraft formation. During a simulated attack on a ship the formation was illuminated by a fighter radar and the aircraft manouevred to break the radar lock. The aircraft struck the sea and was destroyed. It seems possible that the accident was caused by a runaway tailplane powered flying control unit (PFCU). At the speed and height available there would have been little opportunity for the crew to appreciate the danger and to eject.

Flight Lieutenant James Drummond HENDERSON Pilot
Flight Lieutenant Clive Richard LAMBOURNE Navigator

08-Aug-92 ZD350 Harrier GR5 1 Sqn RAF Wittering 0

The aircraft was leading a pair of Harriers and after an apparently normal take off was warned that sparks were coming from his rear nozzles. At this time the pilot heard a loud rumbling noise and felt severe airframe vibration and a marked loss of thrust. He realised that there was a serious mechanical failure and ejected from about 25 feet with the aircraft crashing to the ground and being completely destroyed. The accident was caused by the failure of a second stage stator vane which then passed through the engine causing it to fail.

30-Sep-92 XX334 Hawk T1A 7FTS RAF Chivenor 1

Crashed during turn back after practice engine failure on takeoff. Although the pilot instructor ejected, the student did not and was severely injured

Flight Lieutenant Philip William MARTIN BSc (on 10 October 1992 as a result of injuries received)

17-Oct-92 XX613 Bulldog T1 UAS Northern Ireland 1

Crashed into a wall following a forced landing.

27-Nov-92 XW233 Puma HC1 230 Sqn Northern Ireland 4

Mid air collision with an Army Air Corps helicopter on approach to security forces base

Squadron Leader Michael HAVERSON 39 Pilot Captain
Flight Lieutenant Simon Marcus John ROBERTS AFM 26 Co-Pilot
Flight Sergeant Jan Robert PEWTREES 33 Air Loadmaster
Passenger: Major John Barr 36

15-Mar-93 XH671 Victor K2 55 Sqn RAF Marham 0

The main cabin door and the surrounds were damaged beyond repair in a pressure test. The aircraft was not repaired because the type was approaching the end of its service life

---

19-May-93 WG403 Chipmunk T10 ?

27-May-93 XV193 Hercules C3P LTW Near Pitlochry 9

The aircraft was on a low level sortie with two other Hercules when it began a separate exercise which included a simulated drop of a small cargo pack onto a dummy drop zone in a Valley about 8 miles from Pitlochry. There is no independent evidence but it seems that the aircraft was flown into a valley and that at low speed and height was stalled and unable to recover.

Squadron Leader Graham Paul YOUNG AFC 54 Captain
Squadron Leader Stanley Duncan MUIR 49 Navigator
Flight Lieutenant Stephen Paul MCNALLY 27 Navigator
Flight Lieutenant Graham Robert John SOUTHARD BSc 33 Pilot
Flying Officer Jonathan Huw OWEN 23 Pilot
Master Engineer Terence John William GILMORE 39 Flight Engineer
Sergeant Craig Thomas HILLIARD 23
Sergeant Alan Keith KING 32
Lance Corporal Garry MANNING 23

28-Jun-93 ZD430 Harrier GR7 3 Sqn Heckington Lincolnshire 0

The aircraft was No 2 in a formation of three aircraft en-route from RAF Leeming to Germany. Whilst passing near RAF Coningsby, the pilot felt a small thump which was first thought to be a birdstrike. As the pilot initiated a diversion he was advised that he had a fuel leak and he then noticed the fluid leak himself. A flash fire was then observed and the engine FIRE caption illuminated. As the pilot took appropriate action it became apparent that the blaze was intensifying and at about 3000 feet and 220 knots the pilot ejected. The cause was a massive fuel leak which ignited on contact with the jet efflux nozzles, causing serious internal and external fires. It is possible that the initial leak was caused by a birdstrike to the starboard wing inboard leading edge.

01-Jul-93 XX163 Hawk T1 CFS RAF Valley 0

A CFS instructor and a qualified Hawk pilot were to fly a sortie which included a turnback following a simulated engine failure after take off. Unfortunately, in carrying out the manoeuvre, the aircraft descended rapidly and despite attempts to apply full power the aircraft crashed and burst into flames. Both crew ejected and although they were successful, the second pilot's injuries were major.

12-Aug-93 XR524 Wessex HC2 22 Sqn North Wales 3

Tail rotor drive failure leading to loss of control at critical stage in flight. The pilot had no option but to ditch the aircraft and the three air cadets lost their lives

Air Cadet Amanda WHITEHEAD 17 Air Training Corps
Air Cadet Christopher BAILEY 15 Air Training Corps
Air Cadet Mark Oakden 16 Air Training Corps

27-Aug-93 WP980 Chipmunk T10 UAS RAF St Athan 1

Mishandled practice engine failure and turn back after take off

Group Captain Roger SWEATMAN MA RAF Reserve of Officers Class 'J'

Date Serial Aircraft Unit Place Casualties
Brief Circumstances of Accident
Casualty Details (If Applicable)

09-Sep-93 ZB628 Gazelle HT3 2FTS 18m S Monaco 0

A formation of three Gazelle helicopters was returning from near Rome to RAF Shawbury when it encountered a very heavy rain storm about 60 miles south of Genoa at Cape Nero. In attempting to escape from the severe weather, two aircraft made precautionary landings on a nearby beach but ZB628 was allowed to descend and lose speed and struck the sea. It sank, although the three occupants escaped and were rescued by Italian Coastguard personnel.

10-Sep-93 XV867 Buccaneer S2B 208 Sqn 0

17-Sep-93 XT667 Wessex HC2 22 Sqn

21-Oct-93 ZE858 Tornado F3 43 Sqn Near A66 Road 0

Engine failure. Flight Lieutenant L Taylor and Flight Lieutenant Stu Walker (who was subsequently killed off Cyprus on 8 Jul 94) ejected safely from the aircraft

---

23-Nov-93 ZD432 Harrier GR7 Over Northern Iraq 0

Operation Warden loss. The aircraft was No 2 of the lead pair of six aircraft which took off from Incirlik with a VC10 tanker and climbed to a transit height of 25000 feet. The pilot experienced a series of rapid loud bangs and sharp deceleration. Several attempts to relight the apparently surged engine were made without success and the pilot was forced to eject. Subsequent investigation revealed that the manual fuel control system had made an undemanded activation and that the pilot believed the engine to have surged when it was still in fact delivering power.

14-Jan-94 ZD349 Harrier GR7 233 OCU 5m South-east Evesham Worcester 1

The aircraft was leading a pair of Harriers towards the end of a conversion course and a third Harrier was to provide the 'bounce'. The 'bounce' aircraft manoeuvred to attack the pair and the formation turned to counter the threat but, despite the correct setting of the low altitude warner, the No 1 aircraft flew into the ground with the pilot making no attempt to eject or to take avoiding action even after the LAW sounded.

Captain B K HEARNEY United States Marine Corps

02-Jun-94 ZD576 Chinook HC2 7 Sqn Mull of Kintyre Lighthouse 29

Flew into ground in poor visibility. The aircraft had left RAF Aldergrove at about 1730 hours on a sortie to Fort George. The aircraft struck the ground under control and at high speed at about 800 feet above sea level and 500 feet from the top of a hill. It bounced back into the air briefly and flew over a road for about 100 yards before falling back to the ground and rolling onto its side and continuing for a further 60 yards in a ball of fire. This accident is well reported in Andrew Brookes book 'Flights to Disaster'. Furthermore, the findings of the RAF Board of Inquiry were challenged in the Scottish courts but the facts remain that the crew was flying VMC when it appears that they should have been following IMC regulations. It was suggested that the aircraft was unsafe etc and that it had suffered some failure before the accident but none of this is bourne out by the available evidence.

Flight Lieutenant Richard David COOK 30 Pilot
Flight Lieutenant Jonathan Paul TAPPER 28 Pilot (flying pilot for the sortie)
Master Air Loadmaster Graham William FORBES 36 Air Loadmaster
Sergeant Kevin Andrew HARDIE 30 Air Loadmaster

Passengers:

Assistant Chief Constable Brian FITZSIMONS 53 : Royal Ulster Constabulary
Detective Chief Superintendant Dessie CONROY
Detective Chief Superintendant Maurice REILLY

Date Serial Aircraft Unit Place Casualties
Brief Circumstances of Accident
Casualty Details (If Applicable)

Detective Superintendant Phil DAVIDSON
Detective Superintendant Bob FOSTER
Detective Superintendant Billy GWILLIAM
Detective Superintendant Ian PHOENIX
Detective Chief Inspector Denis BUNTING
Detective Inspector Stephen DAVIDSON
Detective Inspector Kevin MAGEE
John DEVERRELL CB 57 : Home Office
Stephen RICKARD 35
Michael MALTBY 57
John HAYNES 58
Martin DALTON 37
Anne JAMES 42
Colonel Christopher BILES OBE 41 late Devon & Dorsetshire Regiment : British Army
Lieutenant Colonel Richard GREGORY-SMITH Intelligence Corps
Lieutenant Colonel John TOBIAS Intelligence Corps
Lieutenant Colonel George WILLIAMS Intelligence Corps
Major Christopher John DOCHERTY 33 Prince of Wales Own
Major Anthony HORNBY Queens Lancashire Regiment
Major Gary SPARKS Royal Artillery
Major Richard ALLEN Royal Gloucestershire, Berkshire & Wiltshire Regiment
Major Roy PUGH Intelligence Corps

07-Jun-94 ZE809 Tornado F3 11 Sqn 45m North-east Scarborough 0

At about 1300 feet over the sea the crew heard a load bang and the aircraft began to lose speed. The engine fire warning captions illuminated and the rear of the aircraft was quickly ablaze forcing the crew; Flight Lieutenants S Smiley and Chris Chew to eject. The fire was caused by a labyrinth seal around the high pressure shaft, which connects the high pressure compressor to the high pressure turbine, failing. This caused the shaft to fail and the turbine oversped and also failed. There followed an explosive failure which penetrated the engine casing and severed both hydraulic systems and led to a further series of failures!

08-Jul-94 ZH558 Tornado F3 Into Sea off Cyprus 2

After partially completing an air to air gunnery sortie against a banner towed by a Hawk, the aircraft began its recovery to base from a height of about 5000 feet. The aircraft started a gentle descent and the pilot selected full reheat and subsequently a left hand turn towards Akrotiri. As the aircraft passed about 900 feet, the pilot rolled level and the right hand engine reheat was reduced to minimum. At about 400 feet the left turn was recommenced and by time it reached 150 feet the aircraft was banked to 68 degrees and the speed was 590 knots Immediately before impact the aircraft started to roll out of its turn but the rate of descent was not stopped and the aircraft flew into the sea.

Flight Lieutenant Nigel ORME
Flight Lieutenant Stuart John MacDonald WALKER

19-Jul-94 ZA368 Tornado GR1 617 Sqn Moray Firth 0

Aircraft loaned to 15(R) Sqn and circumstances of loss not known. The Luftwaffe pilot; Hauptmann A Stumpf and his RAF navigator Flight Lieutenant S T Petherick ejected

---

28-Jul-94 WB697 Chipmunk T10 10AEF Scarisbrick Lancashire 0

Forced landing in cabbage field

Date Serial Aircraft Unit Place Casualties
Brief Circumstances of Accident
Casualty Details (If Applicable)

01-Aug-94 ZA397 Tornado GR1A 2 Sqn 0

Mid air collision

01-Sep-94 ZG708 Tornado GR1A 13 Sqn Scotland 2

The aircraft had completed an exercise involving a recce of three targets and had entered Glen Ogle in fine weather. Shortly before the accident the aircraft was at 500 feet and flying at 428 knots. It commenced a turn to starboard using 70 to 80 degrees of bank in order to follow the line of the valley and a few seconds before impact full right aileron was applied and the control column moved rearwards together with the selection of reheat on both engines. The aircraft rolled a further 180 degrees through the inverted position and then struck the ground. The cause of the crash was directly caused by the control movements but no satisfactory explanation could be found for why this happened.

Flight Lieutenant Peter John Michael MOSLEY 31 Pilot
Flight Lieutenant Patrick Peter HARRISON 33 Navigator

19-Sep-94 ZG725 Tornado GR1A 13 Sqn Into Sea off Sardinia 0

10-Mar-95 ZE789 Tornado F3 56(R) Sqn North Sea 1

The pilot; Flight Lieutenant D J Hazell ejected safely

Flight Lieutenant Martin Edward OWEN

09-Apr-95 ZE564 Viking TX1 634GS 0

Damaged beyond repair in heavy landing

01-Jun-95 ZG475 Harrier GR7 SOAEU Solway Firth 1

Flown into sea during trials flight after the pilot failed to recover.

Wing Commander Nicholas John SLATER (Officer Commanding Strike Operational Analysis & Evaulation Unit)

01-Jun-95 XW666 Nimrod R1P 51 Sqn off RAF Kinloss 0

Ditched following major engine fire on test flight after Major overhaul. The pilot; Flight Lieutenant Art Stacey was exceptionally skilfull in his handling of this very unpleasant emergency and succeeding in ditching the aircraft thus allowing the crew to escape. He was awarded a well deserved AFC

21-Jun-95 XZ373 Jaguar GR1A 6 Sqn off Sardinia 0

Loss of control during ACMI training forced the USAF Exchange Programme pilot; Captain R L Paradis to eject

---

05-Aug-95 ZE654 Viking TX1 631GS RAF Sealand 2

Mid air collision whilst soaring in the same thermal after taking off from Sealand.

05-Aug-95 ZE677 Viking TX1 631GS RAF Sealand 0

Mid air collision

10-Aug-95 XX288 Hawk T1 4FTS Mona 0

Left runway on landing, pilot ejected and aircraft crashed into rocks

Date Serial Aircraft Unit Place Casualties
Brief Circumstances of Accident
Casualty Details (If Applicable)

03-Sep-95 XV239 Nimrod MR2 120 Sqn Canada 7

Flew into sea at conclusion of air display. The aircraft took off to perform a display at the Canadian International Air Show Toronto in good weather conditions. The display was to include two orbits and two dumb bell turns. Towards the end of the display the aircraft flew slowly past the crowd with the undercarriage down and commenced the second dumb bell turn. It turned under full power and the flaps were retracted to 20 degrees and the undercarriage raised, at which point the nose was pitched up to 24 degrees. The aircraft passed 900 feet and the engine power was reduced substantially so that the speed fell off to 122 knots instead of about 150 knots. The aircraft rolled to 70 degrees of port bank and then reduced to about 45 degrees with the nose being lowered. Speed increased slightly as did the 'g' loading but the aircraft stalled with the wing dropping to 85 degrees and the nose being lowered to 15 degrees below level. Despite the application of full power and the use of starboard aileron, the aircraft could not be recovered in the height available and it crashed into the sea.

Flight Lieutenant Dominic Mark GILBERT 31 Captain
Flight Lieutenant Glenn Howard HOOPER 25 Co-Pilot
Flight Lieutenant Bernard WORTHINGTON 37 Air Electronics Officer
Flight Lieutenant Nicholas BROOKS 26 Navigator
Sergeant Gary Stephen MOXHAM 32
Sergeant Richard Lee WILLIAMS 28
Sergeant Craig BARNETT 32

30-Oct-95 ZE733 Tornado F3 43 Sqn off Tweed Bank 0

Mid air collision. Flight Lieutenant Kev McCarry and Flight Lieutenant Booth the navigator ejected safely

10 Jan 96 ZE166 Tornado F3 56(R) Sqn Near Digby Lincolnshire 0

Mid air collision with ZE862

---

10 Jan 96 ZE862 Tornado F3 56(R) Sqn Near Digby Lincolnshire 0

Mid air collision with ZE166

---

11 Jan 96 ZD846 Tornado GR1 14 Sqn Albachten South West Of Munster Germany 0

Crew abandoned the aircraft after instrument failure

23-Jan-96 XX733 Jaguar GR1B 41 Sqn In The RAF Coltishall Overshoot 1

Crashed taking off on sortie to Lossiemouth. The primary cause of the accident was the failure to select reheat, probably because the pilot was distracted by apparent unusual engine noises. The aircraft left the ground much later than normal and struck the barrier net at the runway end and then flew over the airfield boundary fence before crashing and bursting into flames. The aircraft was one of the first of its type to be modified to the GR1B standard which improved the avionics and provided a TIALD designating capability.

Flight Lieutenant Gregory Mark NOBLE MEng 28

13-Feb-96 XX164 Hawk T1A 4FTS RAF Valley 1

Aircraft rolled on take off and pilot abandoned it but did not survive the ejection. Initial reports suggest that the controls were not properly connected. The pilot had survived an ejection during the Gulf conflict and became a prisoner of the Iraqis.

Flight Lieutenant Simon John BURGES 28

19-Feb-96 ZG476 Harrier GR7 1 Sqn Near RAF Wittering 0

Aircraft abandoned on approach to RAF Wittering whilst returning from Cyprus

Date	Serial	Aircraft	Unit	Place	Casualties
Brief Circumstances of Accident					
Casualty Details (If Applicable)					
26-Feb-96	ZD845	Tornado GR1	9 Sqn	Near RAF Laarbruch	0
26-May-96	XX302	Hawk T1	4 FTS	Near Beja Portugal	0
Destroyed in a mid air collision with Portugese Air Force F16B serial number 15120 during air combat training. Flight Lieutenant Marcus Cook ejected safely					
24-Jul-96	XZ362	Jaguar GR1A	41 Sqn	Alaska	0
19-Sep-96	XX141	Jaguar T2A	16(R) Sqn	RAF Lossiemouth	0
Abandoned on take off					
22-Sep-96		Chinook HC2	7 Sqn	North Wales	1
Crewman fell from the aircraft whilst in transit and was killed.					
Sergeant Michael PATTON 27 Air Loadmaster					

No account dealing with losses to RAF service would be complete without reference to:

Master Air Loadmaster David E BULLOCK GM RAF

killed attempting to save the life of Lieutenant Colonel William Olsen USAF

18 November 1980

His name stands proudly with that of Master Air Loadmaster Peter BARWELL AFC the only other Search and Rescue crewman to lose his life to save others

Index of Aircraft Types and Serial Numbers

Andover	XS609	08-Apr-72
Anson	TX189	05-May-59
Anson	VL312	20-Feb-61
Anson	VM306	05-Aug-59
Anson	VM308	24-Apr-59
Anson	VM322	26-Sep-59
Anson	VM372	21-Nov-61
Anson	VM388	12-Jun-63
Anson	VP535	15-Feb-60
Anson	VV298	01-Jun-60
Anson	VV955	20-May-59
Anson	WD415	17-Oct-60
Anson	WJ514	23-Sep-59
Argosy	XN817	01-Oct-84
Argosy	XP441	04-Jun-70
Argosy	XR105	27-Apr-76
Argosy	XR133	07-May-68
Auster	XP253	11-Mar-65
Balliol	WG217	08-Jun-59
Basset	XS783	05-Jul-73
Belvedere	XG453	18-Mar-69
Belvedere	XG454	30-Aug-61
Belvedere	XG461	31-Dec-64
Belvedere	XG462	05-Oct-62
Belvedere	XG463	30-Oct-64
Belvedere	XG465	30-Jul-62
Belvedere	XG473	04-May-63
Beverley	XB268	13-Apr-63
Beverley	XL132	17-May-62
Beverley	XL150	15-Dec-67
Beverley	XL151	11-Oct-60
Beverley	XM106	21-Jun-67
Beverley	XM110	06-Oct-61
Britannia	XL638	12-Oct-67
Buccaneer	XN975	14-Jun-78
Buccaneer	XN976	09-Jul-92
Buccaneer	XN977	08-Mar-82
Buccaneer	XN978	05-Jun-71
Buccaneer	XV160	20-Sep-82
Buccaneer	XV162	13-Jun-72
Buccaneer	XV166	03-Mar-76
Buccaneer	XV341	14-Jun-85
Buccaneer	XV345	07-Feb-80
Buccaneer	XV347	09-Dec-71
Buccaneer	XV348	31-Oct-77
Buccaneer	XV360	29-Jul-75
Buccaneer	XV867	10-Sep-93
Buccaneer	XW525	04-Apr-77
Buccaneer	XW526	12-Jul-79
Buccaneer	XW531	29-Oct-76
Buccaneer	XW532	25-Mar-71
Buccaneer	XW535	24-Jan-73
Buccaneer	XW536	16-Jul-75
Buccaneer	XW537	23-Sep-81
Buccaneer	XW539	05-Jan-72
Buccaneer	XW540	22-Apr-87
Buccaneer	XW543	14-May-92
Buccaneer	XW548	03-Feb-77

Buccaneer	XX890	18-Aug-77
Buccaneer	XX891	11-Aug-83
Buccaneer	XX898	17-Jun-82
Buccaneer	XZ430	20-May-84
Bulldog	XX514	29-Sep-86
Bulldog	XX517	25-Apr-89
Bulldog	XX542	16-Nov-79
Bulldog	XX545	18-Sep-80
Bulldog	XX557	11-Sep-75
Bulldog	XX613	17-Oct-92
Bulldog	XX618	22-Jul-76
Bulldog	XX660	25-Mar-85
Bulldog	XX662	20-Feb-82
Bulldog	XX703	03-Jun-76
Bulldog	XX712	02-Mar-88
Canberra	WD963	29-Jun-67
Canberra	WD995	26-Oct-61
Canberra	WE111	24-Apr-62
Canberra	WF926	21-Jan-60
Canberra	WH641	27-Jul-70
Canberra	WH667	07-Nov-80
Canberra	WH699	28-Nov-59
Canberra	WH714	19-Jun-68
Canberra	WH715	01-Oct-68
Canberra	WH778	20-Dec-68
Canberra	WH795	23-Aug-68
Canberra	WH857	03-May-66
Canberra	WH874	29-Jan-71
Canberra	WH948	15-Aug-77
Canberra	WH956	15-Jul-69
Canberra	WH958	17-Aug-64
Canberra	WH967	22-Jun-66
Canberra	WH971	24-Apr-68
Canberra	WH972	27-Jun-90
Canberra	WH973	06-Oct-71
Canberra	WH982	14-Sep-59
Canberra	WJ582	21-Feb-62
Canberra	WJ605	16-Apr-62
Canberra	WJ610	26-Jun-72
Canberra	WJ625	03-Aug-83
Canberra	WJ632	01-May-70
Canberra	WJ649	08-Sep-59
Canberra	WJ674	02-Aug-73
Canberra	WJ719	29-Apr-63
Canberra	WJ730	25-Oct-62
Canberra	WJ753	19-Jun-78
Canberra	WJ759	24-Nov-60
Canberra	WJ761	18-Mar-59
Canberra	WJ783	31-Jul-68
Canberra	WJ770	11-Mar-68
Canberra	WJ771	16-Jul-64
Canberra	WJ818	16-Jan-59
Canberra	WJ820	05-Oct-64
Canberra	WJ822	29-May-69
Canberra	WJ824	29-Jan-63
Canberra	WJ862	29-Jan-71
Canberra	WJ877	18-Mar-91
Canberra	WJ988	20-Nov-68
Canberra	WJ994	01-Apr-63
Canberra	WK116	25-Feb-82
Canberra	WK162	08-Aug-85
Canberra	WT209	01-Feb-68
Canberra	WT213	17-Mar-69
Canberra	WT304	02-Jun-59

Canberra	WT310	15-Jan-62
Canberra	WT313	26-Sep-68
Canberra	WT315	15-Jan-62
Canberra	WT321	10-May-60
Canberra	WT322	23-Feb-67
Canberra	WT324	14-Jul-65
Canberra	WT325	19-Aug-68
Canberra	WT330	10-Nov-65
Canberra	WT331	05-Sep-59
Canberra	WT334	16-Feb-60
Canberra	WT335	08-Sep-59
Canberra	WT363	11-Jun-68
Canberra	WT366	05-Oct-71
Canberra	WT370	23-Sep-64
Canberra	WT369	26-Aug-68
Canberra	WT481	02-Jun-65
Canberra	WT489	17-Apr-67
Canberra	WT504	24-Oct-60
Canberra	WT511	08-Nov-61
Canberra	WT515	02-May-66
Canberra	WT530	07-Dec-78
Canberra	WT531	02-Feb-66
Canberra	WT540	26-Aug-59
Canberra	XH130	25-Mar-69
Canberra	XH137	03-May-77
Canberra	XH164	07-Jan-69
Canberra	XH172	06-Oct-72
Canberra	XH176	25-May-78
Canberra	XH204	09-May-67
Canberra	XH207	04-Mar-59
Canberra	XH231	03-Feb-65
Canberra	XK641	04-Apr-66
Canberra	XM266	21-Nov-61
Canberra	XM267	15-Dec-70
Canberra	XM270	05-Jun-66
Chinook	ZA672	06-May-88
Chinook	ZA676	14-Nov-84
Chinook	ZA706	25-Jun-82
Chinook	ZA715	13-May-86
Chinook	ZA716	25-Jun-82
Chinook	ZA717	25-Jul-89
Chinook	ZA719	25-May-82
Chinook	ZA721	27-Feb-87
Chinook	ZD576	02-Jun-94
Chipmunk	WB552	09-Feb-72
Chipmunk	WB555	26-Apr-66
Chipmunk	WB562	29-Jul-75
Chipmunk	WB573	30-Nov-68
Chipmunk	WB697	28-Jul-94
Chipmunk	WD304	16-Nov-63
Chipmunk	WD305	20-Jul-60
Chipmunk	WD364	15-Jun-63
Chipmunk	WD372	04-Nov-62
Chipmunk	WG319	18-Jul-61
Chipmunk	WG403	19-May-93
Chipmunk	WG473	01-Jul-60
Chipmunk	WG488	23-Jul-69
Chipmunk	WK516	02-Jun-62
Chipmunk	WK575	13-Jul-70
Chipmunk	WK610	12-Sep-67
Chipmunk	WK623	22-Dec-61
Chipmunk	WK631	23-Jun-66
Chipmunk	WP774	30-Apr-60
Chipmunk	WP828	25-May-59

Chipmunk	WP834	23-Jun-66	Gnat	XM696	12-Oct-62
Chipmunk	WP836	19-Jul-60	Gnat	XM704	28-Sep-66
Chipmunk	WP838	12-Sep-67	Gnat	XM707	30-Jun-67
Chipmunk	WP841	29-Aug-61	Gnat	XP501	13-Jun-69
Chipmunk	WP854	05-Feb-62	Gnat	XP507	13-Apr-66
Chipmunk	WP865	15-Aug-60	Gnat	XP508	06-Sep-73
Chipmunk	WP895	12-Jul-60	Gnat	XP509	14-Dec-67
Chipmunk	WP922	02-Nov-62	Gnat	XP510	14-Nov-68
Chipmunk	WP968	22-Dec-65	Gnat	XP512	23-Aug-67
Chipmunk	WP976	17-Jun-62	Gnat	XP531	16-Feb-76
Chipmunk	WP979	23-May-82	Gnat	XP536	30-Apr-76
Chipmunk	WP980	27-Aug-93	Gnat	XP539	22-May-79
Chipmunk	WP982	24-Aug-59	Gnat	XR536	18-Oct-63
Chipmunk	WP986	11-Jun-65	Gnat	XR537	12-Oct-73
Chipmunk	WZ857	04-Jul-63	Gnat	XR539	13-May-66
Chipmunk	WZ861	26-Jun-70	Gnat	XR542	09-Mar-65
Chipmunk	WZ864	06-Dec-66	Gnat	XR543	19-Jul-65
Chipmunk	WZ870	01-Nov-59	Gnat	XR544	26-Apr-78
Chipmunk	WZ874	02-May-68	Gnat	XR545	20-Jan-71
Chipmunk	WZ875	05-Mar-78	Gnat	XR567	13-Dec-71
Chipmunk	WZ880	07-Jun-59	Gnat	XR568	14-Jan-65
Dakota C4	KJ810	26-Jan-59	Gnat	XR570	23-May-66
Dakota	KJ955	29-May-65	Gnat	XR573	26-Mar-69
Devon	VP946	23-Sep-61	Gnat	XR948	14-Mar-72
Devon	VP966	05-Jun-67	Gnat	XR949	27-May-64
Devon	VP969	03-May-68	Gnat	XR950	22-Apr-65
Devon	WB532	04-Jan-62	Gnat	XR952	13-Jun-69
Dragonfly	WG662	29-Jun-65	Gnat	XR976	12-Oct-64
Gazelle	XX374	20-Apr-83	Gnat	XR978	22-Jul-64
Gazelle	XX396	30-Jun-81	Gnat	XR979	06-Sep-65
Gazelle	ZA801	18-Nov-80	Gnat	XR981	03-Mar-78
Gazelle	ZB628	09-Sep-93	Gnat	XR983	30-Apr-76

Gnat	XR985	06-Apr-65	Harrier	XV780	27-Jun-72
Gnat	XR986	20-Jan-71	Harrier	XV781	12-Jun-79
Gnat	XR992	16-Dec-69	Harrier	XV784	02-Apr-86
Gnat	XR993	28-Jul-73	Harrier	XV785	26-Mar-74
Gnat	XR994	13-Nov-70	Harrier	XV787	22-Mar-83
Gnat	XR995	16-Dec-69	Harrier	XV788	01-Dec-75
Gnat	XR996	08-Oct-76	Harrier	XV790	02-Nov-87
Gnat	XR997	03-Jan-70	Harrier	XV791	09-Jul-73
Gnat	XR999	08-Jun-68	Harrier	XV792	14-Oct-80
Gnat	XS103	03-Sep-75	Harrier	XV794	04-May-72
Gnat	XS106	16-Oct-75	Harrier	XV795	23-Feb-83
Gnat	XS108	22-Apr-65	Harrier	XV796	06-Oct-70
Gnat	XS111	24-Jun-76	Harrier	XV797	23-Jan-74
Harrier	XV749	26-Apr-72	Harrier	XV798	23-Apr-71
Harrier	XV276	10-Apr-73	Harrier	XV799	12-Sep-72
Harrier	XV739	24-Sep-73	Harrier	XV800	16-May-74
Harrier	XV742	28-Oct-83	Harrier	XV801	15-Dec-78
Harrier	XV743	27-Jan-69	Harrier	XV802	21-Mar-72
Harrier	XV744	08-Jun-82	Harrier	XV803	03-Aug-71
Harrier	XV745	10-Jan-76	Harrier	XV805	30-Jul-73
Harrier	XV746	12-Mar-76	Harrier	XV807	14-Jul-81
Harrier	XV747	11-Nov-87	Harrier	XV809	20-May-88
Harrier	XV750	06-Sep-73	Harrier	XW264	04-Jul-70
Harrier	XV754	19-Jan-76	Harrier	XW272	29-Jun-82
Harrier	XV756	08-Nov-79	Harrier	XW765	12-Mar-80
Harrier	XV757	21-Sep-79	Harrier	XW766	04-Oct-79
Harrier	XV758	11-Oct-74	Harrier	XW767	06-Nov-82
Harrier	XV761	28-Oct-80	Harrier	XW768	28-Jun-86
Harrier	XV762	19-Nov-83	Harrier	XW769	28-Jun-86
Harrier	XV776	09-Apr-75	Harrier	XW770	06-Jul-76
Harrier	XV777	01-May-72	Harrier	XW916	17-Jun-86
Harrier	XV779	16-Dec-74	Harrier	XW918	12-Jan-72

Harrier	XW919	28-Jun-73
Harrier	XW920	20-Jun-72
Harrier	XW921	18-Aug-88
Harrier	XW922	19-Nov-85
Harrier	XW923	26-May-81
Harrier	XW925	20-Jun-89
Harrier	XW926	23-Feb-83
Harrier	XW929	07-Feb-92
Harrier	XW933	18-Feb-85
Harrier	XZ128	21-Sep-79
Harrier	XZ134	03-May-83
Harrier	XZ135	03-Jun-84
Harrier	XZ136	02-Nov-87
Harrier	XZ137	18-Jul-79
Harrier	XZ139	25-Aug-81
Harrier	XZ147	25-Sep-91
Harrier	XZ963	30-May-82
Harrier	XZ972	21-May-82
Harrier	XZ973	12-Feb-82
Harrier	XZ988	27-May-82
Harrier	XZ989	08-Jun-82
Harrier	XZ990	14-May-92
Harrier	XZ992	29-Nov-84
Harrier	XZ999	28-Mar-89
Harrier	ZD349	14-Jan-94
Harrier	ZD350	08-Aug-92
Harrier	ZD355	17-Oct-90
Harrier	ZD412	30-Sep-91
Harrier	ZD430	28-Jun-93
Harrier	ZD432	23-Nov-93
Harrier	ZD473	29-May-91
Harrier	ZG475	01-Jun-95
Harrier	ZG476	19-Feb-96
Harrier	ZG510	29-Jun-93
Harvard	KF314	22-Feb-82
Hastings	TG508	07-Mar-62
Hastings	TG522	29-May-59
Hastings	TG575	04-May-66
Hastings	TG577	06-Jul-65
Hastings	TG579	01-Mar-60
Hastings	TG580	03-Jul-59
Hastings	TG610	17-Dec-63
Hastings	TG624	27-Dec-61
Hastings	WD491	09-Jun-67
Hastings	WD497	29-May-61
Hastings	WD498	10-Oct-61
Hastings	WJ342	23-Jan-61
Hawk	XX163	01-Jul-93
Hawk	XX166	24-Jun-83
Hawk	XX180	07-Nov-84
Hawk	XX182	14-Jun-89
Hawk	XX192	20-Sep-89
Hawk	XX195	08-Jul-83
Hawk	XX197	13-May-88
Hawk	XX223	07-Jul-86
Hawk	XX229	29-Jul-83
Hawk	XX241	16-Nov-87
Hawk	XX243	22-Jan-88
Hawk	XX251	21-Mar-84
Hawk	XX257	31-Aug-84
Hawk	XX259	16-Nov-87
Hawk	XX262	17-May-80
Hawk	XX279	30-Jan-85
Hawk	XX288	10-Aug-95

Hawk	XX291	14-Jun-89
Hawk	XX293	17-Apr-85
Hawk	XX297	03-Nov-86
Hawk	XX298	25-Oct-84
Hawk	XX300	20-Oct-82
Hawk.	XX302	26-May-96
Hawk	XX304	24-Jun-88
Hawk	XX305	28-Jul-82
Hawk	XX333	26-Sep-85
Hawk	XX334	30-Sep-92
Hawk	XX336	29-Jul-83
Hawk	XX340	26-Sep-85
Hawk	XX347	09-May-90
Hawk	XX353	29-Jul-83
Hercules	XV180	24-Mar-69
Hercules	XV193	27-May-93
Hercules	XV194	19-Sep-72
Hercules	XV198	10-Sep-73
Hercules	XV216	09-Nov-71
Hunter	WV253	15-Jul-68
Hunter	WV410	20-Mar-59
Hunter	WW595	23-Jan-67
Hunter	XE531	17-Mar-82
Hunter	XE532	06-May-68
Hunter	XE535	28-Dec-62
Hunter	XE544	17-Sep-62
Hunter	XE552	23-Feb-81
Hunter	XE579	08-Aug-61
Hunter	XE581	22-Nov-61
Hunter	XE583	12-Sep-61
Hunter	XE590	09-Nov-60
Hunter	XE592	16-Oct-64

Hunter	XE593	23-Jan-61
Hunter	XE594	07-Mar-63
Hunter	XE596	19-Mar-70
Hunter	XE600	25-Jun-62
Hunter	XE602	08-Mar-61
Hunter	XE604	02-Mar-61
Hunter	XE607	30-Mar-62
Hunter	XE610	26-Jun-69
Hunter	XE612	17-May-60
Hunter	XE616	21-May-69
Hunter	XE617	07-May-66
Hunter	XE619	17-Jan-59
Hunter	XE621	30-Jan-62
Hunter	XE622	12-Jul-66
Hunter	XE623	11-Aug-64
Hunter	XE628	24-Jun-63
Hunter	XE643	09-Dec-61
Hunter	XE646	30-Dec-66
Hunter	XE647	30-Jun-64
Hunter	XE648	09-Sep-59
Hunter	XE649	13-May-82
Hunter	XE651	13-May-77
Hunter	XE654	20-Nov-67
Hunter	XF384	10-Aug-72
Hunter	XF385	20-Feb-63
Hunter	XF387	10-Aug-72
Hunter	XF388	26-Jun-68
Hunter	XF414	20-Feb-67
Hunter	XF420	27-Jul-73
Hunter	XF421	23-Mar-67
Hunter	XF424	29-Mar-60
Hunter	XF425	25-Aug-59

Hunter	XF433	07-Mar-63
Hunter	XF434	09-Apr-60
Hunter	XF440	20-Feb-67
Hunter	XF443	03-Aug-67
Hunter	XF446	18-Apr-67
Hunter	XF449	06-Jun-63
Hunter	XF451	12-Jul-62
Hunter	XF455	19-Sep-64
Hunter	XF502	25-Aug-59
Hunter	XF507	30-May-60
Hunter	XF508	03-Feb-68
Hunter	XF517	15-Jan-69
Hunter	XF523	24-Jun-63
Hunter	XF940	13-Oct-61
Hunter	XF943	27-Jun-62
Hunter	XF953	10-Nov-59
Hunter	XF986	07-Aug-59
Hunter	XF996	06-May-59
Hunter	XG128	13-Jan-61
Hunter	XG130	07-Jun-74
Hunter	XG131	19-Mar-71
Hunter	XG134	11-Jul-61
Hunter	XG135	06-Apr-73
Hunter	XG136	17-Apr-64
Hunter	XG151	03-Apr-81
Hunter	XG156	09-Oct-71
Hunter	XG157	16-Jun-66
Hunter	XG161	14-Feb-74
Hunter	XG166	17-Feb-64
Hunter	XG169	05-Jun-73
Hunter	XG185	21-Apr-76
Hunter	XG188	15-May-61
Hunter	XG191	16-Aug-76
Hunter	XG192	16-Jan-62
Hunter	XG193	10-Jun-60
Hunter	XG197	06-Jul-79
Hunter	XG198	04-Sep-67
Hunter	XG200	15-May-67
Hunter	XG204	15-Aug-69
Hunter	XG206	01-Jun-65
Hunter	XG208	24-Mar-59
Hunter	XG229	27-Aug-71
Hunter	XG235	15-May-67
Hunter	XG238	04-May-61
Hunter	XG253	28-Oct-62
Hunter	XG256	27-Mar-73
Hunter	XG261	28-May-80
Hunter	XG265	01-Mar-64
Hunter	XG271	13-Jul-61
Hunter	XG273	18-Apr-67
Hunter	XG293	21-Apr-64
Hunter	XJ615	24-Jun-64
Hunter	XJ635	04-May-76
Hunter	XJ636	25-Oct-76
Hunter	XJ637	14-Mar-79
Hunter	XJ641	11-Nov-59
Hunter	XJ673	02-Apr-69
Hunter	XJ674	22-Jul-68
Hunter	XJ675	08-Jan-60
Hunter	XJ691	27-Apr-67
Hunter	XJ693	03-Oct-60
Hunter	XK136	19-Oct-64
Hunter	XK139	30-Jun-64
Hunter	XK140	03-Jul-79

Hunter	XK151	12-Feb-80	Jaguar	XX742	19-Apr-83
Hunter	XL571	08-Sep-77	Jaguar	XX749	10-Dec-79
Hunter	XL575	08-Nov-71	Jaguar	XX750	07-Feb-84
Hunter	XL579	22-Jan-76	Jaguar	XX754	12-Nov-90
Hunter	XL583	01-Dec-81	Jaguar	XX755	10-Dec-79
Hunter	XL593	05-Aug-82	Jaguar	XX755	10-Dec-79
Hunter	XL594	16-Apr-64	Jaguar	XX758	18-Nov-81
Hunter	XL596	02-Nov-73	Jaguar	XX759	01-Nov-78
Hunter	XL597	29-May-80	Jaguar	XX760	13-Sep-82
Hunter	XL610	07-Jun-62	Jaguar	XX761	06-Jun-79
Hunter	XL611	14-May-68	Jaguar	XX762	23-Nov-79
Hunter	XL615	01-Jun-60	Jaguar	XX768	29-Sep-82
Hunter	XL619	21-Oct-81	Jaguar	XX817	17-Jul-80
Hunter	XL622	17-May-71	Jaguar	XX820	11-Jun-82
Jaguar	XX113	17-Jul-81	Jaguar	XX822	02-Jul-76
Jaguar	XX114	19-Sep-83	Jaguar	XX823	25-Jul-78
Jaguar	XX120	17-Sep-76	Jaguar	XX827	12-Feb-81
Jaguar	XX122	02-Apr-82	Jaguar	XX828	01-Jun-81
Jaguar	XX136	22-Nov-74	Jaguar	XX831	30-Apr-75
Jaguar	XX137	05-Feb-76	Jaguar	XX834	07-Sep-88
Jaguar	XX142	22-Jun-79	Jaguar	XX843	29-Aug-91
Jaguar	XX143	??-Sep-96	Jaguar	XX915	17-Jan-84
Jaguar	XX144	09-Sep-74	Jaguar	XX916	24-Jul-81
Jaguar	XX147	26-Mar-79	Jaguar	XX957	21-Oct-81
Jaguar	XX148	29-Jul-77	Jaguar	XX960	18-Jul-79
Jaguar	XX149	27-Apr-78	Jaguar	XX961	28-May-80
Jaguar	XX721	22-Jun-83	Jaguar	XX963	25-May-82
Jaguar	XX728	07-Oct-85	Jaguar	XX964	28-May-80
Jaguar	XX731	07-Oct-85	Jaguar	XX971	21-Mar-78
Jaguar	XX732	27-Nov-86	Jaguar	XX972	06-Aug-81
Jaguar	XX733	23-Jan-96	Jaguar	XX973	14-Apr-81
Jaguar	XX735	15-Sep-76	Jaguar	XX978	14-Jun-77

Jaguar	XZ102	14-Dec-76
Jaguar	XZ105	16-Jun-83
Jaguar	XZ110	16-Jun-83
Jaguar	XZ116	17-Jun-87
Jaguar	XZ120	25-Feb-77
Jaguar	XZ359	13-Apr-89
Jaguar	XZ362	17-Jul-96
Jaguar	XZ362	17-Jul-96
Jaguar	XZ365	09-Jul-85
Jaguar	XZ373	21-Jun-95
Jaguar	XZ376	07-Mar-83
Jaguar	XZ386	24-Jun-87
Jaguar	XZ387	12-Sep-90
Jaguar	XZ388	01-Apr-85
Jaguar	XZ393	12-Jul-84
Jaguar	XZ395	22-Aug-84
Javelin	XA569	18-Jan-59
Javelin	XA640	08-Apr-60
Javelin	XA645	07-Jun-62
Javelin	XA646	25-Jul-62
Javelin	XA661	29-Oct-62
Javelin	XA662	20-Sep-59
Javelin	XA701	04-Oct-62
Javelin	XA706	29-Jun-60
Javelin	XA722	07-Jul-59
Javelin	XA750	20-Jun-59
Javelin	XA752	02-Mar-61
Javelin	XA754	27-Oct-60
Javelin	XA760	10-May-62
Javelin	XA802	09-Mar-59
Javelin	XA803	02-May-61
Javelin	XA813	12-Apr-61
Javelin	XA823	21-May-60
Javelin	XA825	21-Nov-60
Javelin	XA835	21-May-60
Javelin	XH437	19-Aug-64
Javelin	XH645	11-Jul-66
Javelin	XH692	04-May-61
Javelin	XH708	30-May-67
Javelin	XH709	14-Jun-66
Javelin	XH717	26-Apr-66
Javelin	XH720	14-Oct-59
Javelin	XH723	30-Jan-64
Javelin	XH724	03-Apr-64
Javelin	XH747	10-Feb-64
Javelin	XH749	17-Nov-65
Javelin	XH750	09-Jul-59
Javelin	XH755	18-May-62
Javelin	XH758	17-Oct-63
Javelin	XH765	05-Nov-63
Javelin	XH774	20-May-64
Javelin	XH775	01-Sep-59
Javelin	XH781	01-Sep-59
Javelin	XH785	04-Apr-66
Javelin	XH788	11-Oct-67
Javelin	XH789	30-Jul-59
Javelin	XH791	05-Aug-61
Javelin	XH794	09-Mar-62
Javelin	XH800	18-Jan-67
Javelin	XH833	03-Mar-65
Javelin	XH836	03-Dec-62
Javelin	XH838	20-Sep-60
Javelin	XH844	13-Apr-62
Javelin	XH845	28-Aug-64

Javelin	XH847	27-Jun-66	Jet Provost	XM406	12-Nov-65
Javelin	XH848	14-Dec-66	Jet Provost	XM418	25-Mar-71
Javelin	XH876	24-Aug-66	Jet Provost	XM421	13-Dec-63
Javelin	XH877	22-Jun-65	Jet Provost	XM422	08-May-62
Javelin	XH878	27-Nov-61	Jet Provost	XM423	30-Aug-61
Javelin	XH887	08-Nov-65	Jet Provost	XM427	16-Oct-62
Javelin	XH890	02-Jun-66	Jet Provost	XM428	21-Apr-65
Javelin	XH896	30-May-67	Jet Provost	XM452	05-Apr-62
Javelin	XH906	26-Oct-61	Jet Provost	XM453	21-Nov-83
Javelin	XH909	20-Oct-66	Jet Provost	XM456	22-Aug-62
Javelin	XH911	03-Sep-65	Jet Provost	XM460	14-Dec-64
Javelin	XH955	29-Mar-64	Jet Provost	XM469	05-May-61
Javelin	XH958	11-Oct-66	Jet Provost	XM476	29-Jan-63
Javelin	XH959	08-Nov-65	Jet Provost	XM477	28-Mar-61
Javelin	XH962	24-Jun-63	Jet Provost	XN460	01-Feb-61
Javelin	XH971	29-Aug-61	Jet Provost	XN463	26-Oct-60
Javelin	XH977	09-Apr-62	Jet Provost	XN465	24-Feb-71
Javelin	XH988	09-Mar-60	Jet Provost	XN466	29-Jan-63
Javelin	XH990	02-Aug-63	Jet Provost	XN469	22-Jun-70
Javelin	XJ113	11-Sep-63	Jet Provost	XN473	15-Aug-84
Javelin	XJ128	12-Jul-62	Jet Provost	XN495	30-Mar-83
Javelin	XM336	05-Nov-63	Jet Provost	XN504	14-Mar-63
Jet Provost	XM347	23-Mar-61	Jet Provost	XN547	08-Mar-89
Jet Provost	XM360	24-Jan-69	Jet Provost	XN556	17-Mar-70
Jet Provost	XM366	22-Oct-81	Jet Provost	XN558	29-Jun-71
Jet Provost	XM368	29-Apr-63	Jet Provost	XN575	30-Sep-69
Jet Provost	XM373	29-Jun-61	Jet Provost	XN576	04-Sep-69
Jet Provost	XM377	04-Feb-60	Jet Provost	XN580	15-Jun-64
Jet Provost	XM380	29-Jul-63	Jet Provost	XN583	17-Sep-64
Jet Provost	XM382	17-Jun-60	Jet Provost	XN585	28-Mar-79
Jet Provost	XM384	26-May-66	Jet Provost	XN588	18-May-67
Jet Provost	XM385	08-Mar-60	Jet Provost	XN590	31-Jul-80

Jet Provost	XN598	01-Jun-78
Jet Provost	XN599	27-Mar-62
Jet Provost	XN601	16-Oct-62
Jet Provost	XN603	29-Jul-65
Jet Provost	XN604	09-May-62
Jet Provost	XN631	21-Apr-65
Jet Provost	XN642	19-Feb-63
Jet Provost	XN643	30-Jul-81
Jet Provost	XP561	21-Feb-68
Jet Provost	XP564	22-Apr-82
Jet Provost	XP566	30-Apr-70
Jet Provost	XP569	30-Dec-66
Jet Provost	XP576	16-Mar-70
Jet Provost	XP588	02-May-63
Jet Provost	XP616	14-Sep-66
Jet Provost	XP621	15-Nov-65
Jet Provost	XP622	20-Sep-63
Jet Provost	XP623	19-Apr-63
Jet Provost	XP625	27-Jul-66
Jet Provost	XP631	26-May-66
Jet Provost	XP635	18-Apr-63
Jet Provost	XP639	12-Mar-64
Jet Provost	XP670	04-May-66
Jet Provost	XP675	26-Feb-68
Jet Provost	XP682	27-Jul-64
Jet Provost	XR645	04-Oct-66
Jet Provost	XR647	07-May-73
Jet Provost	XR664	30-Sep-64
Jet Provost	XR698	03-Jan-64
Jet Provost	XS211	13-Feb-76
Jet Provost	XS221	05-Feb-66
Jet Provost	XS229	26-Feb-68
Jet Provost	XW288	17-May-82
Jet Provost	XW297	17-Sep-70
Jet Provost	XW300	02-Mar-71
Jet Provost	XW308	28-Jan-81
Jet Provost	XW314	08-May-80
Jet Provost	XW329	16-Jun-81
Jet Provost	XW331	11-Mar-73
Jet Provost	XW356	12-Sep-72
Jet Provost	XW371	03-Jul-79
Jet Provost	XW407	06-Jun-86
Jet Provost	XW411	06-Jun-86
Jet Provost	XW417	09-Dec-82
Jet Provost	XW424	03-Apr-77
Jet Provost	XW426	23-Jan-78
Jet Provost	XW436	12-Sep-72
Jetstream	XX477	01-Nov-74
Kirby Cadet	WT895	19-Apr-83
Kirby Cadet	XA306	24-Apr-83
Kirby Cadet	XE804	17-Aug-65
Kirby Cadet	XN237	15-Apr-73
Lightning	XG334	05-Mar-60
Lightning	XG335	11-Jan-65
Lightning	XM134	11-Sep-64
Lightning	XM136	13-Sep-67
Lightning	XM138	16-Dec-60
Lightning	XM142	26-Apr-63
Lightning	XM174	29-Nov-68
Lightning	XM179	06-Jun-63
Lightning	XM184	17-Apr-67
Lightning	XM185	28-Jun-61
Lightning	XM186	18-Jul-63
Lightning	XM187	19-Nov-63

Lightning	XM188	02-Jun-68	Lightning	XP756	25-Jan-71
Lightning	XM190	15-Mar-66	Lightning	XP760	24-Aug-66
Lightning	XM191	09-Jun-64	Lightning	XR711	29-Oct-71
Lightning	XM213	06-May-66	Lightning	XR712	26-Jun-65
Lightning	XM968	24-Feb-77	Lightning	XR715	13-Feb-74
Lightning	XM971	02-Jan-67	Lightning	XR719	05-Jun-73
Lightning	XM974	14-Dec-72	Lightning	XR721	05-Jan-66
Lightning	XM988	05-Jun-73	Lightning	XR723	18-Sep-79
Lightning	XM990	19-Sep-70	Lightning	XR748	24-Jun-74
Lightning	XM991	03-May-74	Lightning	XR760	15-Jul-86
Lightning	XM993	12-Dec-62	Lightning	XR761	08-Nov-84
Lightning	XN723	25-Mar-64	Lightning	XR762	07-Apr-75
Lightning	XN772	28-Jan-71	Lightning	XR763	01-Jul-87
Lightning	XN780	29-Sep-75	Lightning	XR764	30-Sep-71
Lightning	XN785	27-Apr-64	Lightning	XR765	23-Jul-81
Lightning	XN786	04-Aug-76	Lightning	XR766	07-Sep-67
Lightning	XN788	29-May-74	Lightning	XR767	26-May-70
Lightning	XP698	16-Feb-72	Lightning	XR768	29-Oct-74
Lightning	XP699	03-Mar-67	Lightning	XR769	11-Apr-88
Lightning	XP700	07-Aug-72	Lightning	XR772	05-Mar-85
Lightning	XP704	28-Aug-64	Lightning	XS453	01-Jul-66
Lightning	XP705	08-Jul-71	Lightning	XS455	06-Sep-72
Lightning	XP707	19-Mar-87	Lightning	XS457	09-Sep-83
Lightning	XP736	22-Sep-71	Lightning	XS893	12-Aug-70
Lightning	XP737	17-Aug-79	Lightning	XS894	08-Sep-70
Lightning	XP738	10-Dec-73	Lightning	XS896	12-Sep-68
Lightning	XP739	29-Sep-65	Lightning	XS900	24-Jan-68
Lightning	XP742	07-May-70	Lightning	XS902	26-May-71
Lightning	XP744	10-May-71	Lightning	XS918	05-Mar-70
Lightning	XP747	16-Feb-72	Lightning	XS920	13-Jul-84
Lightning	XP752	20-May-71	Lightning	XS921	19-Sep-85
Lightning	XP753	26-Aug-83	Lightning	XS924	29-Apr-68

Lightning	XS926	22-Sep-69
Lightning	XS930	27-Jul-70
Lightning	XS931	25-May-79
Lightning	XS934	03-Apr-73
Lightning	XS937	30-Jul-76
Lightning	XS938	28-Apr-71
Lincoln	WD144	22-Mar-61
Meteor	VW423	04-Mar-60
Meteor	VW472	11-Jan-60
Meteor	VZ521	05-Sep-60
Meteor	WA669	25-May-86
Meteor	WA681	03-Jul-59
Meteor	WF766	11-Nov-60
Meteor	WF771	29-Jan-62
Meteor	WF791	30-May-88
Meteor	WF835	02-Oct-59
Meteor	WG962	26-Jun-62
Meteor	WH169	26-Sep-60
Meteor	WH206	20-Jan-59
Meteor	WH231	11-Mar-65
Meteor	WH256	16-Jun-59
Meteor	WL106	03-May-66
Meteor	WL142	04-Aug-59
Meteor	WL424	18-Nov-59
Meteor	WL465	17-Jan-62
Meteor	WL470	14-Mar-62
Meteor	WL478	19-Feb-59
Meteor	WL480	15-Jul-59
Meteor	WL481	03-Jun-59
Meteor	WN318	11-May-59
Meteor	WX978	20-Jan-59
Meteor	XF274	14-Feb-75
Mosquito	VP191	17-Jul-62
MRCA	XX950	12-Jun-79
Nimrod	XV236	11-Sep-87
Nimrod	XV239	03-Sep-95
Nimrod	XV256	17-Nov-80
Nimrod	XV257	03-Jun-84
Nimrod	XW666	01-Jun-95
Pembroke	WV737	26-May-61
Pembroke	WV745	09-Jul-59
Pembroke	XK861	25-Oct-61
Pembroke	XL953	16-May-80
Phantom	XT860	20-Apr-88
Phantom	XT861	07-Sep-87
Phantom	XT866	09-Jul-81
Phantom	XT893	24-Apr-89
Phantom	XT904	15-Oct-71
Phantom	XT908	09-Jan-89
Phantom	XT912	14-Apr-82
Phantom	XT913	14-Feb-72
Phantom	XV395	09-Jul-69
Phantom	XV397	01-Jun-73
Phantom	XV403	04-Aug-78
Phantom	XV405	24-Nov-75
Phantom	XV413	12-Nov-80
Phantom	XV414	09-Dec-80
Phantom	XV416	03-Mar-75
Phantom	XV417	23-Jul-76
Phantom	XV418	11-Jul-80
Phantom	XV421	30-Oct-92
Phantom	XV427	22-Aug-73
Phantom	XV428	23-Sep-88
Phantom	XV431	11-Oct-74

Phantom	XV434	07-Jan-86	Provost	WV566	06-Oct-59
Phantom	XV436	05-Mar-80	Provost	WV578	06-Oct-59
Phantom	XV437	18-Oct-88	Provost	WV607	16-Jan-62
Phantom	XV440	25-Jun-73	Provost	WV623	18-Sep-61
Phantom	XV441	21-Nov-74	Provost	WV664	19-Jan-60
Phantom	XV462	08-Jan-91	Provost	WV676	02-Feb-59
Phantom	XV463	17-Dec-75	Provost	XF614	15-Aug-60
Phantom	XV471	03-Jul-86	Provost	XF684	14-Aug-62
Phantom	XV477	21-Nov-72	Provost	XF882	04-May-59
Phantom	XV479	12-Oct-71	Provost	XF884	24-Sep-59
Phantom	XV483	24-Jul-78	Provost	XF893	07-Feb-61
Phantom	XV484	17-Oct-83	Provost	XF901	31-May-60
Phantom	XV491	07-Jul-82	Provost	XF903	14-Aug-62
Phantom	XV493	09-Aug-74	Puma	XW203	15-Nov-74
Phantom	XV501	02-Aug-88	Puma	XW205	23-Jan-78
Phantom	XV578	28-Feb-79	Puma	XW212	22-May-75
Phantom	XV580	18-Sep-75	Puma	XW214	07-Feb-73
Phantom	XV589	03-Jun-80	Puma	XW218	27-Sep-72
Phantom	XV598	23-Nov-78	Puma	XW228	27-Dec-79
Phantom	ZE358	26-Aug-87	Puma	XW230	27-Aug-76
Pioneer	XG560	26-Aug-60	Puma	XW233	27-Nov-92
Pioneer	XG561	23-Oct-59	Puma	ZA941	08-Aug-91
Pioneer	XJ450	04-Oct-60	Shackleton	VP294	15-May-62
Pioneer	XL517	15-Jul-66	Shackleton	WB833	19-Apr-68
Pioneer	XL555	29-Apr-60	Shackleton	WL786	04-Nov-67
Pioneer	XL557	09-Aug-60	Shackleton	WR965	30-Apr-90
Pioneer	XL664	16-Jun-61	Shackleton	WR968	20-Oct-61
Pioneer	XL667	12-May-62	Shackleton	WR976	19-Nov-67
Pioneer	XL699	24-Jul-60	Shackleton	XF702	21-Dec-67
Pioneer	XL700	10-Feb-63	Shackleton	XF704	08-Dec-65
Provost	WV537	05-Jan-60	Shackleton	XF710	10-Jul-64
Provost	WV564	25-Sep-61	Sioux	XT798	01-Mar-67

Sioux	XV310	22-Apr-70
Sioux	XV316	22-Apr-70
Swift	WK278	17-Nov-60
Swift	WK295	16-Mar-61
Swift	WK298	05-Feb-60
Swift	WK299	29-Jun-60
Swift	WK304	26-Oct-59
Swift	WN124	27-Aug-59
Swift	XD913	23-Jun-60
Swift	XD928	09-Apr-59
Swift	XD955	13-Jul-59
Swift	XD961	19-Jul-59
Swift	XD967	28-Feb-59
Swift	XD969	07-Mar-60
Sycamore	XE307	17-Sep-59
Sycamore	XE309	29-Mar-63
Sycamore	XE311	04-Apr-64
Sycamore	XE319	21-Feb-59
Sycamore	XE320	13-Oct-65
Sycamore	XE322	20-Mar-61
Sycamore	XF267	27-Apr-59
Sycamore	XG500	14-Dec-61
Sycamore	XG509	13-Feb-62
Sycamore	XG511	07-Dec-60
Sycamore	XG512	04-Jul-63
Sycamore	XG514	10-Jan-64
Sycamore	XG517	23-Aug-63
Sycamore	XG519	24-Jan-64
Sycamore	XG520	11-Mar-60
Sycamore	XG521	13-Oct-61
Sycamore	XG522	04-Apr-61
Sycamore	XG523	25-Sep-62
Sycamore	XG538	14-Sep-60
Sycamore	XG540	23-Jul-65
Sycamore	XG597	10-Jul-64
Sycamore	XJ382	09-Jul-62
Sycamore	XJ915	12-Feb-66
Sycamore	XJ919	27-Feb-63
Sycamore	XL820	25-Mar-64
Sycamore	XL822	06-May-63
Sycamore	XL825	28-Sep-62
Sycamore	XL826	28-Feb-66
Sycamore	XL828	18-Sep-59
Tornado	43+24	17-Jun-86
Tornado	ZA329	09-Aug-88
Tornado	ZA366	03-Jun-87
Tornado	ZA368	19-Jul-94
Tornado	ZA376	10-May-91
Tornado	ZA392	17-Jan-91
Tornado	ZA394	09-Jan-90
Tornado	ZA396	20-Jan-91
Tornado	ZA397	01-Aug-94
Tornado	ZA403	24-Jan-91
Tornado	ZA408	12-Jul-84
Tornado	ZA412	29-Mar-87
Tornado	ZA448	29-Mar-88
Tornado	ZA451	06-Feb-84
Tornado	ZA454	30-Apr-90
Tornado	ZA464	14-Aug-90
Tornado	ZA466	19-Oct-90
Tornado	ZA467	22-Jan-91
Tornado	ZA468	20-Jul-89
Tornado	ZA493	17 Jun 87
Tornado	ZA494	18-Jul-84

Tornado	ZA540	12-Sep-91	Twin Pioneer	XL966	02-Mar-61
Tornado	ZA545	14-Aug-90	Twin Pioneer	XL994	18-Apr-63
Tornado	ZA555	02-Dec-86	Twin Pioneer	XM287	08-Apr-59
Tornado	ZA558	28-Oct-83	Twin Pioneer	XM288	08-Apr-59
Tornado	ZA561	16-Aug-90	Twin Pioneer	XM290	13-Mar-63
Tornado	ZA586	27-Sep-83	Twin Pioneer	XM941	09-Mar-60
Tornado	ZA593	09-Aug-88	Twin Pioneer	XM942	29-May-64
Tornado	ZA597	14-Nov-83	Twin Pioneer	XM943	16-Sep-64
Tornado	ZA603	08-Nov-84	Twin Pioneer	XM959	19-Sep-67
Tornado	ZA605	10-Dec-86	Twin Pioneer	XN318	14-Feb-63
Tornado	ZA610	12-Dec-85	Twin Pioneer	XN321	28-Apr-67
Tornado	ZA611	10-Dec-86	Twin Pioneer	XP294	11-Sep-64
Tornado	ZD710	14-Sep-89	Valetta	VW803	17-Jun-60
Tornado	ZD717	14-Feb-91	Valetta	VW817	14-Jan-59
Tornado	ZD718	13-Jan-91	Valetta	VW863	11-Jun-64
Tornado	ZD738	27-Jul-87	Valetta	WJ480	28-Aug-62
Tornado	ZD791	17-Jan-91	Valetta	WJ481	04-Dec-59
Tornado	ZD808	10-May-88	Valiant	WP217	06-Aug-64
Tornado	ZD846	11-Jan-96	Valiant	WZ363	06-May-64
Tornado	ZD891	13-Jan-89	Valiant	WZ396	23-May-64
Tornado	ZD893	20-Jan-91	Valiant	WZ399	03-Nov-61
Tornado	ZE166	10-Jan-96	Valiant	XD864	12-Aug-60
Tornado	ZE733	30-Oct-95	Valiant	XD869	11-Sep-59
Tornado	ZE789	10-Mar-95	Vampire	VV640	12-Jun-59
Tornado	ZE809	07-Jun-94	Vampire	VZ302	19-Jan-59
Tornado	ZE833	21-Jul-89	Vampire	VZ357	18-Jun-59
Tornado	ZE858	21-Oct-93	Vampire	WA413	17-Nov-59
Tornado	ZE862	10-Jan-96	Vampire	WA445	07-May-60
Tornado	ZG708	01-Sep-94	Vampire	WE846	18-Jun-59
Tornado	ZG725	19-Sep-94	Vampire	WR194	31-Jan-59
Tornado	ZH558	08-Jul-94	Vampire	WZ417	25-Oct-60
Tucano	ZF316	12-May-92	Vampire	WZ472	04-Aug-60

Vampire	WZ495	15-Oct-59	Vampire	XK626	16-Jun-60
Vampire	WZ513	24-Mar-61	Vampire	XK633	10-Jul-63
Vampire	WZ459	15-Jun-66	Varsity	WF329	25-Aug-64
Vampire	WZ559	23-Oct-61	Varsity	WF334	14-Jun-66
Vampire	WZ578	30-Sep-63	Varsity	WF411	27-Nov-73
Vampire	WZ587	16-Aug-60	Varsity	WJ895	21-Aug-69
Vampire	WZ612	24-Apr-63	Varsity	WJ914	07-Jul-60
Vampire	XD379	01-Mar-62	Varsity	WL680	05-Mar-65
Vampire	XD431	09-Jan-61	Venom	WE377	29-Oct-59
Vampire	XD448	04-Sep-62	Venom	WR400	07-Jul-59
Vampire	XD463	18-Jun-59	Venom	WR421	04-Oct-59
Vampire	XD507	19-Apr-61	Venom	WR475	22-Jun-59
Vampire	XD520	02-Feb-60	Venom	WR504	01-Mar-60
Vampire	XD549	07-Jul-60	Victor	XA929	16-Jun-62
Vampire	XD584	24-Apr-61	Victor	XA934	02-Oct-62
Vampire	XD592	04-Sep-61	Victor	XH613	14-Jun-62
Vampire	XD602	29-Sep-61	Victor	XH617	19-Jul-60
Vampire	XD620	08-Aug-62	Victor	XH618	24-Mar-75
Vampire	XD623	29-Sep-65	Victor	XH646	19-Aug-68
Vampire	XD627	20-Jul-59	Victor	XH668	20-Aug-59
Vampire	XE827	14-Jul-60	Victor	XH671	15-Mar-93
Vampire	XE830	30-Dec-59	Victor	XL159	23-Mar-62
Vampire	XE848	29-Jun-61	Victor	XL191	19-Jun-86
Vampire	XE854	09-Mar-59	Victor	XL230	10-May-73
Vampire	XE882	23-Jan-61	Victor	XL232	15-Oct-82
Vampire	XE883	10-Jun-60	Victor	XL513	28-Sep-76
Vampire	XE897	15-Oct-59	Victor	XM714	20-Mar-63
Vampire	XE936	31-Jan-59	Victor	XM716	29-Jun-66
Vampire	XE944	24-Mar-61	Viking	ZE564	09-Apr-95
Vampire	XE953	24-Oct-60	Viking	ZE654	05-Aug-95
Vampire	XH264	10-Apr-59	Viking	ZE677	05-Aug-95
Vampire	XH304	25-May-86	Vulcan	XA904	01-Mar-61

Vulcan	XA909	16-Jul-64	Whirlwind	XJ412	06-Nov-66
Vulcan	XH477	12-Jun-63	Whirlwind	XJ414	22-Jun-67
Vulcan	XH535	11-May-64	Whirlwind	XJ426	22-Aug-71
Vulcan	XH536	11-Feb-66	Whirlwind	XJ428	10-Sep-63
Vulcan	XH556	18-Apr-66	Whirlwind	XJ432	18-Jan-71
Vulcan	XJ781	23-Apr-73	Whirlwind	XJ433	20-Feb-64
Vulcan	XL361	13-Nov-81	Whirlwind	XJ725	11-Oct-61
Vulcan	XL384	12-Aug-71	Whirlwind	XJ728	20-Jan-60
Vulcan	XL385	06-Apr-67	Whirlwind	XJ757	19-Jun-66
Vulcan	XL390	11-Aug-78	Whirlwind	XJ760	10-Sep-64
Vulcan	XM576	25-May-65	Whirlwind	XJ761	27-Jul-60
Vulcan	XM600	17-Jan-77	Whirlwind	XJ765	01-Jun-61
Vulcan	XM601	07-Oct-64	Whirlwind	XJ766	31-Jul-59
Vulcan	XM604	30-Jan-68	Whirlwind	XK990	27-Oct-67
Vulcan	XM610	08-Jan-71	Whirlwind	XK991	07-May-63
Vulcan	XM645	14-Oct-75	Whirlwind	XL109	17-Oct-70
Wessex	XR500	19-Apr-79	Whirlwind	XL110	06-Feb-73
Wessex	XR510	12-Nov-70	Whirlwind	XL111	01-Apr-67
Wessex	XR524	12-Aug-93	Whirlwind	XL112	20-Nov-70
Wessex	XS518	04-Nov-86	Whirlwind	XL113	05-Aug-61
Wessex	XS678	19-Mar-76	Whirlwind	XN127	08-May-80
Wessex	XT607	13-Jan-88	Whirlwind	XP303	24-Jan-71
Wessex	XT667	17-Sep-93	Whirlwind	XP327	25-Sep-65
Wessex	XT669	25-Oct-85	Whirlwind	XP332	13-May-69
Wessex	XT674	01-Feb-87	Whirlwind	XP342	02-Jun-66
Wessex	XT677	25-Apr-68	Whirlwind	XP343	26-Nov-69
Wessex	XT679	12-Nov-70	Whirlwind	XP347	03-Jun-81
Wessex	XV719	27-Apr-90	Whirlwind	XP348	03-Jun-64
Wessex	XV727	31-Jan-69	Whirlwind	XP349	13-Dec-72
Whirlwind	XD164	25-Nov-63	Whirlwind	XP357	13-Jun-76
Whirlwind	XD183	22-Jun-70	Whirlwind	XP392	20-Jun-62
Whirlwind	XJ410	21-Sep-65	Whirlwind	XP396	07-Jun-69

Whirlwind	XP397	17-Aug-64
Whirlwind	XP402	03-Jul-65
Whirlwind	XR454	27-Jan-75
Whirlwind	XR456	05-Nov-68
Whirlwind	XR477	30-Oct-69
Whirlwind	XR478	07-Aug-67
Whirlwind	XR480	20-Nov-65
Whirlwind	XR487	07-Dec-67
Whirlwind	XS412	18-Jun-68

Abbreviations

A&AEE	Aeroplane and Armament Experimental Establishment
AEF	Air Experience Flight
AFC	Air Force Cross
AFDS	Air Fighting Development Squadron
AFM	Air Force Medal
ANS	Air Navigation School
APS	Armament Practice Station
BCBS	Bomber Command Bombing School
BCCS	Bomber Command Communications Squadron
BEM	British Empire Medal
BTU	Belvedere Training Unit
CAACU	Civilian Anti Aircraft Cooperation Unit
CAW	College of Air Warfare
CCCF	Coastal Command Communications Flight
CFS	Central Flying School
CFS(H)	Central Flying School Helicopter Wing
CGS	Central Gliding School
DFC	Distinguished Flying Cross
DFLS	Day Fighter Leaders School
DSO	Distinguished Service Order
ETPS	Empire Test Pilots School
FCCS	Fighter Command Communications Squadron
FTCCS	Flying Training Command Communications Squadron
FTS	Flying Training School
Handl Sqn	Handling Squadron (part of A&AEE)
LCS	Lightning Conversion Squadron
MBE	Member of the Most Excellent Order of the British Empire
MECS	Middle East Communications Squadron
Met R	Metrological Research Flight

OBE	Officer of the Most Excellent Order of the British Empire
OCU	Operational Conversion Unit
RAE	Royal Aircraft Establishment
RAF Tech College	Royal Air Force Technical College
RAFC	Royal Air Force College
RAFFC	Royal Air Force Flying College
RAFVR(T)	Royal Air Force Volunteer Reserve (Training)
RAuxAFRO	Royal Auxiliary Air Force Reserve of Officers
RNEFTS	Royal Navy Elementary Flying Training Squadron
SAR	Search and Rescue
Sch of FC	School of Fighter Control
Sqn	Squadron
SRF	School of Refresher Flying
TTTE	Tornado Tri National Training Establishment
TWCU	Tornado Weapons Conversion Unit
TWU	Tactical Weapons Unit
UAS	University Air Squadron
Wg	Wing

Aircraft Types and Marks

B	Bomber
B(I)	Bomber (Interdictor)
BK	Bomber Tanker
B(SR)	Bomber (Strategic Recconnaisance)
C	Cargo
CC	Cargo and Communications
F	Fighter
FAW	Fighter All Weather
FG	Fighter Ground Attack
FGA	Fighter Ground Attack (alternative use for certain aircraft types)
FGR	Fighter Ground Attack and Recconnaisance
GR	Ground Attack and Recconnaisance
HAR	Helicopter Air Rescue
HCC	Helicopter Cargo and Communications
K	Tanker
MR	Maritime Recconnaissance
PR	Photographic Recconnaissance
S	Strike
SR	Strategic Recconnaissance
T	Trainer

Bibliography

The main source of basic information came from the British Aviation Research Group (BARG) Journal and its related magazine Roundel.

English Electric Canberra - Ken Delve, Peter Green, John Clemons

Shackleton at War and Peace - John Chatres

The Shackleton - Chris Ashworth

The Lightning - Bryan Philpott

Air Forces Monthly

Aeromilitaria

Flypast

In addition to The Times and Daily Telegraph I used various local newspapers such as the Shropshire Star.

About the Compiler

Colin Cummings was born in Aylesbury and brought up and educated near Bristol. He joined the Royal Air Force in 1963 and was commissioned the following year. He served with the support helicopter force, mainly in the Far East, from 1964 to 1969 and was one of the first RAF officers to be involved with Information Technology projects.

In 1975 he worked at the Directorate of Flight Safety, conducting short studies into the effectiveness (or otherwise!) of Lightning aircraft fire integrity programmes and the impact (unfortunate pun) of aircraft operating patterns on birdstrike damage suffered. He was also a very minor player in the early analysis and design of the first "Pandora" flight safety management system for the RAF.

After a wide range of appointments in the logistics field, he assumed responsibility for support of the Jaguar aircraft fleet in the very week the type was deployed to the Gulf conflict and he managed all aspects of its support and enhancement thereafter. He subsequently added similar responsibilities for the Canberra aircraft to his duties.

After retirement from the Royal Air Force in 1994 he began work for a major management consultancy and currently holds a lowly management position based in London. Besides an interest in all aspects of things military, he is a lapsed rugby union referee and an enthusiastic owner of German Shepherd Dogs.